THE BUSINESS OF SEX

THE BUSINESS OF SEX

Edited by

Laxmi Murthy
Meena Saraswathi Seshu

zubaan

ZUBAAN
an imprint of Kali for Women
128 B Shahpur Jat, 1st floor
NEW DELHI 110 049
Email: contact@zubaanbooks.com
Website: www.zubaanbooks.com

First published by Zubaan 2013

ISBN   978 93 81017 81 4

Zubaan is an independent feminist publishing house based in New Delhi with a strong
academic and general list. It was set up as an imprint of India's first feminist publishing
house, Kali for Women, and carries forward Kali's tradition of publishing world quality
books to high editorial and production standards. *Zubaan* means tongue, voice, language,
speech in Hindustani. Zubaan is a non-profit publisher, working in the areas of the
humanities, social sciences, as well as in fiction, general non-fiction, and books for children
and young adults under its Young Zubaan imprint.

Typeset in 11/13 Bembo by Recto Graphics, Delhi - 100 096
Printed at Raj Press, R-3 Inderpuri, New Delhi - 110 012

Contents

The Business of Sex
An Introduction

LAXMI MURTHY AND MEENA SARASWATHI SESHU

Feminists and sex workers in India have only recently begun to talk to each other; and the dialogue has been difficult. The awkwardness, hesitation and downright hostility from feminists towards sex workers and those working for their rights has been palpable. Sex workers' rights activists have been booed out of meetings and public fora, endured malicious slander campaigns against their work, and they have also had to bear the brunt of personal attacks. With a similar trajectory in the West, it is not surprising that many sex work activists there have ceased to engage with feminism. There is an overwhelming feeling that their voices do not fit the rigid frameworks of feminism, which regards its ideology as almost cast in stone. This antagonism is a conundrum, given that the natural ally for the sex workers' rights movement should have been the feminist movement, since it is precisely this arena of intense thought and action that has revolutionized perspectives on sexuality and labour—the fields that intersect with sex work—and just as importantly, the majority of sex workers are women. For feminists, who believe that sex workers live a life of pain and misery, a gathering of sex workers should exude pain and suffering. But that has not been the experience. The weak and miserable sex workers of the feminist framework simply do not add up. Women in sex work may have a sad story to tell, but they do not get frozen in that sadness. We propose that feminist theory is most comfortable with that unmoving frame because of an underlying discomfort about certain kinds of sexual behaviour within patriarchy. Indeed, the story of the sex worker does not fit into feminist analysis. Several tenets of patriarchy are challenged within sex work, for example reproduction and lineage, over which women have relatively more control.

This volume comes at a time when there is immense negativity regarding sex work. Ironically, feminist thinkers have contributed to this negativity, in particular when sex work is posited as "work". But 'feminists' are by no means a monolith, and this collection, with all the essays written specifically for it, comes from that space. While there is a large body of writing on sexuality, labour, and trafficking, there is comparatively little on sex as work, or the business of sex, as it were, from the perspective of sex workers themselves.

Writing in India on issues of sex work[1] is only just moving beyond the confines of the trafficking and HIV/AIDS dimensions. While there has been some discussion on the rights of sex workers from a human rights perspective, there is a dearth of work that seeks to deepen the understanding of these issues from a feminist perspective, underpinned by the voices of people in sex work themselves, and not entangled in academic jargon. This has perhaps been because of the discomfort in most strands of feminist scholarship in the region towards issues of commercial sex as well as multiple sexual relations. Consistent advocacy by sex workers' rights groups has resulted in issue-based coalitions working towards anti-discriminatory measures which have been effective in improving heath conditions of women in sex work, and some efforts are now focused on decriminalization policies. However, this action-oriented engagement aside, the lack of or skewed feminist discourse on this issue has an impact on the day to day lives of women in prostitution, since scholarship typically influences policy formulation and implementation. The concepts of patriarchy and the construction of power relations which inform feminist theory and praxis have been valuable tools with which to articulate certain forms of discrimination. Yet, these tools have been inadequate to analyse the diversity and complexity of sex workers' lives, a limitation that has had a serious impact on interventions designed to enhance their lives.

This collection of essays aims to complicate this discourse by bringing together thoughtful new perspectives on sex work. The authors bring to bear their specific experience in the women's movement, human rights movements or that against HIV/AIDS. While the focus remains on specific locales, the international experience which impacts the local has been drawn upon. All the writings emphasize the personal and political journeys undertaken by the authors and map their evolution to their current positions. Feminist health activist Adrienne Germain charts her journey in her perspective about sex workers: from pity to power. She speaks of "emotive barriers" that might come in the way of fully empathizing with women who make money out of sex.

In our chapter (Meena Seshu and Laxmi Murthy) in this volume, we show how the overwhelming currency of the victim discourse and underlying dominant morality that privileges heterosexual monogamy within marriage, have hampered an understanding of the myriad realities of sex workers through a feminist lens. At the same time, newly emerging articulations that can broadly be termed "whore feminism", like "queer feminism" have the potential of opening fresh thought on matters pertaining to the sexual terrain and the power equations therein. The understandings in the chapter are drawn from almost two decades of working with people in sex work, foregrounding the richness of their experiences. The chapter emerges out of the lived experience of sex workers, and attempts to present their varied perspectives almost in raw form, keeping secondary references to a minimum.

The mobilization around sex workers was largely propelled by interventions to contain the spread of HIV, which began in the 1980s. The spotlight that fell on sex work as a result of global and national responses to the HIV epidemic could have been an opportunity to draw attention to the health, safety and rights of sex workers. Joanne Csete describes how this picture was complicated by politically powerful faith-based constituencies, an anti-trafficking movement that denied the agency and rights of sex workers, and powerful funders determined to see sex workers only as a means of protecting "respectable" women from HIV. United Nations positions demonstrated some leadership on sex worker rights early in the epidemic but later appeared to acquiesce to prohibitionist views. At the same time, HIV responses liberated resources that in some cases enabled sex workers to organize and to be represented in international fora. Csete's chapter traces advocacy for sex workers' rights through the lens of key developments in the history of HIV/AIDS.

Lobbying for sex workers' rights, however, began long before anyone had heard of HIV/AIDS. Cheryl Overs talks about her first encounters with feminism during her early career as a massage parlour worker in Australia in the 1970s and looks at how that influenced her to form sex workers' rights groups and lobby for law reform. She traces the intersections of feminism and the sex workers' rights movement through the eighties and the advent of AIDS. Finally she addresses the present re-emergence of conservative feminist attitudes which are arranged around a revised theory in which sex work is defined as both indivisible from slavery—inevitably involuntary and inherently violent— and as a driver of the objectification and oppression of women. This notion, given full expression through the Bush years and the President's Emergency Plan for AIDS Relief (the PEPFAR law), the dual labelling of sex workers as victims or criminals inevitably leads sex workers to a contemporary 'choice' between two forms of violence—rehabilitation or punishment. Overs' experience of hostility from the mainstream feminist movement internationally, has resonances in most parts of the world, where sex workers and their advocates have to battle stigma and isolation even from movements that purport to struggle for universal human rights.

Analysing literal notions of isolation, Rohini Sahni and V Kalyan Shankar trace the journey of spaces in prostitution, tracing the movement from centre to the periphery and back. They use the specific case study of Shaniwarwada in Pune. While regional language terms such as *sule bazaar*, *bateekpura*, and *chakla* denote ghettoized spaces where prostitution was practised, the term 'Red Light Area' is more recent in usage while representing a spatial concept that pre-existed. But unlike previous terms, this one has acquired a larger identity as a common spatial calibration for women in prostitution across cities and regions.

In this ethnographic analysis, Sahni and Shankar outline how this transpired, and how it came to supplant the multiplicity of spaces with their distinctive names to evoke a common, larger, homogeneous image of space for prostitution. Mapping the transition from feudal-socio-cultural to colonial to contemporary urban settings, Sahni and Shankar chart the rise of 'space' and its looming importance in prostitution today. In so doing, they bring forth the resilience of prostitution as seen through the dynamism of the spaces it occupies.

The framework of human rights and the discourse around rights in general revolve around the crucial notions of choice and consent, which are coming to be recognized as highly contentious and culture-specific. Srilatha Batliwala's historical review traces the evolution of assumptions surrounding both choice and consent. She examine concepts and practice within feminist, development, and human rights discourses and strategies, beginning with the core of feminist theory and practice from the 70s—in the context of marriage, reproduction, sexual relations, work and employment. She locates choice within the sex work debates revolving around the prohibitionist, protectionist/rights-based positions. Choice as individual decision vs. choice as socio-economic, political or cultural coercion/expectation also comes under her sharp scrutiny. The position of the state with regard to the tricky issue of consent, as expressed through legislation, is also examined. Batliwala examines the complex interplay of choice and consent, borrowing the analogy of intersectionality which transcended and exposed the limitations of the identities discourse. Complicating the discourse on choice and consent is important as the insights of sex workers have deep implications for feminism, human rights, and state policy.

Cath Sluggett and Sandhya Rao, speaking from a vantage point of decades of activism, critique the human rights framework. They point to the need to revisit this framework and conduct a reality check on its successes and failures with regard to promoting the well-being of sex workers. Arguing that the human rights framework is a necessary but not a sufficient condition to address the problems faced by certain populations, such as sex workers, they highlight the contradictions and problems faced by sex workers, when the human rights discourse is used to deal with the problem of trafficking in women and children. This is all the more so when sex work is read *through* the discourse of trafficking, a paradigm that inhibits a comprehensive understanding of the issues at hand. A blurring of the categories of migration and trafficking further confuses the overall picture.

Sonia Correa and Jose Miguel Nieto Olivar's examination of the trajectory of the Brazilian feminist landscape with respect to prostitution vividly highlights its similarities with the global South, particularly India. Dealing with the range of feminist responses to sex work, from abolitionist to reformist and human rights based, Correa and Olivar trace Brazilian feminists' troubled relationship with prostitution, similar to the contentious relationship in India. From the first tentative dialogues between feminists and the emerging leaderships of the sex workers' movements, Correa and Olivar focus on the shift in the 1990s as internationally-led initiatives relating to trafficking gained leverage, and voices within the feminist boundaries gradually adhered to the anti-prostitution position. With dialogues between feminists and sex workers having almost completely stalled, the Brazilian experience holds important lessons for India, where the debates are only recently crystallizing and influencing policy.

Rakesh Shukla analyses the underlying assumptions of Indian jurisprudence related to prostitution and sex-work, showing how the legacy of colonial theory and practice, underpinned by a patriarchal bedrock, continues to play out in current thinking on laws relating to sex work, trafficking and migration, and also in labour law. Feminist interventions in the process of law reform, largely based on the victim discourse, are also examined in order to unravel the ways and extent to which these have proved useful to the lives of sex workers and their access to rights. The gendered view of law and legal reform comes under the scanner to explore the way in which the rigid drawing of "gender" boundaries, used almost synonymously with women's rights, has reinforced the marginalization of male and transgendered sex-workers.

Our book does not claim to be an authoritative or exhaustive text about sex work. Rather, each of the essays zeroes in on the fracture points within and between progressive movements— feminist, human rights, Dalit rights—and the movements for sex workers' rights that are becoming increasingly visible as sex workers mobilize and claim their citizenship. Examining these fissures, both ideological and practical, might unravel some of the obstacles to a broader politics of liberation.

Notes

1. In the individual essays in this volume, prostitution and sex work have been used almost interchangeably. There has been a shift in terminology along with the politicization of the sex workers movement. From "commercial sex workers" (CSWs) of the HIV/AIDS programmes, to "women in prostitution" to "people in sex work", the terminology has evolved to acknowledge the fact that not all people in sex work are women, and also that rendering sexual services need not be the sole defining marker of identity.

From Pity to Power
Musings of a Health Rights Activist

ADRIENNE GERMAIN

There must have been a time, before I met women in sex work, when I would have felt sorry for them, believing that they had no choice, and were always and only degraded and outcaste. At the same time, I have always believed sex workers have human rights and deserve respect as people. This conviction reflects a passion for fairness and justice developed early in my childhood. Regarding my own thinking, I cannot recall the moment or reason that I first developed a political consciousness of sex work.

Because my entire professional life has been centred on women, I focus here on female sex workers, although the human rights imperative I embrace encompasses all sex workers, transgender people and men as well as women. I came to see that while female sex workers experience the same discrimination that all women face in a world where the power lies with men, because their work is usually criminalized and much of it is in private spaces outside of state protection, they are often less likely to exercise their rights. I have felt special rage that it is generally the sex worker who is arrested, denigrated and abused by society. It is not the client and rarely the pimp, but possibly more often the "Madam".

I first started talking with female sex workers 30 years ago in Bangladesh when local calls for action centred on the "rehabilitation" and "relocation" of sex workers. In these conversations, I learned about their strengths as women, as mothers and as organizers. From the organizers I learned about police brutality, abuse by clients and the power of solidarity. From the mothers, how hard they worked for their children's education so that they could make choices in their lives. From the women, I learned about lovers, heartache, disappointments, joy, self-respect, agency and dignity.

At the same time, some feminist leaders in the United States were claiming that the qualities that I had seen in the women I'd met were a charade, and urged all feminists, including me, to join the anti-prostitution campaigns. These leaders included many I'd admired for years and still do. They tolerated no debate about their position, nor in truth did I want to change my position to move toward theirs.

As my professional life has always been international, I was not very engaged in the U.S. feminist discourse about sex work in the seventies and eighties. While I was in Bangladesh speaking with sex workers and learning about their lives, I would hear from the U.S. that there were some who felt that "prostitution" perpetuated and reinforced patriarchy and the oppression of women; that it objectified them and, by implication, reduced them (and other women) to sexual humiliation. This description did not match what I was hearing and seeing in South Asia then, nor does it ring true for me today. Those feminist leaders and I agreed then and still do, that forced sex work (as in trafficking, bondage, etc) and child sex work are unacceptable and we fight those together. But I fear those of us who recognize "sex work" will never be able to persuade some feminists that adults have the right to choose this work. This is, perhaps, the main disagreement between sex workers' rights activists and some feminists today.

Some also see sex work itself as violence, a proposition with which I have never agreed. Rather, I recognize that sex work is one of far too many occupations in which there is very high potential for violence, exploitation, and discrimination. Sex workers, especially where their work is criminalized, experience violence from the state (including law enforcement officials) as well as the potential of violence and exploitation from their clients, pimps, and others. They are discriminated against by health care providers and other social services.

Another prevalent view among some feminists is that women in sex work have somehow been "forced" into it by circumstance, implying that they would choose something else if they could. It seems to me that this position deprives women of their agency and fails to respect their autonomy as individuals. However, it required some years for me to understand and recognize why many women choose sex work. The sex workers I saw in my international work lived in deep poverty, mostly in the red light districts of Asia, or on dark sidewalks of African towns; or they were teens turning tricks on the streets of Latin America. In South Asia in the 1970s, I learned that sex work for poor women is not necessarily any more dangerous or violent than other occupations available to them (domestic service, agricultural labour, low level construction). In fact, sex work had potential for women to take control of the conditions under which sex occurs. For some years, I didn't see sex workers "choosing" their work so much as doing it to survive. As I learned more about how few opportunities to earn a living existed for many women (and too few exist now), and about the nature of work available, I developed a greater understanding of how women might choose sex work despite the stigma and other social costs that can come with it. Even at some higher levels of income, the sex workers I've talked with are in the trade because it is the best source for the income they need. Still others may be closer to actually making an affirmative choice, not simply a survival decision.

I began to think concretely and programmatically about women in sex work only in the late 1980s when the International Women's Health Coalition (IWHC) began to address HIV/AIDS as part of our commitment to sexual and reproductive rights and health. The interface of sex work and HIV was a complex challenge. At that time, epidemiologists and policy makers seemed to see sex workers only as vectors of disease (and arguably still do). They called them (and men who have sex with men) "core group transmitters", and gave relatively little attention to the men who were their clients or the reasons women are in sex work. Their programmatic interventions did not recognize workers as agents of change themselves and actors in their own lives, but as only vehicles for public health. That made me mad, as all responses that objectify women do. It was clear that both human rights and feminist principles needed to be applied to programmes in support of sex workers.

Human rights are absolute and must not be constrained by public health imperatives or by others' approval of a person's choices or circumstances. Feminist principles recognize a woman's right to equal opportunities, including economic opportunities, autonomy, and the right to control her body and make her own decisions about sex and health. The struggle for the human rights of sex workers intersects all of these principles: the right to make one's own decisions, to be protected from discrimination and violence, to exercise control over one's body, and to look after one's own economic interests. After spending time with the members of Sonagachi in Kolkata, with leaders of sex worker organizing in the HIV/AIDS movement, as well as with the Veshya Anyay Mukti Parishad (VAMP) in Sangli district, I've learned a great deal, about the need to also establish and implement sex workers' labour rights.

When I first encountered the non-profit organization Education Means Protection Of Women Engaged in Recreation, better known in Thailand by its acronym EMPOWER, and later Sonagachi and VAMP in India, I saw the agency of sex workers actualized. These experiences, together with my belief in human rights and autonomy for all, have driven my commitment today to fight for the rights of sex workers to mobilize for protection under the law, non-discrimination, decriminalization of sex work, and respect for who they are and what they do in their own right, and not simply as a means to another end, for example the control of HIV/AIDS.

As we think through a strategy to secure the human rights and labour rights of sex workers, as well as programmes and funding to support sex worker organizing and their ability to have their own voice in decisions that affect them, we need to consider language and the positioning of the issues that will be most effective. In my view, it is likely not to be productive to champion or promote sex work per se, particularly because it is, in so many places, still criminalized and socially taboo. Rather, I think strategically we are likely to be more effective if we champion the human rights of sex workers. In order to protect their rights, laws and policies that criminalize, stigmatize or discriminate against sex work must, of course, be changed.

Championing sex work itself, I think requires continuing reflection and analysis of one's own values and perceptions, in my case, not about sex workers as people but about the work itself. Some emotive barriers, or "discomforts" remain for me around sex work even when I feel I have worked out the intellectual dimensions. This is probably importantly due to differences in life experiences. What I refer to as "emotive barriers" may perhaps be primarily that I cannot empathize fully with women in sex work, that is, I cannot fully imagine their choices, as much as I respect their right to be there. Sex and sexuality are highly private subjects for me, yet promoting the human rights of sex workers requires public action on my part. Further, the only way to protect the human rights of sex workers, including their right to work, is to make their work a legitimate matter of public discourse and policy, and to take it out of the realm of social taboos and embarrassment, moral judgments and emotions. This means raising the subject with many people—in government or donor offices, in other NGOs, and in social settings—who will strongly and fervently disagree. Dealing with others' negative attitudes, prejudices, ignorance, and fear around sex work and sexuality, takes skill, self-confidence and persistence, even beyond that required for other sexuality-related issues.

While there are some special political implications to championing the human rights of sex workers, they are not very different from most work concerned with the human rights and the sexual autonomy of women. One must choose carefully the times, places and people to engage. One must moderate messages and be ready to negotiate, to make progress without compromising core values. One must be prepared to champion the representation of sex workers in all forums and make the special investments this requires. Paradoxically, the spectre of HIV/AIDS has opened opportunities to promote support for sex workers' organizing, protection of their human rights and legal changes, but it also poses significant dangers of increasing stigma and discrimination.

There has been and continues to be opposition to defending the rights of women in sex work from the centuries' old power structure dominated by men, as well as from women who fear and reject sex work. Men in power (politicians, law enforcement officials, etc.) have a vested interest in keeping sex workers marginalized and powerless, and they have the power to hide both their needs and their predation (often to maintain marriages with "good" women), to maintain their ability to exploit and abuse sex workers, and to break laws with impunity. At the same time, many women perceive sex workers as a direct threat to themselves, to their marriages, or to a social order in which they feel "safe". More generally, society and individuals impose shame, ridicule, and taboos on most matters having to do with sex, including sex work and anyone who speaks openly about it or defends it. As a result, "prostituted" women have long been seen as villains—hardly the subjects of rights—or as victims whose "rights" can only be protected by removal from the victimizing situation (though I wonder how many of the rescuers have human rights in mind).

Although sexuality is a universal human expression, deep stigma against sex workers marks them as victims of society or economic circumstances, sexual deviants, and vectors of disease. As a result, another "solution" to the problem of sex work is to "rescue and rehabilitate", to restore women to their rightful place, with controlled and private sexualities that are chaste and/or subject to the control of husbands who are socially the only legitimate partners.

Eliminating sex work is also, of course, a means to curtail men's sexual "deviance" though rarely recognized as such. Current policies, therefore, too often aim to eliminate "prostitution". The anti-prostitution loyalty oath demanded by the President's Emergency Plan for AIDS Relief (PEPFAR) is a good example. Far from eliminating sex work, this policy instead constrains funding to sex worker support groups, conflates sex work with trafficking, and makes sex workers more vulnerable to both state and intimate violence. Since work on combating HIV/AIDS cannot be done openly, or through peer workers who are themselves sex workers, this conditionality, in the end, can increase their risk of HIV and AIDS.

Other policies seek to make sex workers "safe" for clients—for example, health screenings, mandatory HIV testing and condom promotion—see the sex worker not as an actor but as someone who is ordered to do something and punished if she does not comply. It is not difficult to transform such programmes into empowering investments. More basically, basic social services need to be made available and accessible to all on the basis of non-discrimination. But the mainstream actors who control policies and budgets for sexual and reproductive rights and health (SRRH) have long had a narrow definition of who is eligible: married women. It is only in the last decade that legitimacy has been given to information, services and rights for the unmarried, especially young people. Other more marginalized groups, including sex workers, have been excluded de facto if not de jure. Hence, efforts to promote and protect the sexual and reproductive rights and health of sex workers face likely dismissal or outright rejection in the SRRH field as "marginal" or worse. At the same time, because of transmission patterns and the risk of HIV/AIDS, some HIV/AIDS power brokers have acknowledged both the human rights of sex workers, and the imperatives to change laws and make health services available.

Actual progress has, however, been extremely limited because health systems have been so discriminatory, work to transform them has not been prioritized, and specialized programmes have been few or weak. Effectively providing health services to sex workers requires sensitivity training and supervision of health workers, in some cases special attention to the location and design of services and the like, all of which may be rejected in the name of the "larger majority" of women in need. This is a persistent struggle in my own mind, as a leader of an organization that has long worked for the availability of sexual and reproductive health services and protection of the rights of all. Focusing on groups of particularly neglected women, other than adolescents and young women, is fairly recent. There are important gains to be made in advancing sexual and reproductive rights and health by involving sex workers and other marginalized groups of women into thinking, strategizing, and acting.

The voices of sex workers have to be heard, and the promotion and protection of their human rights, including their right to work, must be achieved. Having said this, the potential costs of taking on these issues and advocating for them is substantial. You can risk rejection by allies, loss of funds, and marginalization, but the gains are greater. Human rights only have meaning if they apply to all, and it is imperative that we stand up for what is right. As I said earlier, we must be clever about how we do it in order to be effective, but there is no question that we must do it.

The tensions between the feminist and sex worker movements are many, and I have only touched on some of them. However, in the broadest sense, the two movements are founded on commitment to women's autonomy, especially control of our bodies. In this time of insistent, persistent challenges to that right, we should be working in solidarity. The biggest obstacle is the difference of views among feminists, and between some feminists and the sex work movement, on whether sex work is or can be an autonomous choice by women, or is always and only a form of violence and exploitation of women. In my view, the answer lies in sex workers' ability to control the conditions of their work and in the passage and implementation of laws and policies that protect their right to do so. If at least a core part of the feminist movement mobilized to help create these conditions, then perhaps many feminists now opposed to sex work across the board, would change their thinking. The benefit in terms of solidarity would be significant—especially if we work with other segments of women as well. These are times when many more women need to unite across our diversities.

The Feminist and the Sex Worker

MEENA SARASWATHI SESHU AND LAXMI MURTHY

What is it about sex work that arouses so much passion amongst feminists? From outrage over the exploitation of women's bodies to pity for the hapless victims of male lust, it has been difficult to view sex workers as going about the daily business of earning a livelihood by providing sexual services for money. While victimhood and exploitation have been relatively easy to empathize with and mobilize around, money for sex has engendered not just noisy public debate, but quiet squeamishness even among feminists who should argue that rendering sexual services for money must be regarded as a legitimate livelihood option. Even feminists who advocate liberation from restrictive sexual mores have generally not addressed commercial sexual transactions. Where does this unease lie?

The notion is that sex work, or for that matter even surrogate motherhood or breast feeding for hire, by definition debases women and transforms them into objects of control. This thinking is premised on the belief that a cash transaction strips supposedly intimate acts like sex, pregnancy, child birth or breast feeding of their inherent worth. That no "good" woman can actually opt for sex work as a viable livelihood option and the women who "readily" do so do not comprehend the inherent patriarchal sexual exploitation of their body and self is also convincingly argued. At the core of feminist discomfort regarding sex work is the notion that sex with multiple partners, especially casual sex, is inherently exploitative, violent or disgusting. The assumption, of course, is that men want such sex whereas women are exploited and are defiled by it.

But for sex workers, the push to unravel various concepts of sex-related issues—morality, sacredness, pleasure, preference, desire, love, romance, health, rights—have gradually become an important piece of the puzzle of life. Unfortunately, feminists and development activists often consider such discussions to be frivolous and "upper class". Instead, more "important" issues of poverty, caste, environment and violence against women take centre stage. However, as feminist theorist Gayle Rubin pointed out in an essay in 1984:[1]

> To some, sexuality may seem to be an unimportant topic, a frivolous diversion from the more critical problems of poverty, war, disease, racism, famine or nuclear annihilation. But it is precisely at times such as these, when we live with the possibility of unthinkable destruction, that people are likely to become dangerously crazy about sexuality ... Disputes over sexual behavior often become the vehicles for displacing social anxieties, and discharging their attendant emotional intensity. Consequently, sexuality should be treated with special respect in times of great social stress.

Rubin's point becomes clear when we consider that in a world that continues to be threatened by the problems outlined earlier, so much energy and effort is expended on clamping down on and controlling sexuality. Examples abound in fundamentalist campaigns against women: public flogging of adulterers and homosexuals and honour killings and lynching of young people in same-*gotra* marriages. In today's world, sexuality is clearly not an issue at the margins, but is at its very centre. It is an issue which, when viewed through the prism of sex work, poses a challenge to stereotyped ways of thought and activism.

How did we enter into thinking about and working on these issues? Meena,[2] the founder of the Sangli-based voluntary organization Sampada Grameen Mahila Sanstha SANGRAM and a feminist and activist for sex workers' rights, began her journey in the movement against violence against women in the mid-1980s. She started working with deserted women and on cases of dowry deaths in south Maharashtra. Sex workers were always "the other" in every village. The understanding was that married men abused their wives largely because of their interest in "loose" women. She worked with marginalized populations in a rural context through grassroots rights-based organizing, particularly with people in sex work. Her engagement with HIV/AIDS, sexual and reproductive health, violence against women, poverty alleviation and gender and sexual minority rights sharpened her need to work at the intersection of sexuality and marginalization.

What caught her imagination was the notion that casual sex could be a physical act stripped of emotion, could be initiated by women, could be used in a commercial context and even be pleasurable. Besides, many adult women seemed to appear in the communities out of "nowhere" apparently comfortable with this notion of sex within a commercial context with multiple men. This challenged her initial idea that no woman could come into sex work on her own and that all women were forced and trafficked into sex work. It was apparent, however, that many women were not there by force, deception, or debt bondage and were freely walking in and out of the communities.

This picture refused to match the common prevalence of the "prostitute" of one's imagination. But all women were not "happy hookers" either. There was an underlying discontent in this picture that was troubling. Many young girls were in the business and it was unacceptable that minors being trafficked into sex work was a reality. There was an urgent need to unravel and understand these complex contradictions. Numerous conversations revealed that casual multiple sex with the male client was not the core of the problem, but the spaces where sex work was practised were hugely abusive—police violence, petty criminal gang harassment, abusive moneylenders who charged compound interest from the girls and brothel owners, brothel owners who ruthlessly used the system for monetary gain. Debt bondage was a reality, as were petty political leaders who stigmatised and discriminated against women on the one hand and used them as vote banks on the other. Quacks abounded, as did doctors who refused to physically examine the women. The list was endless. This was stark life at the margins. Rights based sex worker organizing and collectivisation as a model to deal with abuse and violence in the community was thus born and grievance addressable mechanisms instituted.

As a feminist engaged in campaigns related closely to population, contraception and control over the body since the mid-1980s, Laxmi was part of discussions about the body (influenced in great part by the iconic *Our Bodies Ourselves* by the Boston Women's Health Book Collective and its Indian versions). Self-help, knowing one's body and its rhythms, and linking the personal to political issues of population control, the body tended to be viewed as a subject over which patriarchal forces fought. However, the simultaneous creation and promotion of the "mother earth" icon—all-nurturing, sexual, and imbued with the power to reproduce—was not a comfortable alternative.

Her work involved campaigning against forced population control and imposition of hazardous contraception and pre-natal sex selection. This, and the conflation of sexuality and reproduction, the reduction of women into uteruses and ovaries and the fragmentation of women in reproductive health policies demanded an engagement with the construction of the female body and "control" over it. Where contraception and fertility control mark the convergence of female sexuality and reproduction, sex work marks the convergence of female sexuality and work. This is a convergence that has demanded a complex response that is still evolving. Morality; double standards; a discomfort with the erotic, accompanied by an unwillingness to listen to sex workers themselves has hindered alliances between what would have been "natural" allies. Feminist theory and practice—a powerful liberatory force challenging inequities in every sphere—seemed to have faltered, and even failed, when it came to the issue of commercial sex.

This essay attempts to examine the troubled relationship between mainstream feminism, the human rights discourse and sex workers" movements for their rights in negotiating the knotty terrain of sexual politics. Over the years, collectivization, community mobilization and fighting for the right to a "voice" has helped centre the debate on sex work by the people in sex work themselves. We address ourselves to issues within the movement and do not talk here of the stigma, discrimination or violence against sex workers that exists in the broader social, legal and political sphere.

The Good, the Bad and the "Other"

Though the distinctions between women who are in sex work and those who are not are sharply and explicitly drawn in social arrangements, the lines between the two categories are fuzzy. Some blurring of the categories of respectable bourgeois womanhood and the woman in sex work, otherwise maintained in sharp disjunction from each other, can be seen in the following:

• The contractual terms of bourgeois marriage
• Many women who admit to "occasional prostitution", or sex for favours
• Some forms of heterosexual "dating" involving a "quid pro quo"
• The description of women accused of departing from the norm as "whores"

The recognition of continuities and commonalities among women is central to a feminist understanding of sex work while analysing the specificities of the phenomenon of sex work.

The dominant feminist discourse today fails to recognize and acknowledge the dynamics of sex work that encompass a wide spectrum of elements, ranging from violence and exploitation to autonomy and agency for negotiating the best possible options. The difficult space of the politics of the female body, female sexual conditioning and sexual control needs to be broadened and its complexities teased out. Feminists must question the very essence of a patriarchal value that shapes and constructs both the "good" women who do not question the dominant norm of propriety and those in sex work who dare to flaunt their "bad" selves, break norms and willingly accept the mantle of the "other" woman. The "good" ideal wife/partner who lovingly services a single man, preferably in a monogamous set up, or the "bad happy hooker" who services several men in a commercial context are both on the same side of a coin. Besides pitting women against each other, this image accords no agency to both the "good" and the "bad" woman. It freezes women into a set format and frame, depriving them of the freedom of framelessness.

Sex work activists and those in sex work have helped immensely in unravelling the mysteries of this framelessness by questioning both the frame and the construction of the bad and good body politic. They have also questioned the understandings of agency, choice and consent. Good or bad, the construction of women as mere recipients of "oppressive" sexual desires from their male partners has created an image devoid of any agency in the spectrum of man-woman sexual relationships. So while good women "bear" the burden of male sexuality, bad women "cater" to this demand, and even make a livelihood off it.

Women in sex work question the simplistic linearity of women being bundled into the good-bad continuum, challenging such a construction as male-centred. The analysis of a burdensome, oppressive sexual desire, which is male-centred, constructs and fuels the image of passive victimhood, again frozen into a timeless frame. They break out of the shackles of the good and bad paradigm, denouncing it as essentially emotional, and claim a space of the "other" which is neither good nor bad. They define *dhanda* (sex business) as a transaction of multiple sexual partnerships within a commercial context. Rendering sexual services for money within this transaction is therefore not only possible but can exist devoid of emotion, whether of love or of guilt.

Women in sex work, as part of a popular whore culture from western Maharashtra and north Karnataka, weave stories that have been passed on through poetry and "sayings" that talk of "control of" rather than "oppression by" the phallus. This is very interesting in that it not only challenges the "grin and bear/ cater to" construction of female sexual conditioning but also introduces a concept that actually trivializes both the phallus and "male sexual control". On the other hand, when discussing power dynamics sex workers—both female and male—share stories of "trivialization of the phallus", reducing of male sexual power to 100 rupees or whatever the going rate is, as commonplace. That male sexual power can be viewed as something to laugh at and even ridicule is fascinating in a world where it is one of the tools of oppression most commonly used to subjugate. Sex workers—female, male and transgender—share a wealth of knowledge and experience of masculine behaviours that defies any one stereotype. That men will pay a lot of money "merely" for sexual pleasure is always a discussion point. The interesting issue of female pleasure is acknowledged but always with a caveat—the money is good, I need to take care of my family and other such practical reasons. But many men who are in sex work also talk about pleasure while servicing a client. These conversations reveal a reality where the popular image of the golden hearted *tawaif* (courtesan) or the vicious vamp is closely entwined with the irreverence around the concept of male sexual power. This is in complete contrast to the popular notions surrounding prostitution as the most abhorrent form of exploitation of women.

Body of Rights

It was only around the mid-19th century that prostitution in India was constructed as a social problem. Prior to this, courtesans, dancing girls and others who provided sexual services outside the confines of marriage were not as reviled as the "common prostitute" who was created out of regulatory laws under the British[3]. The fact that prostitution was perceived to be practised exclusively by women created a category of women who were undesirable and therefore in need of reform. The perception of such women further evolved as "bad" women and they came to be seen as immoral and debauched. The profession itself is thought to have an "evil" influence on society's "good" moral standing, particularly on the character of "good" women. The "loose woman" has been the subject of much public discourse and debate, academic writing, policy-making and campaigns. Several perspectives have been articulated, even within the women's movement. A quick glance at some of the most dominant threads—largely emanating from western feminists who set the tone of the debate in the early years—will help contextualize the current points of friction.

On one end of the spectrum is the view that "prostitutes" are victims of what has been termed "female sexual slavery". In her famous eponymous book, American sociologist Kathleen Barry[4] elaborates on the manner in which prostitution is inherently violent, whether women are kidnapped, purchased, fraudulently contracted through organized crime syndicates or procured through love and befriending tactics. This perspective, echoed by those working to end trafficking in women and children, assumes that all prostitutes are forced into the institution. Further, it assumes that making money from sex is synonymous with sexual exploitation.

Trafficking of women and children also takes place for domestic work, organ transplant, bonded labour, begging or as camel jockeys. But activists, NGOs and the media highlight trafficking for prostitution as the sole issue in fighting trafficking. Trafficking is a criminal offence but the obsession with sex work dilutes the attention that this issue deserves. The violence and injustice faced by those trafficked for a variety of other reasons does not get addressed and the focus remains on sex and morality. Complete abolition of prostitution is thus touted as the logical solution to end such exploitation of women. This approach, which criminalizes the practice of sex work including soliciting, pimping, and brothel keeping, often criminalizes the woman herself. This is also something that is reflected in the official policies of most governments, including in India.

Without doubt, people forced, coerced, duped and trafficked into sex work bear the brunt of a system that uses sex work as a tool of oppression, but they cannot and must not represent all people in sex work. Trafficking for purposes other than sex work should be addressed in the effort to stop trafficking in persons. Activists from the anti-trafficking movement have concentrated on trafficking for sex work almost exclusively, concurrently calling for the abolition of sex work. The tenuousness of this argument would become apparent were there to be calls for the abolition of domestic labour, marriage, factory work or casual labour only because people are trafficked. Yet, this call for the abolition of sex work—mainly because of the conflation between trafficking and sex work—continues to inform the campaigners who insist that *all* women in sex work are victims of trafficking. Ironically, the law that provides that adult women can be "rescued" and detained against their will in "rescue homes" is a gross violation of human rights that has yet to attract the attention of human rights defenders in India.

Such a conflation has contributed immensely to the alienation and marginalization of all women in sex work where force, deception, debt bondage and slavery-like practices are made the ruling principle. The discourse on "trafficking" and "sex work" runs concurrently at the local, national and global levels. Trafficking is conceptualized by authorities and experts as part of the discourse around citizenship and law, and sex work as an articulation generated by the marginalized involved in sex work. The almost exclusive focus on trafficking for sex work leaves little space for sex workers to talk about issues that affect their work—working conditions, state and societal violence against them and safety and health issues. Also, the exclusive narrative of "commercial sexual exploitation" in the paradigm of anti-trafficking obliterates the real life stories of sex workers and the manner in which they negotiate control of their bodies on a daily basis.

Differing notions of who owns the female body or who has the "right" over it have been a rallying point since the early days of feminism. How this "right" is to be interpreted, however, has been deeply contentious. Farida Akhter,[5] a women's health activist and researcher in Bangladesh critiques the notion of "the individual right of woman over her own body" as an "unconscious mirroring of the capitalist-patriarchal ideology… premised on the logic of bourgeois individualism and inner urge of private property." According to Akhter, the idea that a woman owns her body turns it into a "reproductive factory", objectifies it and denies that reproductive capacity is a "natural power we carry within ourselves".

At the other end of the spectrum is a group spearheaded by women in sex work like Margo St James, founder of COYOTE (Cast Off Your Old Tired Ethics) since the early 1970s in North

America who argue that adult women can choose sex work as a viable option. Proponents of this approach view this voluntary decision to make money from sex as akin to selling other forms of labour. They contend that "sex work is work". Viewing prostitution as "work" provides a basis for organizing to solve many of the problems of commercial sex. According to them, distinguishing sex work from other forms of labour reinforces the marginal, and therefore vulnerable, status of a sex worker. Sex workers, they state, should be entitled to labour rights and occupational health and safety regulations like all other workers. Tired of non-sex workers propounding on their lives, women in sex work claim that sex work is a personal choice and demand complete de-criminalisation of voluntary sex work and all related activities. Legalisation of prostitution, demanded by some sex workers' groups, involves taking the subject outside the realm of criminal law, but advocates regulation of sex work through zoning and licensing laws.

Critics of this approach, like political scientist Carole Pateman[6], claim that feminists who invoke "women's right to own their bodies" are reinforcing a language that can just as well validate their "right" to sell their bodies through civil contracts for prostitution, surrogacy, marriage, labour or slavery. For Pateman, saying we "own our bodies" can only mean that we are "free" to sell our bodies (our body parts or sexual or reproductive services) in the marketplace.

According to Pateman, prostitution is the classic case of men as a "fraternity" gaining a "right of access to women's bodies" through the fictive device of contract (voluntary consent). Underneath this contract is another, more insidious fiction that equates women's reproductive and sexual capacities with labour power: as a "service" that can be alienated from the "self" without compromising the self's "moral freedom". According to Pateman, "When a prostitute contracts out use of her body" she is doing something different from a worker getting a job; "she is ... selling *herself* in a very real sense", alienating herself from her sexuality, which is integral to her "womanhood".

A different approach to concepts like autonomy and self-ownership has been taken by feminists of colour in the United States, who are engaged in re-appropriating these concepts. Patricia Williams,[7] for instance, is committed to reclaiming women's ownership of their flesh and blood by reinventing the language of self-ownership, or what she calls "the formulation of an autonomous social self". Those who tend, care for, or carry are by definition those with authentic claims to be named owners of things or people whose growth they nurture. When the "objects of property" speak, they remind us that the language of self-creation, self-propriety and freedom is always a story told and retold, and rejecting that language wholesale is to leave those without property nothing at all to own. As Williams observes, to repudiate formalized claims to personal worth and rights is to trivialise the experience of those who historically have been treated as worthless. She argues that rather than jettisoning the rights discourse, it should be broadened and diversified. The crucial function of the rights discourse—that of giving visibility to those previously invisible—needs to be emphasised.

In recent years, the discourse around prostitution has changed and is now couched in the language of human rights. Feminists, theorists and activists of prostitutes' rights are involved in unravelling the complex and complicated world of sexual autonomy, free choice, sexual exploitation and agency-versus-victim debates. This discourse has helped in that it has shifted the focus from blaming the woman and her sexual life to a continuum ranging from the "inherent victimization of the woman in prostitution" to the "beneficial exploitation of the institution of prostitution", acknowledging the shades in between.

Yet, the human rights framework has been challenged as a limiting strategy for a more radical social transformation that ensures the dignity and self respect of women. Critics do not deny the relevance of "rights" as a survival strategy to negotiate for wider survival spaces within the given system to be more responsible and accountable to all its citizens, but urge that the rights approach be viewed only as a strategy and not shape the vision for possible futures.

In the wake of the HIV/AIDS epidemic, a range of perspectives is being played out in public health programmes and their approach to sex workers, identified as a "high risk" group. It must be noted that most interventions with sex workers are designed to "protect" their male clients rather than the sex workers. A large factor in the ill-treatment of sex workers is the narrow understanding that people have of this work. Traditional perspectives assume that all people involved in sex work are victims who have been coerced, bribed, blackmailed or forced into the trade. Sex work is thus viewed as a dehumanizing business with no space for the assertion of human rights. The only approach to giving sex workers their rights is to "free" them from the trade and abolish prostitution altogether.

VAMP (Veshya Anyay Mukti Parishad), a collective of women in sex work from western Maharashtra and north Karnataka, refused to accept this burden of analysis on their work and self-worth. They have helped build a rare solidarity among people in sex work, and collectivized women who had common experiences of being exposed to multiple discriminations and who had their rights ignored and violated. Women in sex work came to identify themselves as part of a marginalized community who were vulnerable not only to HIV/AIDS but also to social stigma and public violence. VAMP challenges the concept of "exploitation by any male". It defines sex work as adult, monogamous or polygamous sexual partnerships within a commercial context. The contextualization of sex work between consenting adults and where the exchange of money is a contract between two or more individuals is therefore critical. The contract itself signifies the "mutual" nature of the exchange, the more so because the terms of the contract are controlled by the person/woman offering the service.

As Rajeshwari Sunder Rajan[8] observes, the prostitution question(s) "challenges us, as well, to ask whether prostitute interests are being truly represented in these debates. The urgency and force of the disagreements arise not only from the issues relating to prostitution, but also from the fact that the prostitution question has gathered around itself many of the issues that remain unresolved in feminism: the relationship between feminists and female 'victims of oppression'; the construction of the female subject in terms of 'agency' (choice, autonomy, desire, 'voice'); the public/private dimension of work/sexuality; the conceptualization of First World/Third World difference-and-sameness in women's status; the narrativization-as-progress of women's (here, especially, prostitutes') history."

It is apparent that the "prostitution question" will be debated and that arguments for and against, whether voluntary/forced, "agency'/victim, trafficked/socialized, legal/criminal, sexual slavery/sexual autonomy, or exploited/liberated, will continue to occupy theorists, activists and governments. However, the experiences of the women in sex work themselves are not given due recognition in these debates. As Durga Pujari, an activist from VAMP puts it, "Over the years, we have become "commercial sex workers" from "common prostitutes", debates are held about us and we are discussed in documents, covenants and declarations. The problem is that when we try to inform the arguments, our stories are disbelieved and we are treated as if we cannot comprehend our own lives. Thus we are either romanticised or victimised—or worse, our reality gets buried and distorted."

Sex Work as Violence

Is sex work not violence against women? This question has been posed countless times by feminists of various strands in the Indian women's movement. It is not necessarily asked from a moralistic viewpoint, but comes from a genuine need to engage in a contentious space that has pitted women in sex work against mainstream feminist thought and theory. This question necessitates examining feminists' notions of sex itself. In the words of radical feminist ex-prostitute Amber Hollibaugh, "Women in this culture live with sexual fear like an extra skin. Each of us wears it differently depending on our race, class, sexual preference and community, but from birth we have all been taught our lessons well. Sexuality is dangerous. It is frightening, unexplored, and threatening... Many of us become feminists because of our feelings about sex."[9]

Apart from arguments about the violence inherent in sex work, a key issue that feminists raise is that sex work reduces the female body to an object of sexual pleasure for men, bringing it into the marketplace to be exploited. While this view remains strong within feminist and other circles, an increasing number of people are urging a broadening and even outright change of definitions of the fundamental concepts around sex work. For instance, VAMP works to specifically challenge the notion of sex work being inherently exploitative. Instead, sex work is defined as adult, monogamous or polygamous sexual partnerships within a commercial context, including men, women and transgender people. For many, this has proven to be a very contentious position.

Some women in sex work prefer the use of the term "commercial sex" instead of "prostitution" or "sex work" because these terms focus on the seller of sexual services and perhaps contribute to the invisibility of buyers. Yet, they point out that sex workers' priorities vary from one community to another. For example, improving health and safety standards in the workplace may be a realistic goal for those involved in a formal sex industry, but is not helpful for marginalized young people selling "survival" sex spontaneously or housewives who occasionally exchange sexual services for money.

The contextualization of sex work is critical and it needs to be understood as an act between consenting adults involving the exchange of money in return for services. This, of course, does not refer to situations of trafficking, wherein coercion and deception are the dominant features. Within the Indian context sex work is defined as a business or *dhanda* where sex work is a contract with the terms spelt out. Also, there is no equivalent for "selling sex" in any Indian language, possibly because sex or sexual services are not sold, but exchanged for money (or other material benefits). Further, the fact that sex work includes men and transgender people is only recently seeping into societal consciousness, and feminism has to rethink many dearly held positions about male domination over the female body via transactions of commercial sex.

Life at the Margins

Paradoxically, the urge to dismiss the significance of sexuality co-exists with measures by both state and society to control and confine sexual activity according to rigid norms. We can thus discern two distinct worlds: one that would like to control sexuality, couching it in moral terms and societal norms, even in rhetoric of "the good of the species"; and another of resisters, those who break norms and live by rules unacceptable to the moralists. What is forgotten, however, is that life is dynamic, and herein lie the critical grey areas around which most sex workers tend to move and live their lives. In the process they adhere sometimes to the first of these worlds, sometimes to the second, and at other times straddling both.

The patterns that emerge from stories told by sex workers would come as a surprise to those accustomed to the pathetic picture of the whore. These include women's sense of economic power as the head of the household, monetary gains, economic stability and security, mobility, control over their bodies (manifested, for example, in their ability to insist on condom use) and a feeling of liberation from constrictive social norms. Alongside, however, there is also anger, emerging from a feeling of powerlessness against the intolerance and judgements of mainstream society.

Family honour or *izzat* is constantly presented as another issue that most women in sex work have to contend with in South Asia. This, perhaps even more than anti-trafficking or feminist or state constructions of sex work, pushes women underground. Stigma, discrimination and rejection by the family are legendary. Most women in sex work are estranged from their natal families or have furtive relationships with them. While money is accepted by the family, openly acknowledging that a daughter is in sex work attracts ostracism from caste and other community groups. This in some cases has led to violence resulting in the death of the woman in sex work. In townships far away from their natal homes, women start new family structures that include lovers, children and sometimes extended families of older, ailing parents and young siblings. Current lovers become fathers of children whom they have neither fathered, nor claim as their "own" children. Curiously, relationships with their *malaks*[10] often mirror patriarchal relationships within the family. It would seem that "love" and romance could succeed in making even the strongest women vulnerable to the often unreasonable demands of their *malaks*/lovers, a phenomenon that begs further study and analysis. The fact that as clients, *malaks* are multiple and change often is also a reality. But during the "episode of love" they are given the platform of power.

Women who have had the chance to leave the profession have often chosen to remain, accepting sex work as a way of life better than what is offered by the double standards that exist in mainstream society. When convenient, they have also chosen to leave and re-enter the profession when their circumstances changed.

These are indubitably signs of women's control over their lives. Yet, notwithstanding such evidence, and under the guise of protection (of both the individual and of "society at large"), sexuality that does not conform to the norm is widely considered a "vice" and pushed underground. Indeed, self-appointed moral brigades campaign, at times viciously, against a wide spectrum of what they view as sexual deviance, be it single motherhood, pre- or extramarital relationships, same-sex partners, multiple sex partnerships or any non-mainstream form of erotic sexual preference. In India, as elsewhere, many of these choices come under the moral and sometimes legal hammer as "illicit sexual conduct", the punishments for which are as extreme as flogging, forced migration or even death. In particular, sex work and homosexuality have long been considered areas beyond redemption, with stringent laws and their swift enforcement. The linkage between trafficking (a criminal offence) and sex work (which is not an offence per se in India and in some other countries of South Asia) and that of homosexuality with paedophilia, have been repeatedly put forward as reason enough for the moral policing of these presumed "offences".

Much of the debate around sex work has been constructed around one of two polarized positions: either as a human rights violation, a modern form of slavery, or as the exercise of the right to work. But in real life these positions—slavery and victimhood on the one hand, and choice and the right to work on the other—are woven together inextricably. Such ambiguities, however, are in no way reflected in the larger discussion of morality and rights. Before any clarity on this issue can be reached, the complex terrain of the politics of the female body, female sexual conditioning and sexual control need to be understood. Of course, sex work, like marriage and family—which also significantly impact a woman's sexuality—is not a monolithic institution. The degree of autonomy possible, the extent of abuse and violence and the possibility of accessing rights vary widely according to the situation.

As Martha Nussbaum puts it, "...at least some of our feminist theory may be insufficiently grounded in the reality of working-class lives and too focused on sexuality as an issue in its own right, as if it could be extricated from the fabric of poor people's attempts to survive.... When we consider our views about sexual and reproductive services, then, we must be on our guard against two types of irrationality: aristocratic class prejudice and fear of the body and its passions."[11]

The moral value of "chaste womanhood", so beloved by the moral brigades and the middle class, is centred on a monogamous heterosexual relationship within marriage. Further, the sole purpose of this relationship has traditionally been seen as reproduction—an issue considered sacred insofar as the continuance of the species is concerned. In this view, female passion is also vehemently denied, as it is seen as an "impure desire". The flaunting of a woman's sexual parts or the use of such parts for money is also frowned upon, as is any overt use of a woman's sexuality, with such acts deemed cheap or immoral. However, all of this is still permissible if the motive is "love" or marriage, and hence ostensibly in the service of reproduction or pleasuring a husband. Much resistance to sex work emanates from this deep-seated conditioning, which is averse to accepting women's sexuality for any purpose other than reproductive. The unease is compounded by the commercial transaction that characterises sex work. If, in the liberated era, seduction is permissible in certain settings, it must not be tainted by the exchange of cash; which is an underlying but rarely admitted view.

Sex is Sex

Central to re-examining this view is an understanding of sex workers' perceptions of sex itself. In fact, sex workers' daily encounters with sex throw light on an aspect that has been little analysed. As noted earlier, while feminists have long portrayed sex work as a commoditization of the female body, it is important to understand who decides whether such a definition fits a particular transaction. For instance, are monetary exchanges between families, or individuals "in love" commercial? In fact, commoditization needs to be redefined in a world dictated by commerce, where a vast majority of exchanges are defined by some material gain, be it monetary or otherwise.

The assumption that sex is loftier in some situations—between individuals who are in "love" or married, for instance—is problematic. There is absolutely no guarantee that the sexual experience will be pure and elating in a so-called "love" relationship. The opposite also holds good, which is that it is entirely possible to have a sexual encounter with someone one does not love and experience it as elation and pure. One may exchange money or other material goods in either circumstance. One may be in love and need the monetary benefit. Does that make the love unreal and impure? The institution of marriage, of which a feminist and socialist critique exists, is also a framework where exchange of money and goods occurs under various guises and where sexual negotiation also occurs. So why is that not discussed in the framework of "commoditization"? Are we by definition protecting purely commercial exchanges by couching them in "acceptable" terms? Sociologist Wendy Chapkis'[12] contention that sex can be seen not as a representation of the "authentic self" alone, but in performative terms, as an act, might go some way in understanding commercial sex.

Sex is but sex; it is we humans who attribute certain emotions to it, depending on our socialization and our individual experiences.

Moving away from this paradigm, commoditization and commercialization need to be understood from the point of view of "control". Thus, sex should be defined as commoditization only if the body (be it male, female or transgender) is used as an instrument for financial gain without consent.

The Caste Question and Sex Work

Sociologist Andre Beteille[13] articulates the gendered form of social control and perpetuation of caste hierarchies thus:

> There is, firstly, the sexual use and abuse of women, which is an aspect of the inequality of power seen in its most extreme form in the treatment of women on the lowest rank by men of the highest; this is the aspect of the problem that has received the most attention. There is, in addition, the unremitting concern with the purity of women at the top, associated with ideas regarding bodily substance...

The co-existence of prohibition of inter-caste marriages along with sexual unions across castes (usually upper caste men with lower caste women) is what Anupama Rao[14] calls "an important paradox in understanding the profound anxieties about sexuality and caste purity that issues of caste and gender raise..."

Caste, with its rigid strictures related to the body—touch, segregation, ritual purity and pollution—and gender, with its own set of strictures about touch, pollution and segregation, intersect powerfully in the arena of Dalit sex workers. Transgressions and challenges to these strictures, occurring on a daily basis, might provide insights into the functioning as well as fluidity of these systems of control on the ground.

While statistics are difficult to come by, it is well-known that a large number—maybe even a majority—of sex workers are from the Dalit and other backward communities. Yet, the intersection of gender and caste has rarely been explored either by feminists or those within the Dalit movement. The Dalit women's movement in India has largely framed itself around what political scientist Gopal Guru[15] terms "the politics of difference". The attempt to carve out a space independent of the mainstream women's movement dominated by upper caste middle-class urbanized women on the one hand, and dealing with the patriarchal Dalit movement on the other has been an inevitable outcome of the assertion of the politics of identity that dominated the 1990s. Much work (both academic and artistic) has gone into examining violence, particularly sexual violence on Dalit women, the eroticization and "availability" of the Dalit woman's body to upper caste males and the rampant molestation and rape that the Dalit woman is subjected to, both within and outside her community.[16]

In this framework, sex work, especially forms linked to religious/ritual practices like the devadasi or jogappa system,[17] have been analysed as part of systemic violence against Dalit women. Attempts to abolish the devadasi system were also led by former devadasis, who regarded the system as one of utmost degradation. The link between temple prostitution and the backward caste movements, particularly in south India, can be seen in the work of Muvular Ramamirtham (1883-1962), a former devadasi in the Madras Presidency.[18]

Caste continues to be a defining factor in the paradigm within which sex work is practised in India today. Anecdotally, the fact that some Dalit castes are over represented among women sex workers is apparent. While poverty is one of the reasons attributed to this phenomenon, it does not explain why some Dalit women do sex work and others do not. The overall understanding of male control and violence against Dalit women in sex work shapes policies such as the Government of Karnataka campaign (initiated during colonial times) against the devadasi system. It is also the same argument that has gained currency among the young men within the Dalit communities who are now insisting that their women folk stop sex work and remain within the confines of the home. This might not however mirror the situation in reality, where Dalit women sex workers may have more control over their sexuality and their earnings than the men in their families. Continued interaction with Dalit devadasi sex workers in VAMP reveals that they are considered as "males" in the household and given equal status in property and lineage. Indeed, if the devadasi system was not linked to earning money through sexual services it would be studied as a kind of matrilineal system. The problem is that any voice that is raised by the practising devadasis who are in sex work is at worst silenced or disregarded, or at best is deemed as "false consciousness".

An example of this disrespect to sex workers' voices is the disruptive outburst after the VAMP play "My Mother, The Gharwali, Her Malak, His Wife", in Mumbai in 2009. Professor Ramesh Kamble, a prominent Dalit intellectual, raised an objection that a non-Dalit, non-sex worker theatre director and producer had exploited the women in sex work by allowing them to falsely depict their lives. Reality according to him was that sex work is upper caste exploitation of lower caste women. He rebuffed the women, and declared that since they were under the spectre of false consciousness the director and producer should answer his queries. He, however, refused to engage with people who live lives as sex workers as well as identify as women from the Dalit community.

The play was premised on the belief that on seeing sex workers tell their own stories, audiences would finally accept them as human beings entitled to the same set of citizenship rights as others. The play, which aims to give voice to the invisible realities of women, men and trans-persons in sex work, was performed as part of the Women Playwright's International Conference. In his influential book, *Pedagogy of The Oppressed,* the noted Brazilian educator Paulo Friere defined the "culture of silence" as a situation in which oppressed members of society are not heard by the dominant members. Dominant members prescribe the words to be spoken and the images to be seen through control of schools, media and other institutions. In this process, marginalized and oppressed people are both silenced and they internalize negative images of themselves. The result is incapacity to act; to remain only a subject. One way to challenge this incapacitating culture of silence is by turning society on its head. By telling stories bottom-up; talking of reality at the grassroots; making visible life at the margins, where the powerful don't look or listen. Significantly, in the trilogy *Voices of the Poor*[19] World Bank researchers attempting to understand what poverty meant, spoke to some 60,000 people living on less than a dollar a day to identify the biggest hurdle to their advancement. It wasn't food, shelter or health care—it was access to a voice. This is particularly true of voiceless sections like women and Dalits. In the case of Dalit sex workers, their multiple vulnerabilities are rarely voiced.

Vijay Kamble (the son of a sex worker) from VAMP who was at the show referred to above later said, *"Amhi Dalitanchat Dalit ahe. Amcha awaaz kuchalicha haincha kai adhikar?"* (we are the Dalits among Dalits. What rights do these people have to kill our voice?) In VAMP, one of the most valuable lessons learned over the years has been to listen to the women in sex work themselves—rather than to those who speak for them, or about them—and respect the wisdom earned from a life of resistance.

The Falseness of False Consciousness

An inability to see things—especially social relations and relations of exploitation—as they really are is a state of false consciousness, a state that may be the inevitable result of a way of living. It characterizes the generic and chronic kind of servitude that cannot even perceive its own situation and may co-exist with a kind of illusory contentment. The prescribed cure is "consciousness-raising". This is what Sangram set out to do. But the world of the well-meaning activists was turned upside down. An immediate realization was that knowledge from the outside was vastly different from the worldview inside. Caste, class, religion and gender analysis of prostitution and sexual exploitation proved to be very limited in understanding this community of women.

The involvement with this community—now over 18 years old—forced Sangram to address the deep-rooted double standards and biases while dealing with issues related to sexuality and prostitution. It was impossible to "preach" to a group of women who scorned the dominant value systems. The crying victims of the social workers' imagination were not to be seen or heard.

As the understanding of prostitution as "exploitation, victimization, oppression, loose, immoral, illegal" was broken into, it was not merely ideas and beliefs that had to be questioned but the language too had to be transformed. Meena adds,

We had to revise our vocabulary to weed out words that reinforced the stigmatization and marginalization of women in sex work. The need to reclaim womanhood also became necessary since this sanctified moral space refused to acknowledge the fact that the very identity (of being a woman) was obliterated by the "whore", "harlot", "veshya" image. If women were not "good' then they had no right to be considered women.

It thus became a matter of claiming citizenship itself.

This realization dawned in the late 1990s, when one police officer after another declared that they did not consider "common prostitutes" as women. As "bloody veshyas", they were not "normal citizens" hence their complaints could not be registered. But inspectors showering abuses were generally careful; they did not use abusive language referring to caste, as they could have been booked under the law prohibiting denigration of lower castes. Instead, they used sexually explicit language towards a "prostitute". Incidents like this brought home the fact that it was not a question of a woman's caste or religion but the mere fact that she was a "bad" woman in prostitution. She neither had caste nor religious protection as she was stripped of both.

In such a scenario, it was unclear what consciousness could be raised. What was the lesson to be transmitted: should society be educated about using sex for money or about its inhuman behaviour towards a fellow human being because she exchanges sex for money? Where was the inhumanity or exploitation here? Was it in the transaction between the client and the woman? Or was it in our treatment of this woman?

The Ability to Do Sex Work

"There are many kinds of power, used and unused, acknowledged or otherwise. The erotic is a resource within each of us that lies in a deeply female and spiritual plane, firmly rooted in the power of our unexpressed or unrecognized feelings. In order to perpetuate itself, every oppression must corrupt or distort those various sources of power within the culture of the oppressed that can provide energy for change. For women, this has meant a suppression of the erotic as a considered source of power and information within our lives", says Audre Lorde.[20]

"*Dhanda* demands a person who is sharp, intelligent, has the gift of the gab and the ability to retain customers and regular clients", says Shabana Kazi of VAMP. She continues,

> *Dhanda* is not lucrative for people who are merely good looking; they have to be good "performers" both erotic and otherwise. While it is true that economic pressure (*majboori*) is expressed as the driving force of entry into sex work, to understand sex work purely in the economic sense does not present the correct picture. Issues of economic needs supersede religion, morality, family etc. and also provide a convenient frame to position sex work, but this frame is limited. While it shapes the lives of people in sex work it does not determine the way the business is practised. Many women who enter this business are not able to turn it into a viable economic option. It is not necessarily poverty or *majboori* that is the driving force, it is the ability to make money in a certain way.[21] Non-sex workers do not have that ability... thus an analysis about the *ability* to do sex work is usually absent.

The understanding/myth that it is the easiest thing to do (spread your legs) is not true; it is an ability, a skill, to continue the work day in and out. Different skills—the sexy whore, the sympathetic whore, the USP of the housewife, i.e., the "good" woman, etc.—all of these are used as strategies to make money. The ability to negotiate/bargain these spaces is what determines the ability to earn and is translated into economic gain (and not only in terms of hard cash—for food, beer, mobiles, cinema tickets etc). Regular clients are the backbone of the business. How to cultivate a regular client is a skill that is developed by "successful" women in this business. Sex workers challenge the victim image by simply stating the fact that to make money out of sex, a "continuous watering pot" will just not work. Some women will use it effectively to gain the sympathy of the client and hope it will translate into more money, but it is part of the performance.

This is not to say that all the persons in sex work enjoy sex work as work. Some like it on some days and hate it on other days. Some just do not like doing this work and are on the lookout for better working options. As in any other workforce the aptitude to do the work at hand is crucial in order to be successful. Critical evidence—for instance, that a majority of adult women in sex work consent to engage in this work—continues to be largely ignored or disbelieved, since there is little understanding of the difference between "consent" and "choice". Likewise, the issue of "choice" and "consent" is usually stripped of its class and caste context. It must also be noted that consent operates at various stages, not always contiguous. For example, a woman may consent to enter and remain in the commercial sex business. Another might have entered due to various compulsions, but consents to remain in business. It is these realities that can be uncovered only when a judgemental attitude is suspended.

Endnote

The concepts of patriarchy and the construction of power relations which inform feminist theory and praxis have been valuable tools with which to articulate certain forms of discrimination. Yet, the overwhelming currency of the victim discourse and underlying dominant morality that privileges heterosexual monogamy have hampered an understanding of the myriad realities of sex workers through a feminist lens. The other challenge that the sex work paradigm poses is the assertion that sex can be offered as a service for monetary gain. It also contests the belief that women would never willingly offer their sexual services for money, a scepticism that is morphed into societal consciousness.

The condemnatory attitude towards women in sex work has contributed immensely to alienation and marginalization. For sex workers to access and enjoy their rights, misgivings and stereotypes about sex work need to be broken. Sex workers do not necessarily need or want to be rescued. Further, they are not a threat to the greater "chaste" society, nor are they mobile cases and/or transmitters of HIV. In fact, they are capable of advocating for themselves, and of demanding their own rights.

In the last two decades people in sex work have fought back and forced society to create a space for their movement. They have proved that they are capable of advocating for themselves, and demanding their own rights. At the same time, the newly emerging articulation that can broadly be termed "whore feminism", like "queer feminism," has the potential of opening fresh thought on matters pertaining to the sexual terrain and power equations therein.

No one can deny that sex work often involves poor health, financial exploitation and physical and sexual abuse. However, these abuses are not intrinsic to sex work but are the result of the stigmatization and marginalization of sex workers. While sex workers certainly face discrimination and hardship, people in sex work do not need pity. Rather, they need the rest of society to recognize and fight against its own misconceptions, judgements and unfounded fears.

Notes

1. Rubin, G, (1984) "Thinking Sex: Notes for a Radical Theory of the Politics of Sexuality", in Carole Vance (ed.), *Pleasure and Danger*, London: Routledge & Kegan Paul.
2. Meena began working with Sangram in 1992 with peer-based interventions which evolved into VAMP (Veshya Anyay Mukti Parishad) in 1997, a collective of women in sex work from western Maharashtra and north Karnataka and MUSKAN is a collective of men who have sex with men and of men and trans persons in sex work.
3. Tambe, Ashwini (2009) *Codes of Misconduct, Regulating Prostitution in Late Colonial Bombay* New Delhi: Zubaan.
4. Barry, K, (1979) *Female Sexual Slavery* New York: New York University Press.
5. Akhter, F., (1992) "The eugenic and racist premise of reproductive rights and population control" in *Reproductive and Genetic Engineering: Journal of International Feminist Analysis* Volume 5 Number 1
6. Pateman,C, (1998) *The Sexual Contract* Oxford: Polity Press
7. Williams, Patricia J, (1996) "On Being the Object of Property" in Wendy Martin (ed) *The Beacon Book of Essays by Contemporary American Women* Boston, MA: Beacon Press
8. Sunder Rajan, R, (2003) *The Scandal of the State: Women, Law and Citizenship in Postcolonial India*, Durham: Duke University Press, 2003.

9. Hollibaugh, A, (1996) "Desire for the Future: Radical Hope in Passion and Passion" in Jackson, S. and Scott, S. (eds.) *Feminism and Sexuality: A Reader.* New York: Columbia University Press

10. *malak* literally means owner in Marathi, but contrary to popular perception, it is the sex worker woman who "keeps" the *malak* as a lover, and not the other way around. The women are called *malkins* which also means female owner.

11. Nussbaum, Martha C, (1998) "Whether from reason or prejudice: Taking money for bodily services", *Journal of Legal Studies,* vol. XXVII (January)

12. Chapkis, W, (1997) *Live Sex Acts: Women Performing Erotic Labour* London: Routledge

13. Beteille, A, (1992) "Race, Caste and Gender," in *Society and Politics in India: Essays in a Comparative Perspective* New Delhi: Oxford University Press

14. Rao, A, (ed.) (2003) "Introduction" to *Gender and Caste,* Kali for Women

15. Guru, G, (1995)"Dalit Women Talk differently" *Economic and Political Weekly,* October 14-21

16. Dalit poet Namdeo Dhasal's evocative and forceful first collection of poems, *Golpitha,* about the red light district in Bombay that he was brought up in, paints a savage and harsh picture of prostitution.

17. Devadasis (literally, servant of god) and Jogappas (transgender devotees), are part of a system of ritual dedication to the goddess Yellamma. This long-standing tradition in present-day North Karnataka and South Maharashtra equipped girls and women with considerable skills in poetry, music and dance, as well as provided for their livelihood, security, community identity and support. The British in their classification drive, tended to blur and collapse categories of women whose sexuality transgressed rigid restrictions of marriage and caste, thus consolidating a monolithic—but limited and often erroneous—view of Indian culture, for ease of administration in the colonies. As Philippa Levine notes, "These classificatory schemes clearly stripped indigenous women of the ability to name their occupation on their own terms, even while their daily lives challenged colonial definition. But this was an important aim of classification, its insistence on objective knowledge rendering the object of scrutiny passive. Prostitution always complicated that formula, as critics veered uneasily between wanting to see women as victims of abuse or as amoral profiteers." (see Levine (2000) for an excellent analysis of the alienating process of colonial taxonomy).

18. Kannabiran K and Vasanth Kannabiran (translated) (2003), *Muvular Ramamirthammal's Web of Deceit: Devadasi Reform in Colonial India*, New Delhi: Kali for Women
19. World Bank, Voices of the Poor (1999) (three books which bring together the experiences of over 60,000 poor women and men. The first book, *Can Anyone Hear Us?*, gathers the voices of over 40,000 poor women and men in 50 countries from the World Bank's participatory poverty assessments; the second book, *Crying Out for Change*, draws material from a new 23 country comparative study. The final book, *From Many Lands*, offers regional patterns and country case studies.)
20. Lorde, A, (1982) "Uses of the Erotic: The Erotic as Power" in *Zami/Sister Outsider/Undersong* New York: Quality Paperback Book Club
21. Sahni, R and V.Kalyan Shankar, "You know, then why do you still ask? Report on the First Pan-India Survey of Female Sex Workers, 2011". A random sample survey of 3000 women in sex work across 14 states of India, found that 1979 of them had experience of alternative work prior to or alongside sex work. Of these, 925 were in different occupations before sex work but were not engaging with them presently; 1054 were continuing them alongside. These occupations were diverse, though some common ones could be identified across the country (as housemaids, cooks, daily wage labourers, construction labour, farming/agricultural labour, liquor selling/making, petty shops (tea, paan, eggs, cloth, grocery), work (in dhabas, godowns, factories, as sweepers, helpers), selling a host of miscellaneous goods (door-to-door, bangles, candles, socks/hankys in trains, old clothes, traditional medicines, wood, toys, fruits/vegetables/flowers) to mention a few. While the average age of entry in these activities was around 17 years, 468 girls had begun working when they were 14 years or less. The average monthly income for these activities came to be ₹1300 (provisional). In comparison, the average incomes for sex work were ₹4300 (provisional). The average age of entry into sex work was 21 years.

References

Akhter, Farida (1992) "The eugenic and racist premise of reproductive rights and population control" in *Reproductive and Genetic Engineering: Journal of International Feminist Analysis* Volume 5 Number 1.

Barry, Kathleen (1979) *Female Sexual Slavery*, New York: New York University Press.

Beteille, Andre (1992) "Race, Caste and Gender," in *Society and Politics in India: Essays in a Comparative Perspective*. Delhi: Oxford University Press.

Chapkis, Wendy (1997) *Live Sex Acts: Women Performing Erotic Labour*, London: Routledge.

Guru, Gopal (1995) "Dalit women talk differently", *Economic and Political Weekly*, October 14–21.

Hollibaugh, Amber (1996) "Desire for the Future: Radical Hope in Passion and Passion" in Jackson, S. and S. Scott, eds. *Feminism and Sexuality: A Reader*. New York: Columbia University Press.

Kannabiran, Kalpana and Vasanth Kannabiran (translated), (2003) "Muvular Ramamirthammal's *Web of Deceit: Devadasi Reform in Colonial India*, New Delhi: Kali for Women.

Levine, Philippa P (2000) "Orientalist Sociology and the Creation of Colonial Sexualities" in *Feminist Review*, No. 65, *Reconstructing Femininities: Colonial Intersections of Gender, Race, Religion and Class* (Summer).

Lorde, Audre (1982) "Uses of the Erotic: The Erotic as Power" in *Audre Lorde: Zami/Sister Outsider/Undersong*. New York: Quality Paperback Book Club.

Nussbaum, Martha C (1998) "Whether from reason or prejudice: taking money for bodily services", *Journal of Legal Studies,* vol. XXVII (January), The University of Chicago.

Pateman, Carole (1988) *The Sexual Contract*, Oxford: Polity Press.

Rao, Anupama (2003) "Introduction" in Anupama Rao (ed) *Gender and Caste*, New Delhi: Women Unlimited.

Rubin, Gayle (1984) "Thinking Sex: Notes for a Radical Theory of the Politics of Sexuality", in Carole Vance, ed., *Pleasure and Danger*, London: Routledge & Kegan Paul.

Sunder Rajan, Rajeshwari (2003) *The Scandal of the State: Women, Law and Citizenship in Postcolonial India*, Durham and London: Duke University Press.

Tambe, Ashwini (2009) *Codes of Misconduct, Regulating Prostitution in Late Colonial Bombay*, New Delhi: Zubaan

Williams, Patricia J (1996) "On Being the Object of Property." In Wendy Martin (ed) *The Beacon Book of Essays by Contemporary American Women* Boston, MA: Beacon Press.

World Bank (1999) *Voices of the Poor*, Washington: World Bank.

Victimhood and Vulnerability
Sex Work and the Rhetoric and Reality
of the Global Response to HIV/AIDS

JOANNE CSETE

For good or ill, sex work has a different place in the global health world and in the world of human rights than would have been the case without HIV/AIDS. This chapter seeks to trace some of the developments that brought sex work as part of HIV epidemics onto the global agenda, with a view toward understanding the ways in which programme and policy responses to HIV have and have not embodied meaningful notions of sex workers' rights. In short, AIDS emerged as a global issue at a time when the human rights of sex workers were being contested in many ways, particularly in policies related to human trafficking. International policy actors had an opportunity through the emerging AIDS discourse and policy-making to provide leadership and raise awareness of the importance of sex worker rights, both as part of the global HIV response and more broadly. This chapter examines whether or not this opportunity was missed.

My focus is largely on the global level, especially on United Nations policy. Though it is plain that sex workers' lives are not lived at the "global level" in the area of HIV and sex work, United Nations policy inevitably reflected important developments in member states (especially donor countries) and in turn at times influenced policy and rhetoric at the national level.

The HIV epidemic first came to global attention in North America and Western Europe in the early 1980s, before it was widely understood that a much larger epidemic was already under way in sub-Saharan Africa. That AIDS was known for some time as GRID—gay-related immune deficiency—underscores that the disease was associated in both the medical community and the public mind with gay men (Gallo 2006). In North America, there was no shortage of pronouncements from political and religious leaders depicting AIDS as the wages of the sin of sexual deviance. Jerry Falwell, an evangelical Christian leader with a large television following in the U.S. said AIDS was God's punishment not just for homosexuality but also "for the society that tolerates homosexuals" (Johnson and Eskridge 2007). From the beginning, AIDS was met as much with moral judgements as with rational public health discourse. Remarkably, however, gay men in North America refused to accept the "victim" mantle and fought back in ways that demonstrated by example the meaning of "rights-based" approaches:

> ...the community claimed the right to construct the ways in which the disease would be defined and managed. The gay community's decision to take ownership of a stigmatizing disease spread primarily through practices that were morally unacceptable to most Americans was unprecedented (Siplon 1999).

Sex work soon enough figured in discussions of AIDS, even though evidence of its epidemiologic importance was spotty. In the 1980s, a number of US states took up legislation to require HIV tests of all convicted prostitutes (Grover 1987). Out of AIDS-related concern, a court in Florida sentenced a sex worker to wearing an electronic collar that would notify police whenever she left home (ibid.). Epidemiologists noted, however, that HIV prevalence among sex workers seemed to be determined largely by whether they had a history of injecting drugs (Curran et al.1988). Some scientists also concluded that the role of sex work in HIV transmission was overstated because HIV-positive men who were asked in surveys about the origins of their infection would say they had been with sex workers because that was more socially acceptable than admitting they had had sex with men or injected drugs (Castro et al. 1988). In any case, sex work found an easy place in the moralizing about sexual "deviance" that passed for policy discussion on HIV.

The "Good Women" of Africa and HIV

As the burgeoning AIDS epidemic in sub-Saharan Africa came to light, it became clear that heterosexual transmission was dominant in Africa, unlike in North America and Europe, and women and men were almost equally affected (Piot et al. 1988). Heterosexual transmission challenged both the accepted clinical picture from the West and the easy trope of moral blame as an approach to HIV. It did not take long for there to be a mushrooming of "gender analyses" of HIV in Africa that detailed the nature of women's and girls' vulnerability to HIV as a function of multiple kinds of economic and social subordination and victimization. Women's rights experts helped develop the picture of married African women, economically dependent on their husbands, who were often unable to refuse unsafe and coercive sex, were socially or legally disempowered from ending their marriages, and had limited possibilities for economic autonomy because of discrimination in education and employment (Rao Gupta and Weiss 1993).

Again and again, marriage was identified as a risk factor for African women (Zierler 1994; Farmer et al. 1993). This idea heightened sympathy for the innocent, faithful married woman, victim of the promiscuity of her husband, whose philandering was not condemned by society (Hamblin and Reid 1991). Inevitably, women sex workers were figures in this melodrama—contributing to the straying of married men, even though it was likely that men who were clients of sex workers also had other sexual partners who were not sex workers (Parikh 2007). Sex workers, then, had to be targeted as vectors of HIV in order to protect the "good" married women whom they indirectly infected. This idea had real staying power. As Melinda Gates of the Bill and Melinda Gates Foundation, a major donor to AIDS programmes, told the large plenary crowd at the opening of the Toronto AIDS conference in 2006:

> People involved in sex work are crucial allies in the fight to end AIDS. We should be reaching out to them, enlisting them in our efforts, helping them protect themselves from infection, and keeping them from passing the virus along to others. If politicians need a more sympathetic image to make the point, they should think about saving

the life of a faithful mother of four children whose husband visits sex workers. If a sex worker insists that her clients use condoms, that sex worker is helping to save the life of the mother of those children. If you're turning your back on sex workers, you're turning your back on the faithful mother of four (Gates 2006).

The Global Programme on AIDS and Sex Work

Jonathan Mann, one of the doctors who worked in Africa during the emerging epidemic, became head of the Global Program on AIDS (GPA) established by the World Health Organization in Geneva in 1986 as the United Nations' first worldwide effort to address the HIV/AIDS epidemic. Mann brought an unusual approach to this job. To the morass of judgementalism and ignorance that characterized social opinion and policy-making on HIV worldwide, Mann offered a conceptual and practical alternative. Underscoring that HIV mostly affected people who already faced discrimination, social marginalization and often criminalization, he urged for the approach of bringing human rights ideas to bear in developing AIDS programmes (Mann 1999). Before Mann, the intersection of public health and human rights usually occurred in measures to restrict the freedoms of people living with contagious disease to protect the larger public. Mann's idea, rather, was to use human rights to protect those living with HIV, to help remove their fears, shield them from discrimination and abuse, and empower them in their struggle.

Mann's ideas, for the most part, were a generalization of the approach taken by gay men's groups in North America—a refusal to accept "victimhood" as a starting point for conceptualizing the impact of HIV. He asserted that programmes "targeting" gay and bisexual men, people who used illicit drugs, sex workers and others most vulnerable to HIV would fail if they did not see these persons as autonomous non-victimized agents in the fight against AIDS and extend to them the human rights protections they would need to exercise that autonomy (ibid).

Mann built GPA quickly, drawing considerable financial support from UN member states (Fee and Parry 2008). Under his leadership,

GPA distinguished itself both through its focus on human rights and by being one of the first WHO programmes to have meaningful partnerships with civil society organizations (ibid.). Mann hired Priscilla Alexander, a sex workers' rights activist from the United States, as a consultant to GPA on matters related to sex work (Booth 1998, 132). In 1989, he convened a "Consultation on HIV epidemiology and prostitution," the first UN meeting on HIV and sex work, of which the objectives were "to evaluate the potential role of prostitution in HIV transmission and to identify interventions targeted towards prevention of HIV infection among prostitutes and their clients" (Global Programme on AIDS 1989). The consultation included a number of active and former sex workers and sex workers' rights activists (Booth 1998, 127).

Setting an important precedent, the "consensus statement" that emerged from this consultation cited "social stigmatization, legal restrictions and coercive actions against prostitutes, leading to difficulty in engaging their involvement" in responding to HIV (Global Programme on AIDS 1989a, 2). The statement further noted the "lack of political and financial support" for HIV programmes for sex workers and the fact that what programmes there were focused too much on sex workers without also targeting clients. It recommended that programmes "aimed at changing HIV-related risk-taking practices associated with prostitution must urgently be promoted among all prostitutes and their clients" and underscored that such programmes "should be designed in consultation with sex workers...and not impeded by legal structures". It did not speak of decriminalization of sex workers, but for a first statement set out a clear vision of human rights challenges and the rights-based principle of meaningful participation of sex workers in programmes concerning them.

With respect to victimhood, in fact, it appears that sex workers may have fared somewhat better than "good women" of Africa, who seemed to appear in GPA documents as pawns of misogyny, economic disempowerment and social subordination. In the same year as the consultation on sex work, a consultation on "mothers and children" and HIV/AIDS focused, firstly, on women as mothers with a pronounced concern for HIV transmission to children and, secondly, on having to bear children as a part of women's subordination (Global Programme on AIDS 1989b). As Booth notes, the UN's efforts on women and AIDS in the early years were governed by a "mother/whore dichotomy" where Third World women as mothers were constrained by tradition and victimized by ignorance (Booth 1998, 126).

According to Booth (1998), who interviewed principal players in GPA, including Priscilla Alexander, the prostitution consultation's promising start on a rights-based approach to HIV and sex work was soon thwarted for two main reasons.

Firstly, Jonathan Mann resigned in 1990 following a series of conflicts with the director general of WHO, Hayashi Nakajima, who had been appointed in 1988. Whether because of GPA's growth and strength within WHO or because of his conviction, publicly stated, that AIDS was not as important as many other problems on WHO's agenda, Nakajima tried to limit the scope of Mann's activities (Fee and Parry 2008). The loss of Mann's leadership at a crucial time in GPA's mobilization of the global AIDS response was a blow to the emerging human rights-centred paradigm and to the meaningful involvement of sex workers in global AIDS policy-making. Mann's successor dismissed Priscilla Alexander, not seeing eye-to-eye with her views (Booth 1998, 133). (Jonathan Mann's untimely death in a plane crash in 1998 was the permanent loss of an important human rights voice.)

Secondly, there was a division among GPA staff about how to approach HIV and sex work. Booth characterizes this conflict as between (1) career "internationalist" bureaucrats who felt that UN entities had to respect state sovereignty and were therefore relatively constrained in addressing HIV and sex work, and (2) those with a "globalist" perspective who saw GPA's role as challenging national governments to remove legal, social and political barriers to addressing HIV among sex workers (ibid., 132-33). The latter group thought GPA should use its growing clout to advocate for decriminalization of sex work and should push donors to fund programmes that would enable sex workers to organize to fight HIV. In the end, the group designated to formulate gender-related actions for GPA could not overcome these differences and were "unable to translate their shared commitment to gender equality into a single set of policy recommendations that WHO could accept" (ibid., 133).

Sex workers Organize against HIV

Sex workers' organizations, fortunately, did not wait for guidance from GPA to respond to both AIDS and the marginalization of sex work in society. Independent of the emergence of AIDS, sex workers' organizations in some parts of the world organized in the 1980s to assert their human rights. Some of these organizations later extended their activities to address AIDS, and other groups were created with a particular focus on the epidemic (Alexander 1994). By the time of the Second World Whores' Congress in Brussels in 1986, there were already many experiences to share of sex worker-led efforts to fight AIDS (ibid.). These ranged from the work of more established organizations such as COYOTE in San Francisco, which received state money to develop HIV peer education and condom promotion, to the creation of sex worker organizations with varying degrees of success in Africa, Latin America and across Asia (ibid.). In some places, AIDS seemed to galvanize sex workers' rights efforts that were floundering, including by enabling organizations to find funds to attend regional or global meetings. Kempadoo (2003, 147) judges that

> Under-funded sex worker organizations in both the First and Third Worlds who would have been hard-pressed to persuade their funders of the necessity of sending a representative to a "whores' conference" found it easier to get money when public health was, supposedly, at stake (ibid.).

Alexander's assessment from the mid-1990s was similar. While sex worker-driven movements for human rights and workers' rights in many cases did not originate with HIV-related funding or in response to HIV, the epidemic plainly in many ways intensified threats to sex workers' rights but also created some opportunities: "AIDS and the money that has been available for projects for prostitutes have created an opportunity for change" (Alexander 1994, 115).

Some sex worker collectives in South Asia, particularly the Durbar Mahila Samanwaya Committee (DMSC) with its well-documented efforts in the Sonagachi neighbourhood of Kolkata, came to be regarded as effective in their responses to HIV (Jana et al. 2004; Ghose et al. 2008). Founded in 1992, at first around an STD clinic for sex workers, DMSC evolved into a community-based vehicle that enabled sex workers to define and implement condom use in their own interests rather than in the economic interests of the brothel, encouraged them to develop a worker rights framework for their various service activities, and reframed "the problem of HIV from an issue of individual motivation, will or behavioural commitment to a problem of community disenfranchisement" (Jana et al. 2004, 407). This experience was highlighted several times as a "best practice" by UNAIDS—the Joint Programme on HIV/AIDS of the United Nations, GPA's successor—which noted its "integral involvement of sex workers" as the key to its achieving nearly universal condom use among clients and many other successes (Jenkins 2000, 11; UNAIDS 2002, 15).

UNAIDS and Vulnerable Populations

UNAIDS was a different animal from its GPA ancestor. Created by the UN in 1996, it is a multi-agency effort—now comprising ten UN agencies—of which the structure is meant to reflect explicitly that HIV/AIDS is not merely a health problem but a social, economic, gender-related, narcotic drug-related, multisectoral issue. Among other things, UNAIDS issued—and continues to issue but at a slower pace—"best practice" monographs meant to suggest promising interventions and strategies to countries shaping their HIV priorities. Few UNAIDS "best practice" publications have focused on sex work, but most of those that did seemed to reflect espousal of programmes designed to empower sex workers and enable them to direct activities meant for them. In addition to highlighting DMSC, "best practice" monographs also showcased, for example, peer-driven outreach, condom and lubricant provision, and STD service referral among sex workers in Papua New Guinea who were assisted by an established sex worker rights NGO in Australia (Jenkins 2000). The SHAKTI project in Bangladesh was also featured, including both the empowering role of training previously marginalized sex workers as peer educators and the collaboration of sex worker and human rights organizations in response to the murder of a sex worker that eventually led to a ground-breaking court case in favour of sex worker rights (ibid.).

While highlighting these projects, UNAIDS nonetheless seemed to have an analysis of sex work that was separate from its many pronouncements on gender and gender-related rights and was somewhat ambiguous on human rights issues. Statements on gender and HIV and the vulnerability of women barely recognized sex workers (see, e.g., Whelan 1999). A 2002 "technical update" in the "best practice" series on HIV and sex work highlighted the importance of "active involvement of sex workers themselves in all phases of project development, implementation and evaluation" (UNAIDS 2002, 3) but included uncritical espousal of top-down 100 per cent condom use programmes (see below) and was weak on the matter of repressive applications of criminal law. For example, the "update" noted that "a policy framework must establish its legal stance on sex work, be it decriminalization, regulation or prohibition" (ibid., 15), hardly a coherent acknowledgment of the ways in which criminalization and harsh policing undermine HIV programmes and sex worker rights. The "technical update" also included a great deal of unreferenced information on why women enter sex work, including that "many formal sex workers become involved while still children or young adolescents" and that sex trafficking is "increasingly" important as a means of recruitment to sex work (ibid., 4).

In fact, the 2002 "technical update" was something of a backing away from one of the most important United Nations statements on HIV and sex work, the International Guidelines on HIV/AIDS and Human Rights, first issued in 1998 and revised in 2002 (Office of the High Commissioner for Human Rights and UNAIDS 2006). The International Guidelines resulted from deliberations of two expert panels convened by UNAIDS and the Office of the UN High

Commissioner for Human Rights, rather than from member-state deliberations, making them recommendations but not official UN policy. In contrast to the ambiguity of some previous statements, the International Guidelines state:

> With regard to adult sex work that involves no victimization, criminal law should be reviewed with the aim of decriminalizing, then legally regulating occupational health and safety conditions to protect sex workers and their clients, including support for safe sex during sex work. Criminal law should not impede provision of HIV prevention and care services to sex workers and their clients (ibid., para 21c).

In other words, the International Guidelines recognize that:

1. there is sex work without victimization;
2. criminal laws are a central element of risk and vulnerability for sex workers; and
3. occupational health and safety is a useful framework for a human rights-based approach to HIV among sex workers.

All three of these elements were to be continuing points of contention in global policy discussions on HIV and sex work. While the International Guidelines were instigated and "welcomed" by the Commission on Human Rights of the UN (1997), they were never endorsed by the UN General Assembly. At the first UN General Assembly Special Session (UNGASS) on HIV/AIDS in 2001, some member states pushed unsuccessfully for endorsement of the International Guidelines in the formal declaration from the session. The International Guidelines' explicitness about the human rights problems of sex workers was part of this refusal; the United States and other member states were opposed to naming sex workers, people who use illicit drugs and other "vulnerable groups" explicitly in the declaration, and in the end they were not named (Girard 2001; Gruskin 2002).

The US and Prostitution as Victimization

Positions taken by the United States and its allies at the UNGASS in 2001, early in the administration of George W. Bush, were harbingers of things to come as the US under Bush became an important presence in international policy-making and resource allocation for HIV. Not previously known for any particular commitment to international health issues, Bush was influenced at least in part by his evangelical Christian supporters to pay attention to HIV, particularly to the high AIDS mortality in sub-Saharan Africa that persisted even as AIDS deaths were dropping thanks to antiretroviral treatment in the wealthy world (Stolberg 2008). To the surprise of many in the AIDS world, Bush announced in 2003 a major initiative on HIV with a particular focus on Africa that came to be known at the President's Emergency Plan for AIDS Relief (PEPFAR). In near record time, the US Congress cemented the programme in law in June 2003, allocating US$15 billion for the first five years, a significant sum by standards of US official support for health programmes (Kaiser Family Foundation 2010).

PEPFAR turned out to have particular significance for sex workers and global sex work policy with regard to HIV. The 2003 law authorizing the programme underscored that "the US government is opposed to prostitution and related activities, which are inherently harmful and dehumanizing, and contribute to the phenomenon of trafficking in persons" (USDAID 2005). The assertion noted above of the UN International Guidelines on HIV/AIDS and Human Rights that not all sex work is victimization was clearly lost on US policy-makers. The direct consequence of the law was succinctly stated: "No [PEPFAR] funds…may be used to provide assistance to any group or organization that does not have a policy explicitly opposing prostitution and sex trafficking" (ibid.). The law also stated that no US federal funds "may be used to promote or advocate the legalization or practice of prostitution or sex trafficking" (ibid.).

With overtones of the "loyalty oath" that characterized US anti-communism campaigns in the 1950s, organizations wishing to be supported in their work by PEPFAR were required to attest in writing that they did not violate the provisions of the 2003 law. The "anti-prostitution pledge," at first thought to be required only of non-US-based organizations, was later clearly mandated for all PEPFAR recipients, whether US-based or not (CHANGE 2008). Based on interviews with civil society representatives in Asia, the

Center for Health and Gender Equity (CHANGE) concluded that the HIV services of NGOs working with sex workers have been seriously undermined by this provision, whether they previously received US funds or not (ibid.). Some lost resources and support from US-funded organizations that signed the pledge; some curtailed services, such as drop-in centres for sex workers, because they were unsure whether those services would be interpreted as promoting sex work. This included organizations that had been cited as UNAIDS "best practice" examples. One of CHANGE's informants said that that there was similarly confusion about whether programmes to address violence against sex workers by training the police would be allowed because they could be interpreted to be promoting legalization of sex work. In the wake of the law, organizations feared attending rallies for sex workers' rights. Indeed, CHANGE concluded that the fear among NGOs of how the broad wording of the PEPFAR legislation would be interpreted had a chilling effect on activities that may have been as great as the actual withdrawal of funds occasioned by the prostitution provisions.

The PEPFAR provisions on prostitution were not original to HIV policy-making. The US' Trafficking Victims Protection Act (TVPA) of 2000 (Public Law 106-386, 28 Oct. 2000) had similar restrictions as U.S. authorities noted that organizations espousing "prostitution as an employment choice… are not appropriate partners for USDAID anti-trafficking grants or contracts" (USDAID 2003, 4; see also Saunders 2004). The statement from the PEPFAR law that prostitution is "inherently harmful and dehumanizing" and contributes to trafficking reflects the Bush administration's strong adherence to the "rescue" of sex workers and trafficked women—two populations between which little distinction was made (Weitzer 2010). The Bush administration backed up its prohibitionist stance with large grants to organizations such as the Coalition Against Trafficking in Women (CATW)—which declares that "All prostitution exploits women, regardless of women's consent" (see http://www.catwinternational.org)—and to prohibitionist researchers such as Donna Hughes and Melissa Farley (ibid.; Soderlund 2005). As Weitzer (ibid.26) notes, the US Government Accountability Office—a Congress-based watchdog agency—questioned the credentials of some of the recipients of anti-trafficking money, but the money continued to flow.

Though the anti-trafficking work was administratively separate from HIV efforts, Bush administration officials sometimes linked the two. John Miller, the administration's chief of anti-trafficking work in the State Department, said, for example, that "well-intentioned people seeking to limit the spread of AIDS in at-risk populations, especially in the commercial sex industry, often ignore a larger challenge: helping to free the slaves of that industry" (cited in Soderlund 2005, 80).

On the contrary, it is clear that the connection to HIV ensured that anti-trafficking efforts undermined HIV services for sex workers. Many organizations of sex workers that had been conducting effective work in HIV prevention and care were targeted for "raid and rescue" operations that effectively halted their work (CHANGE 2008). The well-established Thai sex workers' organization, Empower, underwent "rescues" in the name of anti-trafficking that disrupted its HIV work; after one particularly damaging rescue, most of the women who had been forcibly displaced escaped the "rescue" centre to return to their work (Soderlund 2005, 68, 80). Sampada Gramin Mahila Sanstha (SANGRAM), an organization in Sangli, India, whose HIV prevention work among sex workers was internationally recognized, refused to sign the anti-prostitution pledge and lost US funding (CHANGE 2008). In 2005, the US-funded Christian organization International Justice Mission (IJM) instigated a violent raid by 200 police officers of brothels benefiting from SANGRAM's services, allegedly to rescue trafficked children. In spite of IJM's not having found any trafficked children in this raid after violating the rights of women in these brothels, IJM undertook a campaign to accuse SANGRAM of sex trafficking. SANGRAM had, on the contrary, enjoyed some success in its anti-trafficking activities. But the heft of big funding and big press operations enabled IJM and organizations like it to sully the reputation and undermine the effective HIV work of SANGRAM and other organizations (Magar, 2008). Thus, in addition to sending the message that sex workers are not worthy of life-saving HIV services, the US policy directly undermined sex worker organizations by denying funding and supporting unjustified and harmful "raids" on them.

UNAIDS under Political Pressure

Where was UNAIDS, with its commitment to rights-based approaches, as these developments unfolded? Throughout most of the Bush administration UNAIDS, led by Peter Piot, was apparently not keen to challenge the US, an important donor, on this matter. Among all of UNAIDS' press statements and statements by Piot available on the UNAIDS website with dates after the 2001 UNGASS and until the end of the Bush administration, there are none that criticize or raise questions about the US anti-prostitution policy. Instead, there are numerous statements highlighting the risks faced by married women in Africa and Asia, some of which also refer to the danger that poverty will drive women and girls to engage in "transactional sex" (e.g. UNAIDS 2004a, 2004b, 2005a). At least one release featured the story of a woman who "turned to sex work" for survival but was helped to get training so she could abandon sex work (UNAIDS 2004c).

The 2004 launch of the Global Coalition on Women and AIDS, which was meant to intensify UNAIDS' work on women's vulnerability to HIV, emphasized the image of the faithful married woman made helpless by subordination and those "resorting to sex for economic survival," but did not mention sex work (UNAIDS 2004d). Several releases praised "faith-based organizations," including organizations seeking to abolish sex work, for their HIV work (e.g. UNAIDS 2005b, 2007). In addition, UNAIDS officials praised the HIV/AIDS national responses of countries with very repressive approaches to sex work, such as Vietnam, where sex workers were interned in "rehabilitation" centres where they underwent forced labour and other human rights abuses (UNAIDS 2004e; ref on VN). In short, in UNAIDS' most public statements during the Bush years, there was both a failure to recognize sex work as a legitimate livelihood option and a failure to endorse or call for the kinds of empowering sex worker-led efforts that had been featured in "best practice" monographs.

Siddharth Dube, who was a senior staff member in Piot's executive office at UNAIDS from 2005 to 2007, characterizes the UNAIDS Secretariat after 2002 as gripped by a "pall of self-censorship" on sex workers' rights following the "best practice" and other rights-oriented publications and statements of the early years (Dube forthcoming, 13). Along with its legislation on PEPFAR, the US enjoined its agencies and grantees to avoid the term "sex worker" because it legitimized prostitution as work. In some of his writing and speaking at UNAIDS, Peter Piot eschewed the term "sex worker" in favour of "prostitute," according to Dube (ibid., 17), even though the UN had long since accepted "sex worker" as the preferred term. It is hard to escape the conclusion that UNAIDS' leadership was pandering to the US at a time when high-level support for the rights of sex workers could have made a crucial difference in their ability to ensure HIV prevention and care services for themselves.

In the absence of meaningful reference to empowering and rights-centred approaches to HIV and sex work, references by UNAIDS to sex work have been dominated over the years by mentioning sex workers together with other "vulnerable populations"—namely (for the most part) people who use illicit drugs, men who have sex with men, and sometimes prisoners and migrant workers. Another term used by the UN for some time for this list of unfortunate groups was the clunky "MARPs" or "most at-risk persons" (Seale 2009). This pattern is exemplified by UNAIDS' major policy paper on HIV prevention from 2005, in which sex workers figure on a list together with what were by then called "key affected groups and populations" (UNAIDS 2005c, 28). These terms tended to identify sex workers (and others) by their vulnerability rather than by terms that highlighted their agency and well-documented ability to manage HIV services for and by themselves.

Some of the UNAIDS co-sponsor agencies on their own should have been forces for advocacy against the US policy and for empowering approaches to HIV and sex work. For example, that the World Bank's landmark 1997 publication "Confronting AIDS: Public Priorities in a Global Epidemic" raised concerns about abolitionist approaches to sex work, suggesting that zealous zero-tolerance actions could undermine provision of HIV services (World Bank 1997). A decade later, however, the World Bank too backed away from criticisms of the abolitionism that was by then the centerpiece of US policy, as well as from its previous reflections on the importance of decriminalization of sex work as part of HIV responses (Dube forthcoming). UNAIDS co-sponsor UNICEF, the United Nations children's agency, has been an active player in anti-trafficking measures in Southeast Asia (UNICEF 2006). The Asia Pacific Network of Sex Workers has criticized UNICEF for supporting anti-trafficking legislation in Cambodia that resulted in violent raids and arbitrary detention and abuse of sex workers (Overs 2009). During the Bush years, it was difficult to find in UNAIDS and its co-sponsor agencies any clear—let alone courageous—support for the human rights of sex workers in the response to HIV.

100 % Condom Use Programmes

An important development related to national and global responses to HIV and sex work has been the expansion of so-called "100 % condom use programmes" (100% CUP), particularly in Asia. First implemented on a large scale in Thailand, 100% CUP as its name implies was an effort to ensure universal condom use in sex transactions in brothels and entertainment venues. The programme was a response to the phenomenon of clients who, if refused sex without condoms, would just go shopping until they found an establishment where sex without condoms was on offer. Under 100% CUP, brothel and nightclub managers, local authorities, police, public health officers, sex workers and clients were all engaged to ensure that all sexual transactions would be offered with condoms so that no one would be free to go off and create a market for condom-less sex (UNAIDS and Thailand Ministry of Public Health 2000). These programmes are now a central part of national AIDS responses in Thailand, Cambodia, China, Vietnam, Mongolia, Laos and Burma, and are supported in many cases by the Global Fund to Fight AIDS, Tuberculosis and Malaria (Rajanapithayakorn 2006).

Existing evaluations indicate that 100% CUPs so far have been implemented largely in a top-down manner (ibid.). This is unsurprising as these programmes essentially consist of making sex without condoms illegal. Enforcing condom use and informing and overseeing all the players involved in establishment-based sex work require no small amount of central coordination by local officials. 100% CUP have so far have also come with built-in requirements for sex workers, including in most cases obligatory medical check-ups, including HIV and STD testing, as well as frequent police inspections of sex-work venues (UNAIDS and Thailand Ministry of Public Health 2000).

Many evaluations suggest these programmes are indeed effective in reducing unsafe sex in commercial sex establishments (ibid.; Zhongdan et al. 2008), though one study found that HIV risk among sex workers post-100% CUPs was still high, partly due to low levels of condom use with non-paying sex partners (Kilmarx et al. 1999). Though these programmes are meant to protect sex workers and their clients, they have generally been designed and implemented without meaningful participation of sex workers (Rajanapithayakorn 2006), and sex workers' experiences have often not figured in evaluations of 100% CUPs (Loff et al. 2003). An exception is an evaluation in Cambodia commissioned by the US-based Policy Project (David Lowe Cons. 2002). This evaluation, which included interviews with 150 sex workers, found that 100% CUPs resulted in forced registration of sex workers with the police and mandatory STI testing and health examinations at health facilities where sex workers were mistreated.

The Network of Sex Work Projects (NSWP) also has highlighted human rights abuses that occur in 100% CUPs, including repressive policing, force-marching sex workers to health facilities with military or police escorts, and publicly posting photographs of sex workers who are accused of having had sex without condoms (Loff et al. 2003). The Asia Pacific Network of Sex Workers has consistently raised concerns about 100% CUPs that include "authoritarian punishment-based HIV prevention and mandatory testing" (Asia Pacific Network 2007). As NSWP and its allies have noted elsewhere:

> Coercive efforts to control or reduce sex work rarely produce good results and have even been associated with abuse of sex workers and their families. Mandatory medical treatment or procedures, raids, forced rehabilitation or programs implemented by police or based upon detention of sex workers are all examples of coercive programming (Global Working Group 2007:7).

It is striking that WHO's regional office for the Western Pacific, the region with most of the countries that have adopted 100% CUPs, has generally praised these programmes with very little questioning of their impact on the rights of sex workers. In discussing sex worker "empowerment" and 100% CUPs, WHO notes that 100% CUPs are "helping sex workers by placing the primary responsibility for condom use in an establishment on the owners and managers" (WHO Western Pacific Regional Office, 37)—a curious notion of sex worker empowerment. UNAIDS, which not only continually professes its commitment to the human rights of "key populations" but also invested in showcasing very different programmes such as the one of DMSC as "best practices," has also not raised its organizational voice to suggest that there may be another way of reaching high levels of condom use. It is a remarkable and well documented result of DMSC's work—and that of many other such networks—that through their solidarity and empowerment and without the assistance of the police and local officials or mandatory HIV tests, they achieved virtually 100% condom use (Jana et al. 2004). It is unfortunate that UNAIDS and its cosponsor agencies have not taken up the cause of human rights abuses in 100% CUPs approaches, including HIV testing without consent, which should always be a concern for UNAIDS.

UNAIDS: Guiding the World on HIV and Sex Work?

UNAIDS, however, did decide in 2006 that it was time to draw up guidelines for members states on how to manage the challenge of HIV among sex workers. To inform this process, it organized a global "technical consultation" on HIV and sex work in Rio de

Janeiro in July 2006. Sex work organizations from around the world were represented, as were a number of abolitionist groups. Nonetheless, sex workers' rights proponents emerged from the consultation feeling that there had been broad agreement on sex workers' rights as a framework for action and that the abolitionist views were in the minority (R. Morgan Thomas, personal communication).

In April 2007, UNAIDS released a "Guidance Note on HIV and Sex Work" in time for consideration by its governing body, the Programme Coordination Board (PCB), in June 2007. Sex workers' organizations and human rights groups were taken aback by the tone and content, which was, to put it mildly, light on the rights of sex workers as human beings and as workers. Several critiques of the Guidance Note were quickly published and disseminated, including one by this author representing the view of the Canadian HIV/AIDS Legal Network (Csete 2007); by the UNAIDS Reference Group on HIV and Human Rights (2007), a body of independent experts meant to advise UNAIDS and its cosponsors on matters of human rights importance in the global AIDS response; and by the Global Working Group on Sex Work and HIV Policy, an ad hoc group of sex workers' organizations and allies formed in response to the Guidance Note process (of which I am a member), which presented its comments in the form of a reworded draft Guidance Note (Global Working Group 2007). These commentaries had certain critiques in common, which are summarized below:

1. Impact of criminalization: The Guidance Note was virtually silent on the challenge posed to both health and human rights of sex workers by criminalization of sex work and repressive policing, even though there was by 2007 a large peer-reviewed literature on this subject and the risks for HIV programmes from harsh criminalization of sex work had been well highlighted in UNAIDS "best practice" documents. The Guidance Note missed the opportunity to show, for example, the human rights gains for sex workers associated with decriminalization of sex work in New Zealand, which

were being documented by 2007 by the New Zealand government (see summary of early results in Prostitution Law Review Committee 2008).

2. Focus on exiting: The Guidance Note strongly emphasized the importance of alternative livelihood programmes and microcredit programmes to help sex workers abandon prostitution without citing evidence as to the effectiveness of these programmes or their desirability among sex workers. Indeed, critics of the Guidance Note pointed out that there is very little empirical evidence of the "success" of any such programmes. The Guidance Note failed to state that skills training and education programmes for sex workers should not be conditioned on a commitment to leave sex work, should be designed and implemented with meaningful participation of sex workers, and should have strong safeguards against coercion of any kind. The focus on exiting in the document seemed to be a major concession to abolitionist perspectives that had not previously figured in UNAIDS documents.

3. Demand reduction: The Guidance Note portrayed reduction of men's demand for sex work, and of the number of partners sex workers have, to be a crucial structural element of "reducing vulnerability" of women in sex work. It did not elaborate on how these goals could be achieved and, again, whether there is any empirical track record whatsoever on reducing demand for sex work other than through repressive means. As the Global Working Group particularly emphasized in its later advocacy, UNAIDS' concern should be the reduction in demand for unsafe sex, not in the demand for paid sex, which is not in its remit.

4. "Rescue" mentality: The Guidance Note's focus on alternative livelihoods for sex workers and reduction of demand for paid sex fed into a "rescue" mentality that the document did not in any way repudiate. The document failed to recognize the ways in which "rescues" in the name of anti-trafficking had compromised HIV services for and human rights of sex workers (as well as trafficked women).

5. Blurring the trafficking/sex work distinction: Again seeming to cave in to abolitionist views, the Guidance Note did not make a clear distinction between sex trafficking and sex work and indeed blurred the line between the two by seeming at points to suggest that all sex workers are victims. It would have been helpful for the Guidance Note to recognize that sex workers' rights organizations were active and effective anti-trafficking agents themselves.

6. 100% CUP: Without naming "100 per cent CUP" as such, the Guidance Note uncritically endorsed approaches that engage "police, brothel owners and managers of sex industry operations, local health authorities and sex workers and clients in introducing codes of practice in sex work settings including condom use" (UNAIDS 2007, 8). It included no cautions about building in human rights protections to such approaches.

7. Women only: The Guidance Note treated sex work as though the only persons in the sex industry were women without recognition of male and transgender sex workers.

Mostly, as particularly noted by the UNAIDS Reference Group on Human Rights, the Guidance Note did not emphasize to its member state audience the urgency of investing in and removing barriers to the scaling up of comprehensive, rights-based, non-stigmatizing HIV services, including treatment, which should have been the central organizing idea of the document. Instead, that message was lost in the distracting agenda of encouraging exiting and demand reduction.

Thanks to critiques such as those of the Canadian HIV/AIDS Legal Network (which was endorsed by 40 organizations) and the Reference Group on Human Rights, as well as prompt advocacy by sex workers' groups and NGO representatives to the UNAIDS PCB, the PCB decided to send the document back to UNAIDS for further work and urged consultation with sex workers' groups (A. Hunter, personal communication). The Global Working Group on Sex Work and HIV Policy convened a consultation in New Delhi in September 2007 to suggest a rewording of the

Guidance Note and invited UN staff, who declined to attend (R. Morgan Thomas, personal communication). It conveyed the result of this work to Peter Piot in a letter and requested a meeting with him. Piot's response some weeks later did not acknowledge the meeting request or shed light on any process of revision of the 2007 Guidance Note.

Whatever revision may have been taking place seemed not to be happening with the civil society consultation requested by the PCB. The Global Working Group wrote to Piot again in February 2008 on this subject, and throughout 2008 many other NGOs and NGO coalitions requested information from UNAIDS on the revision process, but none was forthcoming (Global Working Group 2009). Piot was replaced in December 2008 by Michel Sidibe, who had previously been the UNAIDS Director for Country and Regional Support. In February 2009, UNAIDS released a revised version of the Guidance Note, on which no comment was invited. While some elements of the above critique were addressed, most of them remained problematic in the revised version.

Having largely failed to get Peter Piot to engage with its concerns, the Global Working Group pressed the new UNAIDS executive director for an in-person meeting, which was granted in March 2009 (at which this author was present). Following fairly intense discussions at that meeting, UNAIDS agreed to convene and pay for an Advisory Group on HIV and Sex Work that would, in a departure from other UN structures, be co-chaired by a UN staff member and a representative of a sex worker organization; in this case, the Network of Sex Work Projects was recognized as a global coordinating group to organize the choice of sex worker representatives. Sidibe allowed that there were weaknesses in the final version of the Guidance Note but said that the document could not be revised. He agreed, however, that explanatory annexes to the Guidance Note could be developed and that the formal launch and printing of the Guidance Note could await the development of such annexes.

The membership of the UNAIDS Advisory Group on HIV and Sex Work was established as comprising eight members of UNAIDS and cosponsor agency staff, eight representatives of sex workers' organizations and five independent experts (of which this author is one). At this writing, the group is engaged in the process of developing annexes on four topics: (1) the impact of repressive criminalization of sex work on HIV services for sex workers; (2) the importance of reduction of demand for unsafe sex rather than demand for paid sex; (3) the importance of distinguishing between sex work and sex trafficking; and (4) a critical analysis of "alternative livelihood" activities and recommendations, as opposed to rights-based economic empowerment of sex workers.

Other Developments

With the end of the Bush years in Washington, it was hoped by many that the conditions attached legislatively to PEPFAR might be modified. The PEPFAR reauthorization of 2008, however, happened before the US presidential election and re-established for another five years essentially the same conditions as in the 2003 law, including the anti-prostitution pledge. This re-cementing of the pledge requirement is in spite of two US federal court rulings that the anti-prostitution requirement violated the US Constitution's free speech provision (Brennan Center 2008). In 2009, one of the NGO plaintiffs in these cases petitioned the Obama administration to release a US Department of Justice memo that would shed light on the government's continuing implementation of this requirement, but the request was refused (Abel 2009). At this writing, it is not clear to what degree the Obama administration will be influenced by the court decisions in enforcing—or not—the provision, or whether the government will further appeal the case in the federal courts. It does seem clear, however, that there are few champions in the US Congress who would have the political stomach to initiate a fight to amend the law on this subject.

While UNAIDS in the Bush years backed away from rigorous advocacy for the human rights of sex workers, the Commission on AIDS in Asia showed that this subject can be approached otherwise. The Commission was an independent body of distinguished experts from across Asia that was established in 2006 at the request of UNAIDS, but was not a UN body (Commission on AIDS in Asia 2008). The Commission (ibid.) dealt in a straightforward and evidence-based way with HIV and sex work, raising a number of concerns that were notably absent from the UNAIDS Guidance Note, including:

- A clear recommendation for action in favour of removal of punitive laws and repressive policing as a central element of the HIV response in Asia (e.g. pp 3, 5);
- A recognition that 100 per cent condom programmes were important, but to be sustainable and effective need to incorporate human rights protections for sex workers and to feature meaningful involvement of sex workers in their design, implementation and evaluation (pp 157-58); and
- A clear call for "donors" (i.e. the US) to "remove conditionality or policies that prevent their partners from supporting organizations that work with sex workers' organizations" (p 187).

The Commission's focus on removal of punitive laws and policing of sex work was not lost on its audience. UN Secretary-General Ban Ki-moon, in receiving the Commission's report, emphasized that "we need to review legislation that risks hampering universal access [to HIV services]—in cases where vulnerable groups are criminalized" (Ban 2008). Sex workers' organizations represented at the UN General Assembly Special Session on HIV/AIDS in June 2008, shortly after the release of the Commission's report, displayed a banner citing this quotation from the Secretary-General and thanked him for supporting their rights (Ditmore 2008).

The Commission on AIDS in Asia and the reaction to it may have inspired UNAIDS to do better. In the UNAIDS plan of action for 2009-2011, formulated under the leadership of the new executive director, removing "punitive laws and policies" that impede HIV responses is one of the ten priorities for action (UNAIDS 2009, 8).

The degree to which this priority will result in courageous global leadership remains to be seen.

An area in which leadership is sorely needed, particularly in light of the US anti-prostitution policy, is funding for activities contributing to the health and human rights of sex workers, especially sex worker-led activities. What may be the largest sex worker-oriented HIV intervention in the world, the US\$338 million Avahan programme in India, funded by the Gates Foundation, does not have empowerment of sex workers or protection and promotion of the human rights of sex workers among its objectives in any discernible sense (Flock 2009). Collectivisation is a model that emerged out of organizing sex workers towards self-determination for their rights and claiming a voice in all the programmes that affect them. Such collectives were able to prove that they could enforce consistent condom use among their clients and increase treatment-seeking behaviour among the sex workers. Unfortunately, this successful model failed when transformed into a scaled-up programme where the collective model became "Community Based Organisations". These CBOs are not organically formed but are structures imposed on the community to respond to the need of international and national NGOs as performance indicators. While some international donors such as The Bill and Melinda Gates Foundation do promote collectivisation, their model is instrumental, using collectives of sex workers to achieve certain targets, usually medically oriented. Such programmes encourage sex workers to access health care and services with a narrow focus of "containing" the epidemic. Funding for HIV/AIDS programmes encourages the organizing of sex workers to influence their decision-making on limited public health goals, but frowns on self-determination and their struggle for the recognition of sex work as "work".[1]

100% condom use programmes, not known for strong human rights grounding, also attract large-scale funding in some countries, as noted above, including through large grants from the Global Fund to Fight AIDS, Tuberculosis and Malaria (Rajanapithayakorn 2006).

In November 2009, the New York-based Open Society Institute and the Amsterdam-based foundation Mama Cash convened a meeting of private donors with an interest in supporting sex workers' rights efforts. A background paper prepared for this meeting, informed by interviews with sex workers' organizations and private foundations, concluded that HIV-related funds are "the primary if not the sole source of funding" for many grassroots sex workers' organizations (Greenall 2009, 12). But, according to many of the sex workers' organization representatives consulted, this means that there is very little core organizational funding and very little funding for policy and legal advocacy, legal services, violence prevention and other essential activities (ibid.). Donors reported their own challenges in convincing their boards or other governance bodies of the urgency of sex workers' rights programmes, along with geographical restrictions that may confine them to places where strong sex workers' organizations do not exist (ibid., 23, 25-6).

It is impossible to know exactly to what degree HIV-related funding has benefited sex workers' organizations and whether that benefit significantly offsets the costs to sex workers in "rescue" operations that have been intensified by concerns about HIV or the rights violations that may be associated with well-funded 100% condom-use programmes. The foundations involved in the November 2009 consultation expressed the hope that working together would help them sensitize private donors in the women's rights and labour rights fields as well as bilateral donors into greater support for sex workers' rights (Mama Cash and Open Society Institute 2009).

Conclusions

At the very time that HIV was becoming prominent on the global agenda, concern in some policy circles about human trafficking was shaping strongly entrenched views on the rights of sex workers. As described by Doezema (2005), Weitzer (2010), Outshoorn (2005), Saunders (2004) and others, these views were largely shaped by whether one accepted the view that all sex work is oppression and victimization—most often victimization of women and girls by men—which a centerpiece of abolitionist thought and some versions of feminism. Those accepting this position have pushed hard for eradication of prostitution, often equating it with human trafficking. Counterposed to this position is the view represented by many sex workers' and human rights organizations—that people have the right to sexual and professional self-determination, to work in the sex industry, and to have safe working conditions over which they exercise some control (Outshoorn 2005, 145).

Despite the absence of a large amount of data, Jonathan Mann, the UN's first chief global AIDS policy-maker, understood the latter position in favour of sex workers' rights to be consistent with public health goals, including ensuring access to HIV services for sex workers in respectful and participatory ways. He understood that further repression, criminalization, and stigmatization of people in the sex industry would be counter-productive to HIV service provision. Over time, with the accumulated experience of many sex workers' organizations, in several cases written up and highlighted in UN publications, UN and national policy-makers concerned about HIV/AIDS had strong evidence before them to confirm Mann's instinctive view. While they showcased experiences of sex worker empowerment and paid them lip service, especially before George W. Bush was in the White House, there was a leadership vacuum in the UN on sex workers' rights after Mann's departure and into the Bush years. This leadership void resulted eventually in official guidance on HIV and sex work that had a weak human rights basis, uncritically endorsed programmes that are disempowering to sex workers, and played into the hands of abolitionists. In short, UNAIDS and its co-sponsor agencies missed a chance to weigh in clearly on the side of the human rights of sex workers and thus to provide leadership in a debate of major importance to both public health and human rights. As Saunders (2004, 188) notes:

> In the early days of the epidemic, AIDS activists steadfastly refused to buy into older concepts of victimhood and danger inherent in health discourse, challenging images of infected persons as either objects of

pity...or fear....[A]s US-based organizations increasingly use notions
of the AIDS epidemic as a "security threat" or as a plague on innocent
victims, progressive and effective elements in HIV/AIDS programming
in regards to gender-sexuality and rights are imperilled.

United Nations entities, all founded on human rights principles,
allowed the US to set the parametres of policy-making on HIV and
sex work, and only concerted and courageous advocacy by sex
workers' rights organizations and their allies have begun to turn
this trend around.

Though sex workers have been largely absent from the UN's
efforts on women and HIV, there are parallels to the UN's leadership
failure on sex work and its disappointing results on women and
AIDS. Decades of evidence on the categories of subordination and
"victimization" that contribute to HIV risk and are barriers to HIV
services for women—captured in myriad "gender analyses" of
HIV—have apparently not been translated into significant policies,
programmes and funding for women's rights linked to HIV.
The Global Coalition on Women and AIDS (GCWA), a UNAIDS
initiative, is meant, among other things, to mobilize donors for
funding for HIV-related initiatives for women, but it is difficult
to find evidence of success in this area. The second independent
evaluation of UNAIDS in 2009 concluded that overall, UNAIDS'
leadership on women and AIDS has been weak and lacking in clear
strategy, and that the role of GCWA was unclear with respect to
other United Nations entities such as UNIFEM that work on HIV and
women's rights (UNAIDS Programme Coordinating Board 2009).

The Global Fund to Fight AIDS, Tuberculosis and Malaria,
established in 2001, has funded billions of dollars worth of HIV
programmes through grant proposals submitted by "country
coordinating mechanisms" (CCM), which are meant to represent
government and non-governmental sectors concerned with the
HIV response. Aidspan, an NGO that serves a "watchdog" function
with respect to the Global Fund, analysed funding for women's
issues in the first seven rounds of Global Fund grant making and
found that only three of 211 HIV proposals from CCMs were in any
way related to women's rights issues (Kageni and Garmaise 2008,
8). Others have commented that the HIV-related funds that do exist

for women's rights work tend to push women's organizations into a service-delivery mode rather than supporting policy advocacy and organizational capacity-building (Clark et al. 2006; AWID 2008), a comment reminiscent of the problems noted above with funding available to sex workers' organizations.

It certainly did not bode well for a human rights-centred approach to sex work or women and AIDS that ideologically-driven approaches to HIV gained such a strong foothold with the United States' support. Though it was widely criticized, the ABC approach—that is, A for abstinence outside marriage, B for "be faithful" and C for condoms if A and B were not possible—was a dominant influence in the allocation of significant resources for HIV prevention (Dworkin and Ehrhardt 2007). The simplistic ABC was meaningless for both sex workers and married women and tended to steer donors and governments away from thoughtful understandings of structural factors in women's HIV risk.

Protecting, respecting and fulfilling sex workers' rights as part of HIV responses will never be easy, and neither will the mobilization of women's rights and mainstream human rights organizations toward this end. Keeping multilateral bodies true to their human rights ideals in this regard will be achieved only with sustained vigilance and solidarity. "Victimhood," after all, is always just around the corner.

Note

1. Personal communication with Meena Seshu, Director, SANGRAM, July 2010.

References

Abel, Laura (2009) Obama administration refuses to release Bush-era OLC opinion characterizing "anti-prostitution policy requirement" as unconstitutional. *The Hill's Congress Blog*, 20 October. [http://thehill. com/blogs/congress-blog/healthcare/63837-obama-administration-refuses-to-release-bush-era-olc-opinion-characterizing-anti-prostitution-policy-requirement-as-unconstitutional-]

Alexander, Priscilla (1994) "Sex workers fight against AIDS: an international perspective", in Beth E. Schneider and Nancy E. Stoller. *Women resisting AIDS: feminist strategies of empowerment*, Philadelphia: Temple University Press.

Asia Pacific Network of Sex Workers (2007) Sex workers respond to UNAIDS Guidance on sex work. [http://apnswdollhouse.files.wordpress.com/2007/07/apnswpcb.pdf]

Association for Women's Rights in Development (AWID) (2008) Where is the money for women's rights: funding to fight HIV/AIDS through the promotion of women's rights—a case study from South Africa. [http://www.awid.org/eng/About-AWID/AWID-Initiatives/Where-is-the-Money-for-Women-s-Rights/What-s-new-from-this-initiative/Funding-to-fight-HIV-Aids-through-the-promotion-of-women-s-rights-A-case-study-from-South-Africa]

Ban Ki-moon (2008) Remarks on the handover of the report of the Commission on AIDS in Asia, 26 March. [http://www.un.org/apps/news/infocus/sgspeeches/search_full.asp?statID=206]

Booth, Karen M. (1998) "National mother, global whore and transnational femocrats: the politics of AIDS and the construction of women at the World Health Organization", *Feminist Studies* 24:115-39.

Brennan Center for Justice (2008) Broad range of humanitarian groups must benefit from injections against speech restriction in HIV/AIDS program, says federal court (press release). [http://www.soros.org/initiatives/health/focus/sharp/news/victory_20080808/aosi_20080808.pdf]

Castro, Kenneth G., Alan R. Lifson, Carol R. White, Rimothy J. Bush, Mary E Chamberland, Anastasia M. Lekatsas and Harold W. Jaffe (1988) "Investigations of AIDS patients with no previously identified risk factors", *Journal of the American Medical Association* 259:1338-42.

Clark, Cindy, Ellen Sprenger, Lisa VeneKlasen, Lidia Alpizar and Joanna Kerr (2006) Where is the money for women's rights? Assessing resources and the role of donors in the promotion of women's rights and the support of women's organizations. Mexico City: Association for Women's Rights in Development. [http://www.springstrategies.org/storage/1st_fundher_report.pdf]

Commission on AIDS in Asia (2008) *Redefining AIDS in Asia: crafting an effective response* New Delhi: Oxford University Press.

Commission on Human Rights of the United Nations (2007) The protection of human rights in the context of human immunodeficiency virus (HIV) and acquired immunodeficiency syndrome (AIDS).

CHR res. 1997/33. Geneva: Office of the United Nations High Commissioner for Human Rights (E/CN.4/RES/1997/33).

Csete, Joanne (2007) A human rights-based commentary on UNAIDS Guidance Note: HIV and Sex Work (April 2007). Toronto: Canadian HIV/AIDS Legal Network. [http://www.aidslaw.ca/publications/interfaces/downloadFile.php?ref=1196]

Curran, James W., Harold W. Jaffe, Ann M. Hardy, W. Meade Morgan, Richard M. Selik, Timothy J. Dondero (1988) "Epidemiology of HIV infection and AIDS in the United States," *Science* 239:610-16.

David Lowe Consulting (2002) Documenting the experiences of sex workers: report to the Policy Project. [http://www.nswp.org/search?SearchableText=100%25+condom+]

Ditmore, Melissa (2008) Punishing sex workers won't curb HIV/AIDS, says Ban Ki-Moon. *RH Reality Check*, 24 June. [http://www.rhrealitycheck.org/blog/2008/06/23/sex-workers-grateful-banki-moon]

Doezema, Jo (2005) "Now you see her, now you don't: sex workers at the UN trafficking protocol negotiations", *Social and Legal Studies* 14:61-89.

Dube, Siddharth (forthcoming) *Sex workers, the World Bank and UNAIDS* (manuscript to be published by AIDS-Free World). (On file with the author.)

Dworkin, Shari L. and Anke A. Ehrhardt (2007) "Going beyond "ABC" to include "GEM": critical reflections on progress in the HIV/AIDS epidemic", *American Journal of Public Health* 97:1-6.

Farmer, Paul, Sirley Lindenbaum and Mary-Jo Delvecchio, "Good. Women, poverty and AIDS: an introduction.", *Culture, Medicine and Psychiatry* 17:387-97.

Fee, Elizabeth and Manon Parry (2008) "Jonathan Mann, HIV/AIDS and human rights", *Journal of Public Health Policy* 29:54-71.

Flock, Elizabeth (2009) Bill Gates' Indian education. *Forbes* vol. 184, 3 August. [http://www.forbes.com/forbes/2009/0803/avahan-aids-prostitution-bill-gates-indian-education.html]

Gallo, Robert C. (2006) "A reflection on HIV/AIDS research after 25 years", *Retrovirology* 3:72, doi:10.1186/1742-4690-3-72.

Gates, Melinda (2006) Keynote address to opening session of the International AIDS Conference, Toronto. [http://www.kaisernetwork.org/health_cast/uploaded_files/Bill%20and%20Melinda%20Gates%20Opening%20Speeches.pdf]

Ghose, Toorjo, Dallas Swendeman, Sheba George and Debasish Chowdhury (2008) "Mobilizing collective identity to reduce

HIV risk among sex workers in Sonagachi, India; the boundaries, consciousness, negotiation framework", *Social Science and Medicine* 67:311-20.

Girard, Françoise (2001) Reflections on the Declaration of Commitment on HIV/AIDS adopted by the UN General Assembly Special Session. New York: International Women's Health Coalition. [http://www.iwhc.org/index.php?option=com_content&task=view&id=2169&Itemid=555]

Global Fund to Fight AIDS, Tuberculosis and Malaria (2008) The Global Fund's strategy for ensuring gender equality in the response to HIV/AIDS, tuberculosis and malaria ("the gender equality strategy"). [http://ilfondoglobale.org/documents/strategy/TheGenderEqualityStrategy_en.pdf]

Global Programme on AIDS of the World Health Organization (1989a) Consensus statement from the consultation on HIV epidemiology and prostitution, Geneva, 3-6 July. [whqlibdoc.who.int/hq/1989/WHO_GPA_INF_89.11.pdf]

Global Programme on AIDS of the World Health Organization (1989b) The health of mothers and children in the context of HIV/AIDS. [http://whqlibdoc.who.int/hq/1989/GPA_INF_89.19.pdf]

Global Working Group on HIV and Sex Work Policy (2007) Draft reworking of the UNAIDS Guidance Note on HIV and Sex Work, April 2007. [http://sexworkpolicy.files.wordpress.com/2007/09/final-response-to-unfpa-safer.pdf]

Global Working Group on HIV and Sex Work Policy (2009) Materials prepared for meeting with UNAIDS executive director Michel Sidibe, March 2009. (On file with author.)

Greenall, Matthew (2009) Strengthening global commitment to sex worker rights—background paper for a proposed donor collaboration. [http://www.soros.org/initiatives/health/focus/sharp/events/sexworkers-donorcollaboration-20091111/donor-background-20091111.pdf]

Grover, Jan Zita (1987) "AIDS: keywords", *October* 43:17-30.

Gruskin, Sofia (2002) "The UN General Assembly Special Session on HIV/AIDS: were some lessons of the last 20 years ignored?" *American Journal of Public Health* 92:337-38.

Hamblin, Julie and Elizabeth Reid (1991) "Women the HIV epidemic and human rights: a tragic imperative", New York: UN Development Programme.

Jana, Smarajit, Ishika Basu, Mary Jane Rotheram-Borus and Peter A. Newman (2004) "The Sonagachi project: a sustainable community intervention program", *AIDS Education and Prevention* 16:405-14.

Jenkins, Carol (2000) "Female sex worker HIV prevention projects: lessons learnt from Papua New Guinea, India and Bangladesh—UNAIDS case study", (Best Practice Collection). Geneva, UNAIDS.

Johnson, Hans and William Eskridge (2007) "The legacy of Falwell's bully pulpit", *Washington Post* (May 19):A23.

Kageni, Angela and David Garmaise (2008) Do Global Fund grants work for women? Nairobi: Aidspan. [http://aidspan.org/documents/aidspan/aidspan-gender-paper-en.pdf]

Kempadoo, Kamala (2003) "Globalizing sex workers' rights", *Canadian Women's Studies* 22:143-150.

Kaiser Family Foundation (2010) The US President's Emergency Plan for AIDS Relief: fact sheet. [http://www.kff.org/globalhealth/upload/8002-02.pdf]

Kilmarx Peter H., Thanit Palanuvej, Khanchit Limpakarnjanarat, Anupong Chitvarakorn, Michael E. St Louis, Timothy D. Mastro (1999) "Seroprevalence of HIV among female sex workers in Bangkok: evidence of ongoing infection risk after the '100% condom program' was implemented", *JAIDS* 21(4):313-316.

Loff, Bebe, Cheryl Overs and Paulo Longo (2003) "Can health programmes lead to mistreatment of sex workers?" *Lancet* 361:1982-3.

Magar, V, Center for Health and Gender Equity (CHANGE), (2008) Implications of U.S. policy restrictions for HIV programs aimed at commercial sex workers (policy brief). Takoma Park, MD (USA). [http://www.genderhealth.org/pubs/APLO.pdf]

Mama Cash and Open Society Institute (2009) Donor dialogue: donor collaboration to advance the human rights of sex workers—report of a meeting in Amsterdam, 11-12 November. [http://www.soros.org/initiatives/health/focus/sharp/events/sexworkers-donorcollaboration-20091111/donor-dialogue-20091111.pdf]

Mann Jonathan M (1999) "Human rights and AIDS: the future of the pandemic", In Jonathan M. Mann, Sofia Gruskin, Michael A. Grodin and George J. Annas, eds. *Health and human rights: a reader.* New York: Routledge, pp 216-26.

Network of Sex Work Projects (2008) Sex workers at UN high level meeting on HIV/AIDS

Office of the High Commissioner on Human Rights and UNAIDS (Joint United Nations Programme on HIV/AIDS), 2006. International guidelines on HIV/AIDS and human rights (consolidated version). Geneva: United Nations. [http://data.unaids.org/Publications/IRC-pub07/jc1252-internguidelines_en.pdf]

Outshoorn, Joyce (2005) "The political debates on prostitution and trafficking of women", *Social Politics: International Studies on Gender, State and Society* 12:141-55.

Overs, Cheryl (2006) "Violence and exposure to HIV among sex workers in Phnom Penh, Cambodia", Washington, DC: Policy Project.

Overs, Cheryl (2009) Caught between the tiger and the crocodile: the campaign to suppress human trafficking and sexual exploitation in Cambodia. Phnom Penh: Asia Pacific Network of Sex Workers. [http://apnswdollhouse.files.wordpress.com/2009/03/caught-between-the-tiger-and-the-crocodile.pdf]

Parikh, Shanti A., (2007) "The political economy of marriage and HIV: the ABC approach, "safe" infidelity, and managing moral risk in Uganda", *American Journal of Public Health* 97:1198-1208.

Piot, Peter, Francis A. Plummer, Fred S. Mhalu, Jean-Louis Lambourey, James Chin and Jonathan M. Mann (1988) "AIDS: an international perspective", *Science* 239: 573-9.

Prostitution Law Review Committee, Government of New Zealand. Review of the Prostitution Law Review Committee on the operation of the Prostitution Reform Act of 2003. [http://www.justice.govt.nz/policy-and-consultation/legislation/prostitution-law-review-committee/publications/plrc-report/documents/report.pdf]

Rajanapithayakorn W. (2006) "The 100% condom use programme in Asia", *Reproductive Health Matters* 14(28):41-52.

Rao Gupta, Geeta and Ellen Weiss (1993) "Women's lives and sex: implications for AIDS prevention", *Culture, Medicine and Psychiatry* 17(4):399-412.

Saunders, Penelope (2004) "Prohibiting sex work projects, restricting women's rights: the international impact of the 2003 US Global AIDS Act", *Health and Human Rights* 7:179-92.

Seale, Andy (2009) "Heteronormativity and HIV in sub-Sarahan Africa", *Development* 52:84-90.

Siplon Patricia (1999) "A brief history of the political science of AIDS activism", *Political Science and Politics* 32:578-79.

Soderlund, Gretchen (2005) "Running from the rescuers: new U.S. crusade against sex trafficking and the rhetoric of abolition", *NWSA Journal* 17:64-87.

Stolberg, Sheryl Gay (2008) "In global battle on AIDS, Bush creates legacy", *New York Times*, 5 January. [http://abidjan.usembassy.gov/uploads/images/8ytvSl6mjzA4_kJOMVmC9w/AIDSGlobalBattleNYT.pdf]

UNAIDS (Joint United Nations Programme on HIV/AIDS), (2002) Sex work and HIV/AIDS: UNAIDS technical update. Geneva. [http://data.unaids.org/Publications/IRC-pub02/jc705-sexwork-tu_en.pdf]

———, (2004a) Number of women living with HIV increases in each region of the world (press release). [http://data.unaids.org/Media/Press-Releases02/pr_epilaunch_23nov04_en.pdf]

———, (2004b) UN Secretary General's report calls for action on women, girls and AIDS (press release). [http://data.unaids.org/Media/Press-Releases02/pr_sglaunch_safricataskforce_06jul04_en.pdf]

———, (2004c) Action against AIDS must address epidemic's increasing impact on women, says UN report (press release). [http://data.unaids.org/Media/Press-Releases02/pr_women-aids_14jul04_en.pdf]

———, (2004d) HIV prevention and protection efforts are failing women and girls: many young women are becoming infected by long-term partners—female-controlled HIV prevention methods urgently needed (press release). [http://data.unaids.org/Media/Press-Releases02/pr_gcwa_02feb04_en.pdf]

———, (2004e) UNAIDS praises Viet Nam for adopting national AIDS strategy (press release). [http://data.unaids.org/Media/Press-Releases02/pr_vietnam_18oct04_en.pdf]

———, (2005a) Flemish government and UN launch women and AIDS programme in Mozambique (press release). [http://data.unaids.org/Media/Press-Releases03/pr_flemishmozambique_06may05_en.pdf]

———, (2005b) Faith-based organizations in Mozambique rise to the AIDS challenge (press release). [http://data.unaids.org/Media/Press-Releases03/pr_mozambique_fbo_08jun05_en.pdf]

———, (2005c) Intensifying HIV prevention: UNAIDS policy position paper. Geneva. [http://data.unaids.org/Publications/IRC-pub06/jc1165-intensif_hiv-newstyle_en.pdf]

———, (2007) UNAIDS Executive Director Peter Piot praises religious groups" actions on AIDS at Saddleback Church Global AIDS Summit (press release). [http://data.unaids.org/pub/PressRelease/2007/071129_saddleback_en.pdf]

———, (2009) Joint action for results: UNAIDS outcome framework 2009-2011. Geneva. [http://data.unaids.org/pub/Report/2010/jc1713_joint_action_en.pdf]

UNAIDS Programme Coordinating Board (2009) UNAIDS second independent evaluation, 2002-2008: final report. Geneva, UN doc no. UNAIDS/PCB(25)/09.18. [http://data.unaids.org/pub/ BaseDocument/2009/20091002_sie_final_report_en.pdf]

UNAIDS and Thailand Ministry of Public Health (2000) Evaluation of the 100% condom programme in Thailand: UNAIDS case study. Geneva. [http://data.unaids.org/publications/IRC-pub01/ jc275-100pcondom_en.pdf]

UNICEF (United Nations Children's Fund) (2006) Trafficking (child protection information sheet). [http://www.unicef.org/protection/ files/Trafficking.pdf]

US Agency for International Development (USDAID), (2003) Trafficking in persons: the

USDAID strategy for response. Washington, DC. [http://www.usaid. gov/our_work/cross-cutting_programs/wid/pubs/pd-abx-358- final.pdf]

US Agency for International Development (USDAID), (2005) Implementation of the United States Leadership Against HIV/AIDS, Tuberculosis and Malaria Act of 2003—eligibility limitation on the use of funds and opposition to prostitution and sex trafficking. AAPD directive 05-04. [http://www.usaid.gov/business/business_ opportunities/cib/pdf/aapd05_04.pdf]

Weitzer, Ronald (2010) "The mythology of prostitution: advocacy research and public policy, *Sex Research and Social Policy* 7:15-29.

Whelan, Daniel, (1999) Gender and HIV/AIDS: taking stock of research and programmes. Geneva: UNAIDS. [data.unaids.org/Publications/ IRC.../JC419-Gender-TakingStock_en.pdf]

World Health Organization Western Pacific Region (2009) Responding to questions about the 100% condom use programme (2nd ed.): a job aide for programme staff. Manila. [http://www.wpro.who.int/ NR/rdonlyres/789F079F-96DE-463F-9D4D-F62501884596/0/ RespondingtoQuestionsaboutCUP_forupload.pdf]

World Bank (1997) *Confronting AIDS: public priorities in a global epidemic.* New York: Oxford University Press.

Zierler, Sally (1994) "Women, sex and HIV", *Epidemiology* 5(6):565-67.

Sex Workers and Feminists
Personal Reflections

CHERYL OVERS

In this chapter I share some of my thoughts and experiences of the women's movement and feminism, from my perspective as a sex workers' rights activist. Being a sex workers' rights activist means continually negotiating a complex relationship with the women's movement and the various branches of feminist thought. I am not alone in this. I doubt even one of my colleagues would disagree with that statement. Some of us identify as feminists and some do not, but all have reflected at length on notions of consent, exploitation, safety, danger, pleasure and identity in the context of commercial sex. Here, I will not analyse feminist theory or the movement for sex workers' rights, but instead offer a series of snapshots and reflections about relationships between the two that have sometimes been productive, sometimes ambivalent and too often painful.

I think most of my activist colleagues would agree upon the existence of this ambivalence, whether or not they identify as feminists. Clearly, feminism is not a single stream of thought and the women's movement is also not monolithic. Many in my peer group of sex workers' rights advocates talk about themselves as the 'real' feminists, in contrast to those whose feminism is seen as oppressive, misguided and even violent. On the other hand, it is also true that the sex workers' rights movement has been supported and at times even driven by committed feminists. These are polarities, but undue focus on these extremes can divert attention from the important middle ground of mainstream or popular feminism. Where extremists have focused on pornography and 'sex trafficking', mainstream feminism has been more associated with the women's health movement. Its influence is visible, for example, in gender-sensitive economic development and responses to rape and violence against women. Both ends of the spectrum and everything in between began to affect my life well before I knew of the existence of such nuances.

In Australia's prosperous 1970s, when I was 17, I moved from a Melbourne suburb to the inner city near the university. I lived and had a wonderful time in shared households of artists, actors and musicians. I dedicated myself to rock bands and nightclubs but managed, relatively effortlessly, to go to school and support myself with menial jobs. Whenever there was a clash between work and my social life, I would leave the restaurant or bar and only think about finding a new job much later. I wasn't exactly desperate to avoid the hours spent in kitchens and sandwich bars earning the small amount of money I needed, but those hours did detract from my social life and so I was pleased to join some fellow clubbers who worked in a massage parlour a couple of nights a week. A receptionist post was vacant; I guess I did that rather than massage because I was so young. I am not sure I gave it any thought at all.

In the few moments I bothered to think about the conditions at the parlour it was only because they annoyed or bemused me. The management fined us for being late and charged workers a dollar for the laundry for each towel (in 1975, a half-hour massage was only AUD 10). Eventually we decided that instead of paying these charges, as well as 50 per cent to the 'house', a small group of us would rent a house to work as a collective. We would simply contribute to rent and bills just like in shared student housing. We did, and that is another story. Indeed, it is a story that I would have a hard time believing if someone else had narrated to me. To this day, I don't know why the dangerous criminals and corrupt police that I now know were running Melbourne brothels at the time ignored a bunch of upstart girls setting themselves up as a 'workers collective'. Maybe it was the axiom that gangsters only go after each other. Maybe we weren't taking enough of the market share. Who knows? All I know is that I am glad I survived such absurd naiveté.

I had to take bookings for massages and in my script I was to make it clear that no prostitution was taking place, because undercover cops would enter these legal massage parlours to check if a brothel was operating within them. They would try to get a massage girl to agree to provide 'hand relief', which was the only 'extra' service on offer. Later when I worked as an outreach worker, I heard lots of stories about police raids; but even then the teary 'girls' caught providing 'extras' were charged under false names and small fines were paid. I suppose this served to illustrate that the police were doing their job of keeping prostitution out of massage parlours. I knew that it was pretty benign as police-prostitute interaction goes and I was only a bit apprehensive of the risk of a police visit.

Within the next year, I went from caring much more about the next party than conditions in the sex industry, to being a fully committed sex workers' rights activist. Was I raped? Was a friend brutally murdered by a client? Was I hurled into a dank police cell? Exposed in the media and disowned by my family? No. What happened was that I gradually realised that my social life and status were being limited by my lack of popularity with local feminists who were influential enough to make me controversial and stop me getting the invitations I thought I should. It seems ridiculous to think now that I was so affronted by the risk of not getting to the 'A' list! But acceptance is a precious commodity at that age and was almost an obsession for me. I had been prepared for some disapproval directed at me for working in a massage parlour but I expected it to come from moral or religious people, and not my contemporaries. I had a vague sense that feminism was somehow transgressive, and to this day I believe that in almost all its forms, it remains insufficiently so.

I couldn't understand why I was so unpopular until a feminist man helpfully told me that everyone in his very hip feminist household saw me as colluding with sexist oppression, commoditisation and abuse of women. It was useful of him to fill in the blanks, and blanks were certainly what were being directed at me from 'wimmin' (as some feminists called themselves then to avoid the 'man' suffix).

These are soupy memories from a distant era of feminism. Anti-pornography feminists were influential at the time, so I scoured their texts to understand this analysis of gender and power that labelled me a collaborator and oppressor. I remember Susan Brownmiller's *Against Our Will*[1] delivering one of the first jolting disconnects between my reality and the emerging feminist orthodoxy: the gap between the notion of client as rapist and the polite, ordinary men of my reality.

> Man's discovery that his genitalia could serve as a weapon to generate fear must rank as one of the most important discoveries of prehistoric times, along with the use of fire and the first crude stone axe. From prehistoric times to the present, I believe, rape has played a critical function (...) It is nothing more or less than a conscious process of intimidation by which all men keep all women in a state of fear.

Reading passages such as the one above, I was forced to wonder: are all men rapists?

This brand of feminism was not confined to America. Elizabeth Reid, a prominent feminist and driving force behind some of the Australia's most visionary reforms on women's rights, explained to me the concerns of the 'women and development' branch of feminism about prostitution: "It threatens livelihoods and oppresses women in developing countries because husbands spend household money on sex and infect their wives with diseases acquired from prostitutes." Was she saying that sex workers should support local economies by not selling sex? Gender and development discourse seemed to me to veer dangerously toward sexual essentialism, the idea that heterosexual monogamy is the best and highest form of sex. Where was the transgression I had expected from feminism? Susie Jolly addresses this question more than 20 years later in her 2009 article "Why is Development work so straight? And what can we do about it?"[2]. "Some development work has reinforced inequalities around sexuality and gender. Sometimes even the interventions seeking greater justice and equality—such as those associated with Gender and Development, the Men and Masculinities field, Rights-Based Development, empowerment and participation—inadvertently reinforce oppressive sexuality and gender norms," she points out. Her statement emerges from her earlier efforts to bring to the table a discussion on sexual pleasure. In her 2007 paper "Why the Development Industry Should Get Over its Obsession with Bad Sex and Start to Think About Pleasure"[3] she says:

> The development industry has emphasised the dangers of sex and sexuality. This negative approach to sex has been filtered through a view of gender which stereotypes men as predators, women as victims, and fails to recognise the existence of transgender people. It is time to go beyond this negative and gender stereotyped view of sexuality, to recognise that pleasure and danger are imbricated in the ways people experience sexuality. We need to move to more positive framings of sexuality which promote the possibilities of pleasure, as well as tackling the dangers at the same time.

Ten years previously in 1997, a practical dimension to my amateur navigation of feminist theory and sex work law had emerged. Despite politically correct speech about being a workers' collective and lack of contact with police, I was aware that my colleagues could now be seen as brothel keepers in the eyes of the law, and liable to tens of thousands of dollars fines and jail. At the time, prostitution laws in Australia were the same as those in most other parts of the world. Though the prostitution laws differed according to states and territories, the common features were that prostitution-related activities such as soliciting and brothel keeping were illegal, but the act of selling or buying sex itself was not. There was division among feminists over whether the criminal law should be used against both sex workers and sex businesses, or just against sex businesses or 'pimps'. When law reform came on to the agenda locally, a vocal minority of feminists and religious groups called for the law to be used to abolish prostitution by punishing everyone. Most feminists probably thought that female sex workers shouldn't be punished, but that 'pimps' were fair game. Initially, few grasped that it wasn't possible to criminalise the 'pimp' without the consequences being passed along to sex workers. Crucially, feminists who thought things would be better for women without prostitution, but didn't support criminalisation of sex work, were largely silent. This silence from moderate feminists continues to deafen me until today.

The feminist agenda at the time was focussed on addressing law and policy on abortion, family law, rape, domestic violence, sexual harassment and employment law, but the ambivalence among feminists about sex work was enough to keep prostitution law low on the list of priorities. I resolved to help draw attention to it and began to look for allies who might have a clue about where to begin.

Happily, this apparent absence of concern about the unfair prostitution law had come to the notice of a small group of feminist lawyers, who worked in shopfront legal services that bought them into contact with actual sex workers. We started a collective called the Prostitutes Action Group in the early eighties. As it turned out, the divide between the feminists and sex workers in that group was not as significant as it first appeared. Several of the feminists and lawyers had worked in the sex industry as students and several of the sex workers were in tertiary education. The group evolved into the Australian Prostitutes Collective. In 1984 we opened an office, funded not by health but by a justice initiative, that distributed money seized from drugs and organised crimes to worthy causes. We began building excellent relationships with feminists, civil libertarians, church groups, humanists, trade unions and others. Those alliances and the high quality of our law reform advocacy had, by the end of the eighties established us as the acceptable voice for decriminalisation of sex work. I am thrilled to say that a quarter of a century later these relationships have been sustained and expanded by successive generations of sex workers in Australia.[4]

When HIV was identified, we used our outreach skills to set up the very first condom distribution and needle exchange programmes in 1987 and to establish what is now known as 'peer education'. This meant that we now gained the support of public health institutions and gay organisations that were also moving into work combating HIV.

Internationally too, the prostitutes' rights movement was developing within a branch of feminism. Gail Pheterson (Associate

Professor of Social Psychology at the University of Picardie and a psychotherapist in private practice in Paris), Priscilla Alexander (a member of COYOTE, one of the oldest prostitutes' rights groups), and other American and European feminists joined with sex workers across the world to form the International Committee on Prostitutes' Rights in the 1970s, based on the ideology that Pheterson would go on to articulate in several works that have now become classics (such as "A Vindication of the Rights of Whores", 1989 and "The Prostitution Prism", 1996). Pheterson's 1993 book *The Whore Stigma: Female Dishonor and Male Unworthiness*[5] argues that all women are controlled by the ideology surrounding the whore. Indeed, Pheterson, just three years earlier, had questioned the category of "prostitute" itself:

> Social science research is infected with prejudices against prostitute-branded women. Even the category "prostitute" is based more upon symbolic and legal representations of the bad woman, or whore, than upon an actual set of characteristics within a population of persons. Two recent articles in *The Journal of Sex Research*, one which concludes that prostitutes are a devastating health menace to men, women, and babies and the other which concludes that prostitutes experience greater sexual satisfaction than other women, illustrate the problem. Researchers are criticized for limiting their study of sexual-economic behaviour to prostitutes and for relying upon a status variable, "prostitute," in designing a broad range of needed research in which status is either irrelevant or one variable among many. Deconstruction of the category "prostitute" is necessary to counter prejudice and to conduct scientifically valid inquiry.[6]

These ideas were refreshingly tolerant of sex workers compared to other feminist ideology of the time, and we needed allies that understood international organising. The landmark moment was a conference in Brussels in 1985 at which the World Charter for Prostitutes' Rights was developed and agreed upon.

This was the onset of the HIV pandemic and it was not surprising that abolitionist feminists offered nothing helpful about HIV. They did not go so far as to say that AIDS was punishment for prostitutes, as the anti-homosexuality groups did about homosexuals, but it was seen as further evidence that limiting (male) sexuality was a worthwhile goal to pursue, and also a reiteration that the behaviour of the female prostitute constitutes a threat to other women. However, I was surprised that the American and European feminists who supported us drifted away. I can't say why, and it was never documented, but it seemed to me that some lacked interest in public health and some did not want to devote energy to a mixed gender movement, as the prostitutes movement was becoming by then.

Also disappointing at the time was the sex workers' movements' position on HIV/AIDS, which was to deny links between sex workers and HIV and distance female sex workers from gay men who were deeply affected by HIV. Slogans such as 'We are safe sex sluts' and 'Sex workers use condoms – do you?' aimed to illustrate the valid point that sex workers were not to blame for HIV. Some groups (including the Dutch Red Thread) went so far as to denounce other sex workers' groups that accepted funds to provide information to sex workers about HIV as 'selling out ' for funding to do work that would further stigmatise sex workers as 'vectors of disease' . This was understandable, given the historical blaming of sex workers for disease, and it was logical for a group predominantly of women from the Global North. Indeed, the patterns of HIV that emerged in subsequent decades showed that non-drug-using female sex workers in the Global North did largely escape the virus. However these ideas were a denial of the reality of the millions of men, women, and transgender persons, of injectors and of all other people selling sex in places without adequate sanitation or food security, let alone condoms and access to sexual and reproductive health services. It was a mistake to say 'Don't blame us for spreading HIV' instead of 'Don't blame people with HIV for the transmission of HIV'. That mistake divided the sex workers' rights movement and made it largely irrelevant in the face of AIDS. It was an easy task for feminists to discredit the sex workers rights' movement as a bunch of "White Happy Hookers" whose ideas had no relevance in situations where women who sell sex face disease, and where sex work is seen as a route out of extreme poverty.

As responses to HIV developed in the early nineties, people concerned about HIV—male and transgender persons, sex workers, and allies from developing countries— began to swell the ranks of the sex workers' rights movement. The political environment changed as the post-modern era dawned. The HIV activist agenda was articulated by ACT–UP, queer theory was all the rage in gender politics, Michel Foucault was de rigueur and popular culture saw the rise of the sexy empowered woman as exemplified by the icon of the day, Madonna.

Readers may have noticed that I have stopped using the term prostitute and begun using 'sex workers.' This is because I am up to the late eighties when we stopped being 'prostitutes' and became 'sex workers'. Carol Lee, an American sex worker, coined the term and Priscilla Alexander wrote a book called Sex Work[7]. The first director of the Global Progamme on AIDS Jonathan Mann, incorporated this usage into UN language. The rest is history. I regard this shift in language as the greatest achievement of the sex workers' rights movement, partly because it is unchangeable. No-one—no law, no army, no ideology, no religion, and no state—can roll back a change in language once it has taken root.

As our political and cultural alliances grew to include gay men, people with HIV and emerging sex worker groups in poor countries, the feminist analysis of gender and sexuality of the early movement became less prominent. Embarrassingly, the record shows that in 1995 I really believed that the currency and influence of abolitionist feminism had declined and would no longer influence sex work policy. I optimistically announced, "Redefining prostitutes from evil women to passive victims is a blip on the historical landscape... its greatest 'achievement' was criminalising clients." In the same interview however I worried that "middle class women in developing countries are taking up the old ideas of Western, puritan feminism. This is expressed in the plethora of anti trafficking organisations which posit the prostitute as victim and call for criminal sanctions to stop her working or moving about freely".[8]

How wrong, and then how right, those two observations turned out to be. Throughout the 1990s while HIV was still fatal, my engagement with feminism was mainly through the women's health movement, which had been instrumental in articulating the importance of sexual and reproductive health as well as the struggle for abortion rights. Meanwhile, anti-prostitution feminist academics like Donna Hughes (professor of women's studies at the University of Rhode Island), Janice Raymond (professor emeritus of women's studies at the University of Massachusetts in Amherst), Melissa Farley (Executive Director of the non-profit organisation Prostitution Research and Education) and others were publishing what Ronald Weitzer, Professor at the Department of Sociology, George Washington University, describes as 'pre-scientific' papers with a 'prohibitionist' (also called abolitionists or radical feminists) stance to push the ideology that "prostitution exploits women, regardless of women's consent...and...affects all women, justifies the sale of any woman, and reduces all women to sex". Weitzer goes on to critically analyse the claims based on what he shows to be flawed research: sweeping generalisations, faulty sampling, opaque and biased data collection and inconvenient findings.[9]

> In such studies, bias is also evident in a neglect of the scientific canon of falsifiability. If they comment at all on results that they did not expect, prohibitionist writers go to great lengths to discredit such findings. This discrediting includes downplaying or questioning the voices of sex workers themselves when they disagree with the author's opinions. For example, Raymond (2003) has written: "There is no doubt that a small number of women say they choose to be in prostitution, especially in public contexts orchestrated by the sex industry" (p. 325). By claiming that the number is small and by using the words 'say' and 'orchestrated', Raymond clearly sought to cast doubt on the veracity of the women's testimony.
>
> In Farley's (2007) interviews with some workers at eight of Nevada's 30 legal brothels, she stated, "I knew that they would minimize how bad it was" (p. 22). Respondents who did not acknowledge that working in a brothel was bad were considered to be in denial, and Farley sought to penetrate this barrier: "We were asking the women to briefly remove a mask that was crucial to their psychological survival"

(p. 22). Farley also has asserted that most of the women working in the legal brothels had pimps, despite the fact that the women were "reluctant to admit that their boyfriends and husbands were pimping them" (p. 31).

Farley found that "a surprisingly low percentage—33%—of our interviewees in the legal brothels reported sexual abuse in childhood" (p. 33), a percentage that "is lower than the likely actual incidence of sexual abuse because of symptoms of numbing, avoidance, and dissociation among these women" (p. 33), or discomfort discussing such experiences.

These are studies conducted in the 2000s, but a decade earlier I took little notice of these extremist anti-men, anti-sex, anti-whore feminists who had little or no influence in my world. I didn't know then that these people would become the hired guns to provide the pseudo-evidence to justify the avalanche of anti-sex-work law and policy generated by the Bush administration.

I couldn't have imagined that what I saw as obsolete heterosexist feminists would stage a comeback in cahoots with fundamentalist Christianity, to provide the justification for waves of violence being rained down on sex workers in dozens of countries the world over. Nor did I imagine that the influence of fundamentalist feminists and Christians would influence the UN to recommend diverting funds from proven HIV prevention for sex workers like condoms and care of Sexually Transmitted Infections (STIs), to spurious 'gender' programmes to help women avoid selling sex. But this is exactly what has happened.

In 2004 the Bush Administration introduced legislation that forbade any US development aid money from going to organisations that did not have a policy condemning sex work. This was known as the "Prostitution Pledge" and its wording commits any organisation that receives US money to defining prostitution as "exploitation and abuse of women." Any person or organisation bound by the Pledge who could entertain the idea that sex workers have rights—including simply using the term sex work— was in breach.[10] The US has done this before too, with the Global Gag rule on abortion.[11]

I was working in an international NGO that was mainly funded by USAID at the time. My life suddenly became hell. The entire basis of my work—HIV prevention through empowerment of sex worker communities—was suddenly prohibited by our main donor. I and other activists, were stalked on the Internet by anonymous Americans who denounced us for breaches of the "Pledge". Staff members who had always silently resented the organisation supporting sex workers suddenly had free reign to openly bully and marginalise me and others like me. The US has done this before,when it has incentivised denunciations and social exclusion of communists, civil rights activists and draft dodgers. It works very well because it draws on apparently well-stocked reservoirs of cowardice, dormant malice, and opportunism.

While the Pledge was the main mechanism for closing down civil society's rights-based services and squashing sex workers, an even more effective mechanism was used by governments to entrench violence against, and abuse of, sex workers. The Trafficking in Persons Report is an annual US report that ranks countries for their efforts to end human trafficking. 'Ending human trafficking' involves introducing laws that smash the sex industry and jail people identified as traffickers. Countries that do this are fiscally rewarded and those that do not co-operate with the US are punished under the system of 'Tier Ratings'[12]. The enormous implications of this are too complex to discuss here, but the point to note is this: the rationale for eliminating the category 'sex worker', and redefining sex workers as either traffickers or victims of trafficking, has been provided by extremist, conservative feminists from university posts that are either directly funded by the State Department, by fundamentalist Christians or by other even more anonymous (and presumably more nefarious) sources. They are sustained and given respectability by the complicity of more moderate feminists in, for example, the UN and EU systems.

What happened in the UN was less predictable.

Throughout the HIV epidemic, the UN had been at the forefront of identifying and advocating for evidence-based HIV services for sex workers. Condoms, friendly STI services, peer education, social support and so on were proven to be effective in raising condom use in commercial sex to levels that significantly slow HIV epidemics. Suddenly a new position on sex work was to be developed by the UN, and a consultation led by UNFPA would be held. This meeting would be different from meetings we had attended for the previous 15 years. The US State Department had sent in the notorious Melissa Farley, author of pseudo-research that illustrates that sex workers are forced into sex work and traumatised by it.[13] Several agencies had sent their "gender" experts. Sex workers' advocates all shiver in our boots when the word "gender" is even mentioned. We know that what's coming won't be good for us. And it wasn't.

As the meeting progressed, it became clear that the formerly marginal idea that most women are prostituted by others against their will as a result of trafficking or poverty, and raped by their clients, was suddenly the status quo. With such an analysis there are only two available solutions: law enforcement (raid and rescue) and poverty reduction through small enterprise (rehabilitation). Through this analysis, the women's movement—extremists and the more moderate women's health movement alike—were effectively suggesting that to reduce HIV, money should be diverted from effective HIV prevention and care to projects that would prevent poverty and criminal abuse, and therefore entry into sex work. Money, they said, should go to 'girls education' to prevent them growing up to sell sex, as well as to rescuing trafficked women and providing training and loans, in the completely untested assumption that women will abandon sex work if they can access other work. Clients (of consenting adults) should be arrested for forcing sex on trafficked women. Sex workers' rights activists (and off-the-record many UN staff) were collectively gobsmacked by the appearance of all this in a UNAIDS Guidance Note on Sex Work, which emerged from the process in 2007. We launched a process to develop an alternative set of recommendations and invited the UN to consider it, which they did not do until several significant shifts had occurred in the political landscape, including Obama's arrival in the White House. Thankfully the UN has changed tack now. Under the leadership of UNAIDS director Michel Sidibe, SG Ban Ki Moon and others, the emphasis seems to have shifted back from ideologies shared by right wing Christians and feminists toward rights and evidence-based approaches. A new and reasonable Guidance note (based on the recognition that sex workers need a comprehensive package of services and a policy environment that reduces vulnerability and ensures access to treatment) was eventually issued in 2009 and sex workers are on board to help make it work.

The international sex workers' rights movement was burnt by their experiences around the Pledge, the conflation of trafficking and sex work, and the UN Guidance on Sex Work. These are not the only examples of policy that harms sex workers that are being driven by feminists. The women's movement continues to mobilise to attack the sex industry, often literally[14] (see UK Feminist for an example of feminist violence and vigilantism against sex workers in the UK).

The sex workers movement seems to be turning now to the human rights movements for support and alliance building, since clearly the potential is great and we have already seen NGOs take on sex workers' and human rights issues. It remains to be seen if and how feminism blocks this route to justice for sex workers. It won't be difficult. There is little in the human rights conventions to help sex workers of any gender. Many of the conventions aim to prevent abuse and define sex work as abuse—no matter how voluntary or consensual it is. For example, the Cambodian government passed laws to close down the sex industry and stop human trafficking, and brought in Christian groups to raid the sex industry in 2008. Cambodian sex workers turned to human rights advocates but were surprised to discover that the only support on offer addressed a sex worker's right not to be illegally detained or beaten and raped when arrested. There was no support for the right that affected the majority—the right to make a living from sex work in a safe and legal way.

As I said at the outset, this is not a systematic analysis, but observations by a sex workers' activist that different feminists are variously our worst enemy, not helpful allies of our movement. Feminist scholars, especially the sensible non-violent ones, are understandably quick to point out that feminism is not monolithic and seek to understand the logic of how each strain of feminism links, or de-links, with the sex workers rights' agenda. But from my perspective of living those links it is not as neat as that. If it was, I could have learned to predict which feminists will attack us and which will help us. But this has not happened. We see chapters of the same women's organisation attacking sex workers in one country or city and supporting them in the next, or attacking one year and supporting the next. Perhaps the most worrying is those who are consistent—consistently silent. Silence, as the eighties ACT–UP slogan says, equals death.

The matter of silence was raised by a long-time sex workers' activist and friend who I spoke with when I was considering writing about my reflections on feminism and sex workers' activism. Over a bottle of wine, punctuated with chuckles, we shared stories of the highlights: "Remember the time we were attacked by feminists at such-and-such conference in 1993?" "Remember when you were called a trafficker at the US Senate Hearing?" "What about when Shiela Jeffries called you a 'prostituted woman' and you made her apologise in print?" "Hah! It's still on top of the list when you Google my name!". We laughed, ordered more wine and concluded that there is no simple answer to the question of whether feminisms and feminists have helped or hindered the sex workers' rights movement, as per the previous paragraph. Then my friend, whose research on trafficking and sex work policy is well respected and who has been much more active than me in feminist circles, commented, "The right wing feminists will always come back, will always lie, will always hate us and will always produce new faux research to justify violence and oppression of sex workers. If it's not a Dworkin it will be a Hughes or Farley. Their stuff will or won't get traction according to the politics of the day. But reminiscing like this, I feel grateful to the great feminists who are truly part of our movement. It's not the abolitionists alone who have let us down but the feminists who should be our allies but say nothing. You know the ones. They support 'expanded opportunities' and 'career development' but they know perfectly well it means rehabilitation for the poor sex worker dumped behind the sewing machine who they know is never going to get an 'alternative income' or 'life skills'. They express concern for young girls but don't give a toss about a sex worker's right to work as a sex worker. Or the rights of old sex workers to retire. They know that criminalising clients is rubbish. They visit sex workers' groups, they come to our meetings, they sympathise with us in the hallways and tea breaks at conferences. They even bemoan the anti-sex work stand of their own organisations to us. They say to us that the category 'women' includes sex workers, but they forget all that the minute the tea break is over and plans to divert resources from sex workers to 'women' get under way again. They fall silent. They don't speak out, or mobilise to challenge the vicious abolitionists or the powerful lobby of developing country elites in gender, development and women's health. It's simply not a good career move to side with sex workers and these days feminism has sure been reduced to a career."

Her observation certainly rang a bell. Undeterred – and if there is any one word to describe us it is undeterred – we ordered more wine and reminisced about the wonderful feminists who I've described as the backbone of our movement. From Priscillla Alexander (author of *Sex Work*), to CHANGE who have lobbied vigorously against the anti Prostitution Pledge. to Gail Pheterson whose work inspired us to action, Rosanna Barbaro whose legacy in Cambodia is an invincible sex worker movement, Meena Seshu who advocates for sex workers in important Human Rights forums, to Bishaka Datta whose film 'Zinda Laash' says it all—and Bebe Loff. Bebe was the feminist lawyer who, more than three decades ago, first said to me that prostitutes have human rights. She founded our first prostitutes' group in Melbourne and has written and edited work for sex workers' rights groups ever since. She convinced me to go to university to become an effective law reform advocate and has been my mentor and is now my boss. So here's a conclusion and a dedication rolled into one - if only all feminists were like Bebe Loff.

Notes

1. See   http://www.susanbrownmiller.com/susanbrownmiller/index. html. Coincidentally, I read this in the British *Observer* newspaper just today as I was writing this article I read a commentary on the proposed anonymity for rape defendants "This is not about twanging 1970s dungarees and hysterically screaming 'All men are rapists.'" That this is sufficiently well recognised to appear in a newspaper column now illustrates the traction that the early feminists claims about men gained. At the same time it illuminates the role that claim and that time now has as a benchmark of feminist excess from which support for good policy on women must be distanced to have credibility. Observer 11.7.10 Barbara Allen page 15.

2. http://www.piri.org/resoruce/why developmentwork-so-straight-and-what-can-we-do-about-it.

3. http://www.ntd.co.uk/idsbookshop/details.asp?id=936

4. see www.scarletalliance.org.au/

5. Pheterson, G (ed.) (1993), *The Whore Stigma: Female Dishonor and Male Unworthiness*, Durham: Duke University press.

6. Pheterson, G, "The category 'prostitute' in scientific inquiry", *Journal of Sex Research*, Volume 27, Issue 3 August 1990 , pages 397–407

7. Delacoste, Frederique and Priscilla Alexander (eds.) (1987), *Sex Work: Writings by Women in the Sex Industry*. San Francisco: Cleis Press.

8. Kempadoo Kamala and Jo Doezema (eds) (1998), *Global Sex Workers: Rights, Resistance, and Redefinition*. New York: Routledge.

9. Ronald Weitzer, "The Mythology of Prostitution: Advocacy Research" (Sex Res Soc Policy (2010) 7:15–29). Available online at: http://www.plri.org/resource/mythology-prostitution-advocacy-research

10. See http://blip.tv/file/181155 and How Ideology Trumped Science: Why PEPFAR Has Failed to Meet its Potential http://www.plri.org/resource/new-how-ideology-trumped-science-why-pepfar-has-failed-meet-its-potential

11. The Mexico City Policy, also known by critics as the Mexico City Gag Rule and the Global Gag Rule was an intermittent United States government policy that required all non-governmental organisations (NGOs) that receive federal funding to refrain from performing or promoting abortion services, as a method of family planning, in other countries. (Wikipedia)

12. see http://www.state.gov/g/tip/rls/tiprpt/ for an explanation of the Tier Ratings system

13. See for example Farley, Melissa, Isin Baral, Merab Kiremire and Ufuk Sezgin (1998), "Prostitution in Five Countries and Post-Traumatic Stress Disorder (South Africa, Thailand, Turkey, USA, Zambia)", *Feminism & Psychology*, Volume 8 (4): 405–426.

14. http://www.ukfeminista.org.uk/blog/2010/06/17/55-protest-against-strip-club-appeal-to-the-bcc.html)

From Centre to Periphery and Back
Tracing the Journey of Spaces in Prostitution

ROHINI SAHNI AND V. KALYAN SHANKAR

The term "Red Light Area" integrates, within it, two distinct identities. Spatially, it defines a specific location within the confines of an urban space, while functionally, it hints at the nature of services on offer within that location. Existing research on sex work in India has mainly focused on how women function in the space of a Red Light Area. Turning this question on its head, this essay explores how the very spaces affect the functionality of sex work itself.

At what juncture did the term "Red Light Area" come into use in India? Presuming that there is a colonial context to its emergence, it is pertinent to ask if the term was used in reference to the historical, pre-existing spaces for prostitution or more specifically to denote the newer spaces that were emerging in colonial cities. It would require further investigation into colonial archives to shed more light on this issue. However, the existence of spaces similar to Red Light Areas is not unknown in India. References to terms such as *sule bazaar, bateekpura, chakla* in the Indian languages suggest that something similar existed in earlier times. Thus, in the description of spaces where prostitution is practised, the term "Red Light Area" is more recent in usage, although it represents a spatial concept that already existed. But unlike the previous terms, this one has acquired a larger identity as a common spatial calibration for women in prostitution across cities and regions. How did this transpire? How has it come to supplant the multiplicity of spaces (with their distinctive names) to evoke a common, larger, homogeneous image of space for prostitution? Tracing the transition from feudal–socio–cultural to colonial to contemporary urban settings, this essay charts the concept of "space" and its looming importance in prostitution today. In doing so, it brings forth the resilience of prostitution as seen through the dynamism of spaces it occupied.

Historic Centrality

How did prostitution begin to get defined in terms of spatial identities? Understandably, a certain continuity of fixed, recognized space is essential in order to bestow prostitution with a definitive spatial identity, something that a red light area embodies. This would not have been possible if prostitution had functioned only from shifting or temporary locations, as can still be found in the migrating hamlets of the *Nats* in Rajasthan (Swarankar, 2008).

Having become relatively stationary, the next spatial characteristic that red light areas display is the constancy with which they have persisted over time, even as the institution of prostitution operating from within them has altered in form and practice. Taking the case of courtesans, regarded as the "primary exponents of *gazal* (and *thumri*) through the first decades of the twentieth century" (Manuel, 1988-89), "their performance took place regularly in the red light district (*ćakla*)". Manuel writes further of how the *ćakla* eventually became the refuge of the less skilled in fine arts, who were then obliged to rely increasingly on prostitution. The term red light district thus gets constructed as a generic space that remained constant while assimilating the changing versions of prostitution.

The red light area, as a strong spatial entity, also results from the visibility it offers for women in prostitution. In the light of the tryst of prostitution with modernity which is gaining ground, there has been a gradual loss of alternative spaces where women "in prostitution"[1] (dancers, artists, entertainers, women considered on the fringes of morality) could engage. For example, in the late 19th century, the *kalavanthulu* or the Andhra form of the *devadasi* system interacted with the public sphere through their performances at diverse sites such as the temple (which included the sanctum ritual, procession ritual and the *pandal* entertainment), the royal courts and the homes of feudal landlords (Soneji, 2008). These spaces have shrunk with the result that the *kalavanthulu* are today identified as "brothel prostitutes", akin, presumably, to those living and working in red light areas. Thus, the continuing existence of the area can also be read as the survival of a space of visibility that compensates for the loss of other traditional spaces.

How have the red light areas of today acquired these characteristics of being consistent, visible, surviving spaces for women "in prostitution"? In order to answer this question we need to place contemporary red light areas in the context of their precedents, to trace the sequence of how these spaces rose in importance.

In the feudal systems that existed in pre-colonial times, there was a certain diversity of the threads that fed into the connotation of "fallen" women. The category included performers, dancers and artistes; religious prostitutes; keeps, mistresses and servants. This diversity of identities and occupations manifested itself further in the kind of spaces the women occupied. For instance, the Peshwa period (that lasted till the mid-19th century in Maharashtra) exhibited its own differentiations across various classes of women who were either keeps or servants (Shirgaonkar, 2001; Rege, 1995). Barring a few exceptions, inter-hierarchies of relationships would come into play defining the space a woman occupied, based on the patron's status. Within each profile, there were intra-hierarchies as well. In Veena Oldenburg's work on colonial Lucknow (in the province of Awadh), she brings out the hierarchies among the courtesans in the city, with their own distinctive spaces (Oldenburg, 1990). There is a tawaif, patronized by the ruling classes, followed by the thakahi and randi, who lived in the bazaar areas and catered to the labouring classes and the common citizens. This is an intra-hierarchy of skills, which can also be traced in case of devadasis across the provinces of South India (Kersenboom, 2002).

The (skills and relation based) hierarchies were instrumental in determining who operated from where, that is, what location a woman "in prostitution" inhabited within the city. In case of older, pre-colonial cities (like Pune, Hyderabad, Lucknow, Agra, Allahabad), where clusters of prostitution pre-existed, we can trace the centrality of spaces occupied by a specific class of women. This was particularly true of mistresses and women of entertainment (singing and dancing girls), who were spatially positioned to be in close proximity to their feudal patrons. In the case of the latter, the level of skills was key in gaining access to central or prime urban places. Among the courtesans of colonial Lucknow, the tawa'ifs were ensconced in lavish apartments in the city's main Chowk Bazaar and in the Kaiser Bagh palace (Oldenburg, 1990). The less skilled ones or common prostitutes did not qualify for such patronage and were more scattered in their operations, and might have operated from city peripheries. The devadasis too functioned from the central spaces of temples in several temple towns, performing "a range of ritual services, derived incomes from endowments associated with their offices and enjoyed considerable prestige within traditional Hindu society" (Parker, 1998). The term devadasis encompassed a broad spectrum of women (referred to diversely as *aradhin, bhavin, bogum, jogin* or *jogtin, sani, basavi, devlee, suli,* with each having a distinctive space and functions) in the Bombay and Madras presidencies, and such a status was not homogeneous across all of them. At one level, their status and function would get formed by the nature of temples (and deities) they were dedicated to. For example, the *devadasis* from the northern Karnataka belt were dedicated to Yellamma/ Renuka, *muralees* to Khandoba and *bhakteen* to Bhairoba (see Apte and Sahni, 2008). The extent of patronage that these women would derive would differ socially and economically from that enjoyed by those dedicated to the more affluent temples further down South that flourished with royal patronage (see Kersenboom, 2002). Even within temples, there existed a hierarchy of women performing different functions and their economic position was defined by where they were placed on this ladder. The hierarchy of the women is what gave rise to the hierarchy of spaces, thereby making the occupancy of spaces secondary to the profession

In the Indian context, spatial importance in prostitution grew in colonial times with the emergence of the *lal bazaars,* "the red light or brothel area of the regimental bazaar" (Ballhatchet, 1980) in military cantonments. For prostitutes to operate in the precincts of the cantonment, a registration mechanism was in place subsequent to which they would be given "a descriptive ticket which was practically a license to ply their trade" (Kaminsky, 1979). The classification of prostitutes into the registered versus the non-registered was a colonial measure for controlling the spread of venereal diseases. But it led to segregation among prostitutes based on spatial occupancy, which in turn resulted in the creation of a hierarchy of spaces which supplanted previous hierarchies. Within the spatial confines of the *lal bazaars* in the cantonments came the structural emergence of brothels to house the registered prostitutes. For a closer description of such a development, "in Kamptee in 1873, the army went to the extent of building accommodation for registered prostitutes in the *lal* (or regimental) *bazaar*, described as two rows of buildings, divided into twenty compartments" (Hodges, 2005). The establishment of lock hospitals adjoining the cantonments could also be considered supporting infrastructural spaces that emerged for the treatment (or servicing) of the women lodged within them.

While colonization impacted prostitution in India through the imposition of regulatory frameworks and medical surveillance (Satish Kumar, 2005), it also changed the paradigms of spatial distribution of prostitution within the country. Prostitution came to be "regulated and licensed at more than 70 places in the country" (Dang, 1993). Understanding these places to be the British military cantonments, these sites came up as alternative forces dictating the fixing of spaces for prostitution, something that was previously the prerogative of the feudal patrons. In the case of smaller cities, the cantonments engulfed a sizable number of the prostitutes; as can be found in the city of Kanpur, where the census of 1848 estimated the number of prostitutes at 420, of which 110 were working out of the bazaars in the cantonment (Peers, 1998).

Mapping the establishment of cantonments across the country, we can also gauge the spatial spread of pockets of prostitution that had emerged in their fold. Here, we can differentiate between (a) cantonments established in the vicinity of pre-existing cities and (b) those established in strategic locations across the country without urban proximity. In the former case, prostitution pre-existed, and therefore its spaces too were pre-defined. With the establishment of a cantonment, a parallel clustering of women in prostitution got created in such centres. In the latter case, the presence of cantonments brought with it a certain concentration and ghetto formation that might not have existed before. The cantonments, thus, played the dual role of decentralization of fixed spaces and creation of additional spaces for prostitution even as they brought about the concentration of women in the *lal bazaars*.

Previously, the skilled women occupied central urban spaces and the less skilled/unskilled ones were in the periphery. How did the pre-colonial hierarchies among women in prostitution get re-oriented in the face of the new hierarchies of spaces? Firstly, taking the case of the less privileged, the very presence of cantonments constructed in the city outskirts now became the focal point of convergence for them. Ballhatchet's descriptions substantiate this process. He speaks of how the "cantonment was crowded with diseased women of the very lowest caste" (p. 26), and how "only the poorest and the most wretched could be induced" to enter the lock hospitals (p. 17). While the cantonment housed a mix of dancing girls and prostitutes who were the registered ones; it also became the centre of gravity attracting a host of unregistered women to operate from its vicinity. In all probability, these were prostitutes. Ballhatchet uses the term "vagrant" to describe such women. He also writes of "unauthorized women haunting the barracks and infesting the neighbourhood after dark" at Madras (p. 52) and that "prostitutes were flocking in Bellari from neighbouring villages" (p. 54), possibly to service the cantonment. The effort here is to make use of this archival information in a different context, and highlight a certain spatial reorganization that had already set in with regard to the sites of "common" prostitution. Our understanding of spaces for prostitution has historically been informed by the sites inhabited by those at the higher rungs of the hierarchy. It is through the above-mentioned instances, emerging in the colonial archives, that we find an increased mention of the larger mass of the "less skilled" and the spaces they thronged.

Swept to the Margins

A spatial displacement was also in store for some of the sections of women occupying the higher echelons in feudal hierarchies. The growing pressures of colonial regulatory frameworks worked in tandem with middle class morality to oust these women from the central spaces they had come to occupy. Public pressures were mounting to oust women in prostitution from central, visible locations within cities. The Cawnpore Gazette of 23 September 1892 reports how the "Municipal Board of Kanpur was rebuked for allowing prostitutes to live in the centre of the town" (as cited in Gupta, 2001). In the case of Agra, bylaws attempting to regulate the location of residence for prostitutes had been initiated by the municipal authorities (ibid, 120-121); the intention being to shift them from their established central locations in Saib-ki-Bazaar, Kinari Bazaar, Cashmere Bazaar to the other side of the river, where new (less visible) residences were proposed. The byelaws were eventually issued not only in Agra, but in several other places like Khurja, Rurki, Banaras etc., "giving details of areas from where prostitutes and brothels were to be *excluded*" (ibid, 121 italics ours).

What were the implications of defining the zones from where prostitutes were to be excluded? The main objective, undoubtedly, was the sanitization or cleansing of the cities. From the perspective of the women though, what would be the inclusive spaces from where these dislocated women could operate? The exclusion from spaces led to a de facto spatial convergence of women in commonly shared areas, leading to a dismantling of the hierarchies that previously existed among them. It can be speculated here that such a convergence could either (a) have materialized in the peripheries of the same city or (b) involved an element of migration into the larger urban centres that had begun to emerge in colonial times. In their work on prostitution in Bombay, when Punekar and Rao cite from the *Bombay Gazetteer* and describe how "the dancing girls drifted into Khetwadi and Byculla, the scarlet women to Kamathipura" (Punekar and Rao, 1967) by the 1880s, it can be interpreted as a result of migratory undercurrents that were triggered elsewhere.

Other studies support this surmise. "Census figures from 1921 reveal that the majority of Indian brothel workers in Bombay were not born in that city. Of the 2995 reported female prostitutes, only 460 listed their birth district as being Bombay. The others hailed from regions such as Deccan, Ratnagiri and Goa to the south; Hyderabad state to the east; and Delhi, Punjab and Kashmir to the north. 25 women listed Jodhpur as their birthplace, which suggests "organized procuring" from there" (Tambe, 2004).

Thus, a loss of old, traditional centres of prostitution in the old cities was being supplemented by the rise of newer destinations, resulting in a process of reorganization of spaces for prostitution, not just intra city but also inter city.

Spatial convergence can also be linked to a social and occupational homogenization of the women as well as the changes in the markets for prostitution. The loss of exclusive spaces also led to the loss of differentiated markets, giving rise to the predominance of monetary transactions as the form of exchange within prostitution. The differentiated spaces and markets across regions acted as the non-standardizing elements within prostitution; their convergence led to a standardization of prostitution at two different levels. Among the women, it led to a gradual uniformity of what was on offer, with sexual services gaining precedence over other functions. In geographic terms, it led to a decline of city or region specific characteristics in prostitution leading, over time, to a sort of similarity in the spaces for prostitution across cities.

Colonial India witnessed a shift in the centres of gravity within spaces for prostitution. The *lal bazaars* were deliberate spatial creations to this effect. A larger, sustained impact could be identified in the new colonial cities, which invariably became the converging hubs for a wide range of migrants, including women in prostitution. After feudal spaces in older cities and later in colonial cantonments, the new cities emerged as the operating bases for women in prostitution to thrive. Towns like Bombay, Calcutta and Madras were all schematically designed to have segregated spaces for the British and the native Indians (Kosambi and Brush, 1988). As part of the population of natives, the prostitutes had to find a space for themselves within these boundaries of "native towns" that emerged in the colonial cities, which were peripheral by their very nature. From the centrality of feudal spaces to the periphery of colonial spaces, a distinct sequential shift in spatial occupancy of prostitutes came into effect.

Red Light Areas Emerge

It is to these colonial cities that the origins of contemporary red light areas can be traced. In fact, even as the native towns were getting formed in the colonial cities, spaces for prostitution were already getting incorporated into their fold. Taking the case of Mumbai (then Bombay), the native town of colonial times roughly corresponds to the current area of Kalbadevi that includes Khetwadi, Mandvi, Central Bombay and Masjid (Grant and Nijman, 2002). Of these places, the *Bombay Gazetteer* mentions Khetwadi and Kamathipura (now part of central Bombay) as part of prostitutes' settlements in Bombay by the 1880s (as cited by Punekar and Rao, 1967). It also suggests that prostitutes had already established themselves in Kamathipura by then, or even earlier. Circumstantial evidence can be marshalled to argue for the presence of prostitution in the confines of the native town, thus making it an integral part in the history of the city's spatial emergence and expansion.

A similar case can be argued for Kolkata (then Calcutta). In British Calcutta, the main "Indian town" had become centred in the north (Marshall, 2000), outside the British establishment of Fort William and Esplanade. These "native" areas in a 1911 map of Calcutta (see Kosambi and Brush, 1988) get identified as the suburbs of Chitpore and Maniktolla. Banerjee, in his work on the geographic diffusion of brothel formations in colonial Calcutta states how by the end of the 19th century, new red light areas were developing in other parts of the city (like Harkata Lane in central Calcutta) even as "the *old* brothels of the *traditional* Sonagachi area (in Chitpore and its by-lanes of Sinduriapatti) continued to thrive" (Banerjee, 1998 italics ours). Thus, even while we cannot put a precise date to the emergence of prostitution in Sonagachi and Chitpore, it did have an older presence in the native town, and in the urban–spatial history of Kolkata.

Today, the colonial cities of Mumbai and Kolkata stake claim to the largest red light areas in the country. The spaces occupied by sex workers here are old urban pockets bearing witness to urban growth, having managed to retain their presence in what was then the "periphery". Over time, the understanding of what can be classified as "centre" and "periphery" has become somewhat blurred, with many of the peripheral suburbs (or the erstwhile native towns) now qualifying as city centres. In addition, urban peripheries have begun to spill over into adjoining areas, thereby creating larger spatial continuums of urban populations. Having lost their original centrality and forced to find a place in the peripheries, a certain reversal is occurring with regard to the spatial occupation of women in prostitution. The red light areas in these cities find themselves in the heart of the towns once again. *The centrality of spaces that was lost to women in prostitution has been handed back to them, this time via the process of urbanization.*

Historical in origin and existence, and having come to occupy city centres, the red light areas today have to strike a balance between two contrasting forces. On the one hand, the growth of the city generates a greater demand for paid sex, creating a push for the expansion of the red light area. On the other, the centrality of the area restricts its spatial spread, being encircled by the growing pressures of "mainstream" urbanity around it. How have these areas been shaped by these dual pressures? Even with a limit to spatial expansion they have grown in demographic terms. Consequently, a massive spatial constraint has come to characterize them. If we take the case of Kamathipura in Mumbai, the 1951 census reports that it was 0.08 square miles in area with 9,578 houses occupied by 12,608 families (as cited in Punekar and Rao, 1967). Today, its description would be similar, the numbers higher, and the congestion much greater. Indeed, Kamathipura is now described as a slum area, which among other things also implies a great deal of irregular and transitory housing (Shah, 2008). This has given rise to a new spatial conundrum for women in prostitution. While earlier it was a question of finding inclusive spaces, gradually it has been about finding a place within the existing, increasingly congested spaces.

Colonial cities, with their longer experience of urbanization, provide better examples of this progressive spatial squeezing of red light areas. This is already visible in Mumbai, where the area in Kamathipura is now being looked upon as prime real estate considering its central location. As reported recently in a Mumbai newspaper:

> In an earlier time, builders had stayed away from this part of central Mumbai. Ownership and tenancies were notoriously difficult to establish and in any case nobody wanted to shift out. But changing trends have made the area a veritable gold mine for its location. No one will confirm this, but the word is that the current quoted rate on the periphery of Foras Road is already between ₹10,000-12,000 per sq ft and this could go up when the buildings come up (Kolhatkar, 2008).

Such a phenomenon is by no means restricted to Mumbai. Across several pre-colonial cities (like Pune, Hyderabad), a similar trend is discernible. Mehboob-ki-Mehendi, the historical lane of courtesans in Hyderabad has already been demolished. As stated in a news item in *The Times of India* describing this event; "We've lost it due to road widening! It's sad that heritage structures are sometimes looked at in terms of real estate value" (Sangeetha Devi, 2005). Once it was reclaimed for mainstream housing, the women were quickly ousted from the lane and soon even the structural remnants of the past were erased. Today, the dynamics in which spaces for prostitution find themselves caught are increasingly urban or urbanization related, rather than the socio-cultural settings of earlier times.

Across the urban centres of India, a red light area has grown to be a commonly recognized spatial entity. Typically associated with larger urban agglomerations (Mumbai, Kolkata), the term evokes a similar understanding when referring even to a lane or street in smaller urban centres (Kolhapur, Sangli). Thus, the term fluidly traverses several scales of urbanization, differing only in the real dimensions and size of operations. What is on offer has grown to be consistent across the centres, which makes it easier to look at inter-city comparisons. In feudal times, the visibility of spaces for prostitution was associated with those at the higher rungs of the social ladder. There is little documentation of the kind of spaces inhabited by those at the lower rungs - the non-elite or "ordinary" women in prostitution. Over time though, with the dismantling of earlier hierarchies, the order of visibility has reversed. It is the spaces for these women that are now the most conspicuous ones, as seen in the red light areas. The higher rungs of sex workers (call girls) do not get identified with any fixed spatial locations. Their operations have an element of invisibility to them (see Majumdar and Panja, 2008) that works against the assigning of spatial associations.

Red Light Area and its Intra-Spatial Dynamics

As cities across India, both colonial and pre-colonial, undergo rapid urbanization, how do their respective red light areas evolve as urban spaces? To trace this transformation, we focus on the spatial dynamics of a red light area in Pune, drawing resources from extensive social mapping and fieldwork conducted across 2004-2007. The choice of Pune as a microcosm for analysing the long-term spatial dynamics of red light areas has certain advantages *a priori*. With its feudal origins and its more recent metamorphosis into a metropolis, the transformations in its spaces for prostitution cover a wide time period. In addition, the rapid urbanization of the city over the past decade makes it suitable for assessing its impact on the red light area; and to see how the area, in turn, responds as a dynamic space.

Today, Pune is the second largest city in the state of Maharashtra, after Mumbai. From a smaller cluster of 0.16 million people in 1901, its population rose to 0.7 million in 1961 (Nalawade, 2007); the 2001 census registering 3.76 million (Census of India, 2001). The geographical expanse of the city grew to accommodate these numbers—spread over a mere 7.6 sq. km in 1860, the city had grown to 440 sq. km in 1997 (Nalawade, 2007). The red light area of Pune needs to be placed in the context of these spatial and demographic changes.

In the urban history of Pune, how old are the spaces (or lanes) that house sex work today? Have they always been associated with the provision of sexual services? These questions are crucial if we wish to understand why the city's red light area comes to be located where it is. They will also give an insight into how the area has transformed over time, within its existing spatial dimensions. Historically, the fortunes of the city were integrally linked with the Peshwas—chief ministers of the Maratha kingdom—"who for all practical purposes began to rule the territory from their seat at Pune" (Guha, 1995). Shaniwarwada, a two-storied citadel and the official residence of the Peshwas, was built around 1730–1732 (Gokhale, 1985). Residential and commercial spaces emerged and flourished around this central construction, alongside existing old, and emerging new *peths* (literally meaning markets), named after the days of the week. Two of these *peths*, namely Budhwar Peth and Shukrawar Peth, which house sex work today date from the 1600s and 1700–1749 respectively (see Mehta, 1969). Thus, the locality where the current red light area is lodged had a presence that dates back to the early period of urbanization in Pune.

a. Spatial Expanse of the Area

Tracing the presence of prostitution in the city both spatially and structurally, the earliest reference point is Shalukar Bol (see figure 1), a lane situated along the boundary walls of Shaniwarwada (in Budhwar Peth). One of the backdoor entries to the palace, suggestively titled *Jambhul Darwaza* (or the concubine's gate) opened directly into this lane. Recognized as the oldest of lanes housing mistresses and dancing girls (along with artisans), it derived its patronage from the political and administrative centres in the city. With Shaniwarwada as the central urban edifice, a host of dependent structures spawned off it, and the lane was a part of this. During the Peshwa period the ranks of entertaining women had spilled over into the nearby lanes of Daane Aali, Pasodya Vitthal Galli, Dhamdhere Bol, Murgi Galli and Tabla Galli. A cluster of dancing girls and "mistresses" replaced women of the "mainstream", thereby leading to the lanes being identified as centres of entertainment and prostitution. Gradually, the entertainment aspect began to disappear and the spaces thus came to be identified only with prostitution.

In contrast there are some old lanes which subsequently acquired new names such as Welcome Galli, Bata Galli, Shreenath Galli and Medical Galli. A few houses of "mistresses" did exist here among the larger number of "good" households. But the stigma of the presence of the "mistresses" eventually led to the withdrawal of "good" households. So while the lanes are old, and have long been recognized as places for prostitution, their names today are derived from more recent commercial entities operating in these lanes; like the Bata shoe shop at the entrance of the lane, or the movie hall named "Shreenath", or the medical shops or from the presence of a new building named "Welcome".

Branching out and inter-connected, these very lanes (alternatively referred as *galli, bol, aali* in Marathi) form the red light area in the city today (see figure 1). The figure shows the relative isolation of Shalukar Bol, the earliest of the lanes and the clustering of the area around Daane Aali. Changes in density have occurred over time in terms of the concentration of women in the area, a consequence of the shifting patronage. Shalukar Bol originated to service the seat of political patrons, Shaniwarwada in this case. But with the defeat of Peshwas by the British in 1818, and the eventual decline of this principal urban structure, it was imminent that Shalukar Bol too diminished in significance. With the loss of patronage making it imperative that the dependent structures adapt by themselves for survival, the spatial positioning of Shalukar Bol didn't easily lend itself to such a change. This should have been the fate of other lanes as well, but the presence of markets in their fold made them more conducive to accessing new patrons. Daane Aali, other than housing the women entertainers, was also a thriving market centre for grain. Similarly, Tabla Galli was known for its musical instruments and Cholkhan Aali for its *cholis* and *khanas* (traditional cloth material).

The further expansion of commerce around the area came in colonial times, with the construction of Laxmi Road (the first east-west route in the city) by the Poona Municipality after World War I. By 1935, the road had emerged as an important retail business area (Brahme, 1962). The spatial evolution of the area was impacted by these changes. Firstly, it caused a drift of

Figure 1: Map of the Red Light Area in Pune

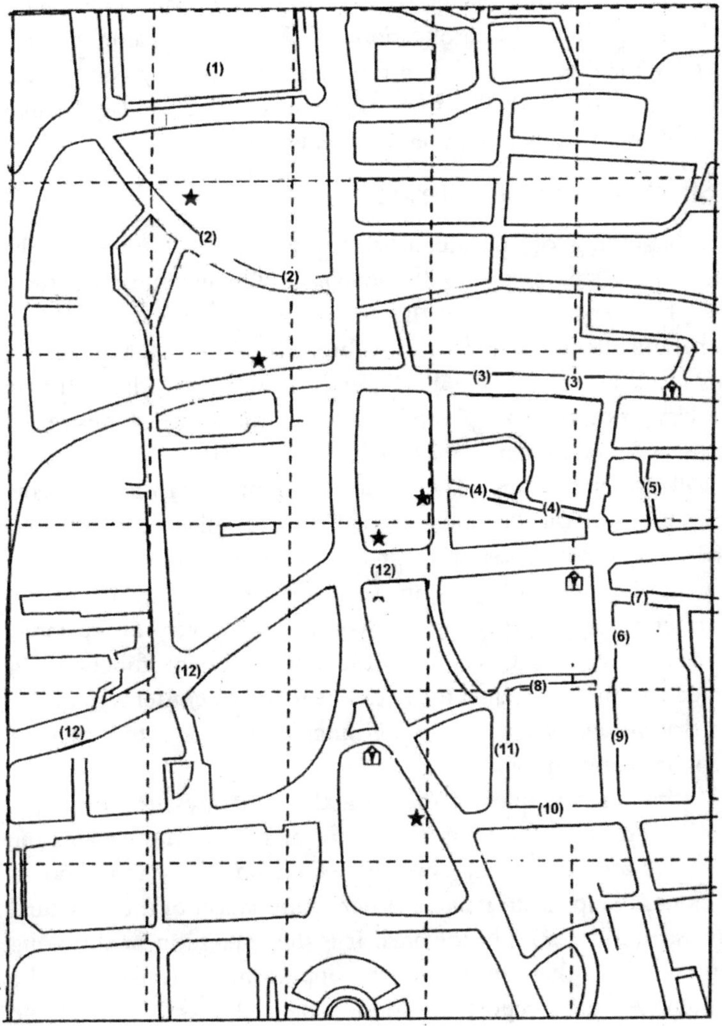

{Sourced from Apte (2002)}

Description of the Area:

(1)	Shaniwarwada	(2)	Shalukar Bol	(3)	Pasodya Vitthal Galli
(4)	Dhamdhere Bol	(5)	Bata Galli	(6)	Daane Aali
(7)	Medical Galli	(8)	Murgi Galli	(9)	Welcome Galli
(10)	Tabla Galli	(11)	Shreenath Galli	(12)	Laxmi Road

concentration of brothels and women from their original place towards the commercial centres in the city. Secondly, after having drifted, the spatial consolidation of the area became centred near Laxmi Road. Located in the midst of this busy commercial centre, the area gradually drew its patronage from the large transit population, from where potential clients emerged.

b. Structural Evolution of the Area

The beginning of commercialized prostitution in Pune can be traced to a structure called *Bavankhani* (literally meaning fifty-two chambers), located in the centre of the city (in Shukrawar Peth) and dating back to the eighteenth century (Date, Karve, Chandorkar, Datar, 1936). Though prostitution did exist in the city prior to that, predominantly in the form of mistresses, keeps and entertainers (Shirgaonkar, 2001), the introduction of *Bavankhani* symbolizes a case of the "economics of cash" markedly different from the "economics of kind" prevalent earlier. With other forms of entertainment-linked prostitution continuing to exist, *Bavankhani* represents a case of identifying a centre for commercial sex and placing the women collectively in separately defined structures. Over time, the entertainment function has waned and the entire area today can be seen as a cluster resembling the *Bavankhani*. What *Bavankhani* singularly represented then has become the norm today.

Within the confines of the area, the structures (the buildings housing brothels) form the next rung of spatial entities after the lanes. Understanding the ways in which buildings and brothels are housed helps us to make a closer examination of the structural expanse and densities in the area. It is the expansion or shrinking of these spaces that determines the opportunities available to the women. Avchat's report on commercialized sex work in Pune states that there were "in all about 500 prostitutes" operating in the area (Avchat, 1986). Our social mapping and fieldwork (conducted during 2004–07) estimates a minimum of 5,004 sex workers, a manifold increase in numbers. In the context of the fact that no new lane was added to the area, how did such large numbers get accommodated? What are the spatial reorganizations that are permitting such an expansion? To answer these questions, we identify three factors: (i) structural transformations (ii) occupancy of spaces and (iii) the changing composition of women influencing the evolution of structures.

(i) Structural Transformations and Density

In the area, 87 buildings were identified, which housed a total of 380 brothels spread across the ten lanes. However, the growing numbers of women are not evenly spread across the lanes.

What are the factors affecting this distribution? The lopsided concentration could be better understood by constructing a "building to brothel" ratio per lane. Using this, the area can be segregated as a three-tiered zone (See table 1). Daane Aali and Murgi Galli would form Tier I, with a very high concentration of brothels. These two lanes put together account for 35 buildings, but house an overwhelming 218 brothels, more than half in the area. Dhamdhere Bol, Tabla Galli and Welcome Galli would form Tier II, with moderate levels of concentration. In these by-lanes, the number of buildings and brothels is substantially lower, but with density almost on par with Tier I lanes. At the lowest rung would be the rest of the lanes like Shalukar Bol, Pasodya Vitthal Galli or Bata Galli, further lower in numbers and concentration.

As seen from table 1, Daane Aali has 117 brothels operating across 21 buildings (close to 6 brothels per building). Shalukar Bol on the other hand has 5 brothels operating from 5 buildings. Thus, Daane Aali is concentrated not only with a very high number of brothels, but also in terms of a high clustering of brothels per building. This lopsided spatial distribution is the consequence of structural differentiations across the two lanes as seen below.

Two types of constructions could be identified in the area:

(a) *Wadas* (literally meaning mansions) or old constructions: These structures are usually single storied, square shaped and comprising of small rooms arranged along the periphery of the square, and with an open central courtyard. They date back to the 19th century and are naturally dilapidated. Their spatial capacities to house residents are limited. They

Table 1: Number of Lanes, Buildings and Clustering of Brothels

Name of the lane	Total number of brothels	One side of the lane		Opposite side of the lane		Number of sex workers
		Number of buildings	Number of brothels	Number of buildings	Number of brothels	
Tier I:						
Daane Aali	117	10	56	11	61	1821
Murgi Galli	101	7	35	7	66	1147
Tier II:						
Dhamdhere Bol	49	8	21	6	28	>498
Tabla Galli	41	5	28	4	13	587
Welcome Galli	34	4	14	3	20	> 524
Tier III:						
Bata Galli	16	7	16	0	0	126
Medical Galli	8	2	8	0	0	>140
Pasodya Vitthal Galli	5	3	4	1	1	58
Shreenath Galli	4	4	3	0	0	60
Shalukar Bol	5	3	3	2	2	43
Total	380					>5004

have common toilets, and are without a municipal water connection, with a common tap being used by the tenants (sex workers).

(b) Buildings or modern constructions: These are usually 2-3 storied comprising of 3-4 apartments per floor with a brothel per apartment. These buildings are comparatively more spacious, with better amenities.

Originally, the residential architecture in the area (as part of the old city) comprised entirely of *wadas*, a constructional pattern continuing from the Peshwa period. Over time, some of the *wadas* were demolished and replaced by modern, concrete buildings, making the area a mix of the past and present. This vertical expansion has been the dominant mode of increasing space within the area. In the more concentrated of lanes (like Daane Aali), there are a larger number of newer buildings. The *wadas* here have been replaced by subsequent waves of newer constructions. With more space available, a higher number of brothels operate from them. In brief, the uneven distribution of the old and new structures across the lanes is the key to deciphering the skewed numbers of women in prostitution across the lanes.

(ii) Occupancy of Spaces, Ownership and Rentals

In terms of real estate, the area can be termed as a conglomeration of two types of structures:

(a) Primary structures: These comprise the brothels which are residential-cum-commercial spaces.

(b) Complementary structures: These are commercial spaces not associated directly with sex work, but deriving their customers from the sex workers and their clientele. They include restaurants, eateries, laundry shops, beauty parlours, garment shops, wine shops etc., as well as makeshift commerce in the lanes including hawkers selling flowers, quack doctors, roadside vendors selling pirated CDs of pornographic material etc.

Across the lanes, the brothels have come to occupy spaces by replacing residential households that were here till even a decade ago. Alongside structural transformations, this substitution of occupancy has been the pattern for expansion within the area; by gradual assimilation of all non-sex-work based residential spaces.

The non-sex-work based residential spaces in the area have been driven out, by those for whom these spaces are more profitable. In the case of brothels, the higher monetary realizations through sex work have prompted the purely residential spaces to be gradually rented out at higher rates or bought over. Similarly, considering that it would be difficult to find customers for non-sex-work related business; the commercial spaces have also been occupied by sex work supporting commerce.

The high profitability of spaces reflects in the high realty valuations of the area, both in terms of:

(a) Capital values of the real estate:

Considering the average price of ₹2,200 per sq. ft in this area of Pune (in 2007), the real estate valuations here are comparable with premium residential spaces in the city (Trammel Crow Meghraj, 2007). The valuations are in line with rates quoted across the old city (Trammell Crow Meghraj, 2006), of which the red light area is a part. Significantly, the stigma of sex work hasn't led to a lowering of its real estate valuations. There is strong sustaining demand from the brothels arising from the high productivity of the spaces that works to keep the prices high.

(b) Rentals derived from the spaces:

The area in Pune witnesses exorbitantly high rentals being derived out of the structures. The asking rental rates start from ₹1,100 per day per room (in the *wadas*) and could be as high as ₹5,000 per day per room (in the new buildings). This translates into a range of ₹33,000–1,50,000 per month as rent. In comparison, the average residential rentals in the old city of Pune fall in the range of ₹5,785-7,465 per month for a 2 bedroom, hall and kitchen (BHK) apartment and ₹7,934-11,665 per month for a larger 4 BHK apartment (Trammel Crow Meghraj, 2006; the figures quoted in the original are in US dollars, converted at 1 $=₹42). Thus, within the same geographical limits of the old city, the rents in the red light area are much higher and that too, for much smaller floor spaces and amenities.

(iii) Changing Composition of Women

The third dimension of the skewed distribution in the area emerges from the evolving composition of residential and flying sex workers across the lanes. In his report, Avchat states that:

> There seemed to be "good" households above the business rooms. These "good" households rent their cots to these businesses. All the women do not belong to a building or a "mother" (herein inferring the woman acting as the brothel keeper/manager). Some are just street walkers, some are actually married women from other parts of the town, who come here in the afternoons to earn some extra money and make ends meet. These households upstairs keep one room for such women and charge a couple of rupees per visit (Avchat, 1986).

The current research reveals developments that contradict the above observations. Firstly, it is the withdrawal of the mainstream or "good" households from the area, and with it the decline in the operations of the non-residential or flying sex workers. For "residential" households, renting out a room to a flying sex worker was a supplementary activity for earning money. For a brothel manager however, the high rentals would have to be compensated by greater occupancy of spaces; the opportunity costs being high in allowing a flying one to operate from the same space. Increasingly, the rise in numbers in the area has resulted from replacement of flying sex workers with the residential ones.

This is particularly true for the Tier I and II lanes, where the structural replacement of the *wadas* by buildings has taken place. The increasing residential population here is also younger in age. The flying ones, usually from a higher age bracket, are now confined to the Tier III lanes, where the average age is higher and competition less intense. It can be inferred that the structures by themselves become representatives of the women operating in their folds, influencing who fits into what space and earns what range of incomes.

Sex in the City

In urban settings, as cities grow in area and population, the demand for paid sex is driven by numbers. Questions however remain on how the red light area, with its centrality and spatial constraints, will cope with this pressure. Even as the area still continues to be a concentrated zone for sex work, its eminence would be a trifle undermined by the emergence of alternative centres of unorganized sex work across the breadth of the city. Such transitory activities are more dynamic and considering that no fixed cost of structures is involved, they could easily move into locations where the demand might exist. In a way, this is how sex work circumvents the spatial constrictions faced by the area.

Within the area itself, the focus is on spatial utilization and who can generate maximum returns from the available, limited space. It is the incomes that are earned from those spaces that dictate who gets to occupy which space. For example, we find a combination of ethnicity and age where the Nepali girls invariably occupy the new or better constructions; as also the younger Indian girls. The older women (and eunuchs) occupy the older structures, even as they face the risk of being pushed towards the dilapidated fringes of the area. It is these fringes that are also more susceptible to being absorbed into the mainstream residential/commercial spaces. Rather than perceiving this as a "cleansing" trend within the area, it would be pertinent to comprehend the factors that lead to such transitions. The peripheries are less dense in terms of the number of women they accommodate compared with the very central spaces *within* the area; therefore less profitable for the owners of *those* spaces (it is very difficult to ascertain the real owners of the buildings). This makes the shift of ownership more economically feasible as compared with the core areas where the returns from sex work are substantially higher.

The area today does not exhibit any skill- or relationship-based hierarchies, and thus creates a uniformity of what is on offer. And yet, we continue to find newer hierarchies emerging within its folds that are visible in spatial occupation. The segregation of women into less concentrated versus more concentrated lanes, into *wadas* versus apartment blocks suggests the rising spatial hierarchies. This is where the complex of structural transformations, occupancy and composition of women get intricately connected with each other, driving home the rising importance of "space" in prostitution.

We would like to acknowledge the contributions of Kawakami Foundation (Pune), Meena Seshu, Nitin Bora, Prakash Yadav and Puja Yadav to this paper.

Note

1. To what extent these women could be deemed to be "in prostitution" is fraught with its own subjectivity considering that they were known more for their "professional" or "working" identities. Chatterjee (2008) goes to the extent of terming the history of the prostitute in India as an important chapter in the history of work and women. "The more they lost their right to work, the more they had to resort to "prostitution". They are *patita* or fallen women – what they have fallen from is actually their professional status. Early facts and realities are all obliterated now, replaced by a ghettoization of "all such women" into being only sex workers and the rise of social and moral discourse around them."

References

Apte A. (2002) "*Punyaateel Veshyaa Vyavasaay: Sarvekshan 1998*", Pune: Vanchit Vikas

Apte Hemant and Rohini Sahni (2008) "What does a Language have to Say? Words for Prostitution in Marathi Vocabulary" in Rohini Sahni, V. Kalyan Shankar and Hemant Apte (eds.) "*Prostitution and Beyond: An Analysis of Sex Work in India*", New Delhi: Sage, pp. 307-08

Avchat Anil (1986) "Prostitution in Pune and Bombay: A Report", *Economic and Political Weekly,* March 22-29, p. 479.

Ballhatchet Kenneth (1980) "Race, Sex and Class under the Raj: Imperial Attitudes and Policies and their Critics, 1793-1905", New York: St. Martin's Press, p. 11

Banerjee Sumanta (1998) "Dangerous Outcast: The Prostitute in Nineteenth Century Bengal", Calcutta: Seagull Books, p. 85

Brahme Sulabha (1962) "Distribution and Consumption of Cloth in Poona", Gokhale Institute Studies No. 42, Gokhale Institute of Politics and Economics, Poona: Asia Publishing House, p. 5

Census of India (2001), Online: http://censusindia.gov.in/default.aspx (Accessed on May 12, 2007)

Chatterjee Gayatri (2008) "The veshyā, the ganika and the tawaif: Representations of prostitutes and courtesans in Indian language, literature and cinema", in Rohini Sahni, V. Kalyan Shankar and Hemant Apte (eds.) *"Prostitution and Beyond: An Analysis of Sex Work in India"*, New Delhi: Sage Publications, p. 280

Dang Kokila (1993) "Prostitutes, Patrons and the State: Nineteenth Century Awadh", *Social Scientist*, Volume 21, No. 9/11, Sep–Oct 1993, p. 190

Date Y.R., Karve C.G., Chandorkar A, Datar C.S. (1936) "Maharashtra Shabdakosh—Part 5", Pune: Maharashtra Koshmandal Ltd

Gokhale Balkrishna (1985) "The Religious Complex in Eighteenth Century Poona", *Journal of the American Oriental Society*, Vol. 105, No. 4, Oct-Dec 1985, New Delhi: Oxford University Press

Grant Richard and Nijman Jan (2002) "Globalization and the Corporate Geography of Cities in the Less-Developed World", Annals of the Association of American Geographers, Vol. 92, No. 2, June 2002, p. 330

Guha Sumit (1995) "An Indian Penal Regime: Maharashtra in the Eighteenth Century", *Past and Present*, No.147, May 1995, p. 102.

Gupta Charu (2001) "Sexuality, Obscenity, Community: Women, Muslims, and the Hindu Public in Colonial India", New Delhi: Permanent Black, 2001, pp. 118, 120-121

Hodges Sarah (2005) "Looting the Lock Hospitals in Colonial Madras during the Famine Years of 1870s", *Social History of Medicine*, Volume 18, No. 3, The Society for the Social History of Medicine, p. 387

Kaminsky Arnold P (1979) "Morality Legislation and British Troops in Late Nineteenth Century India", *Military Affairs*, Vol. 43, No. 2, April 1979, p. 79

Kersenboom Saskia C. (2002) *Nityasumangali: Devadasi Tradition in South India*, Delhi: Motilal Banarsidass

Kolhatkar Neeta (2008) "Builders eye red light area", *DNA*, Monday, April 14th, 2008 Website: http://www.dnaindia.com/report.asp?newsid=1159675 accessed on 24th July 2008

Kosambi Meera and Brush John E. (1988) "Three Colonial Port Cities in India", *Geographical Review*, Vol. 78, No. 1, Jan 1988, pp. 34, 44

Kumar, Satish M. (2005) "'Oriental Sore' of "Public Nuisance": The Regulation of Prostitution in Colonial India, 1805-1889", in Proudfoot L.J. and Roche M.M. (eds) *(Dis)Placing Empire:*

Renegotiating British Colonial Geographies London:Ashgate Publishing, pp.155-174

Majumdar Ishita and Panja Sudipta (2008) "The Invisibles: A Study On Kolkata's Call Girls" in Rohini Sahni, V. Kalyan Shankar and Hemant Apte (eds.) *Prostitution and Beyond: An Analysis of Sex Work in India*, Sage: New Delhi, pp. 156-165

Manuel Peter (1998-1999) "A Historical Review of the Urdu Ghazal Song in India", *Asian Music*, Vol. 20, No. 1, (Autumn 1998—Winter 1999), pp 93-113, University of Texas Press, pp. 97-98, 100, 102

Marshall P.J. (2000) "The White Town of Calcutta under the Rule of the East India Company", *Modern Asian Studies*, Vol. 34, No. 2, May 2000, p. 317

Mehta Surinder K. (1969) "Patterns of Residence in Poona, India by Caste and Religion: 1822-1965", *Demography*, Volume 6, No. 4, November 1969, pp 474

Nalawade S.B. (2007) "Geography of Pune Urban Area" Online: http://www.ranwa.org/punealive/pageog.htm accessed on May 12, 2007

Oldenburg Veena Talwar (1990) "Lifestyle as Resistance: The Case of the Courtesans of Lucknow, India", *Feminist Studies*, Vol. 16, No. 2, Speaking for Others/Speaking for Self: Women of Color, Summer 1990, p. 263

Parker Kunal (1998) "A Corporation of Superior Prostitutes: Anglo-Indian Legal Conceptions of Temple Dancing Girls, 1800-1914", *Modern Asian Studies*, 32, 3, p. 559

Peers Douglas M. (1998) "Soldiers, Surgeons and the Campaigns to Combat Sexually Transmitted Diseases in Colonial India, 1805-1860", *Medical History*, 1998, 42, p. 148

Punekar S.D. and Rao Kamala (1967), *A Study of Prostitutes in Bombay: With reference to Family Background*, Second Revised Edition, Bombay: Lalvani Publishing House, p. 9

Rege Sharmila (1995) "The Hegemonic Appropriation of Sexuality: The Case of the Lavani Performers of Maharashtra", *Contributions to Indian Sociology*, 29: 23-38, p. 26

Sangeetha Devi K. (2005) "Preserve for Posterity", *The Times of India*, 31st May 2005 Website: http://timesofindia.indiatimes.com/articleshow/1128274.cms accessed on 24th July 2008

Shah Svati P. (2008) "Producing the Spectacle of Kamathipura: The Politics of Red Light Visibility in Mumbai", in Rohini Sahni, V. Kalyan Shankar and Hemant Apte (eds.) *Prostitution and Beyond: An Analysis of Sex Work in India*, New Delhi: Sage Publications: p. 350

Shirgaonkar V. (2001) *Peshvyanche Vilasi Jeewan* Pune: Continental Publication

Soneji Davesh (2008) "Memory and the Recovery of Identity: Living Histories and the Kalavantulu of Coastal Andhra Pradesh", in Indira Viswanathan Peterson and Davesh Soneji (eds.) *Performing Pasts: Reinventing the Arts in Modern South India*, New Delhi: Oxford University Press, pp.283–312

Swarankar R.C. (2008) "Ethnographic Study of Community-based Sex Work among *Nats*", in Rohini Sahni, V. Kalyan Shankar and Hemant Apte (eds.) *Prostitution and Beyond: An Analysis of Sex Work in India*, New Delhi: Sage Publications pp 118-125

Tambe Ashwini (2004) "Hierarchies of Subalternity: Managed Stratification in Bombay Brothels, 1914-1930", presented at the 18th European Conference on Modern South Asian Studies, Lund, Sweden, 9th July 2004

Trammel Crow Meghraj (2007), "Pune Real Estate Market Profiling" Online: http://chestertonmeghraj.com/downloads/profiles/pune.pdf. (Accessed on: May 22, 2007)

Trammel Crow Meghraj (2006a, b), "Marketscope: Pune Residential Market", Midyear 2006 Online: http://www.chestertonmeghraj.com/downloads/pmu/pmu_latest/Pune/Pune_Res_2Q06.pdf (Accessed on: May 22, 2007)

How Sex Workers Expand Feminist Concepts of Choice and Consent

SRILATHA BATLIWALA

From the earliest days of "second wave" feminism,[1] whether in the global North or South, the issue of choice has been central to the feminist project. This emerged logically from the realization that the differential power of choice awarded to men and women was one of the pillars of patriarchy,[2] with varying manifestations in different cultural and political contexts. Much of early feminist analysis focused on how patriarchies manifested themselves in terms of male control or dominance—often policed and regulated by women themselves—over women's lives: their sexuality and reproduction, their mobility, their work, employment, and assets, and their access to and participation in the public realm. This control not only constricted the range of women's choices, but often denied their right to make choices at all. Consent—connoting acquiescence, willing acceptance, or even active support—was perhaps a less significant theme in early feminist analyses, and one fraught with greater political complexity. Most feminists viewed the notion of consent with some suspicion, since it was widely used by ideologies of male dominance or religious obscurantism to justify gender discrimination. Feminist thinking on consent therefore appeared more often in the context of women's "false consciousness", as a manifestation of their co-option into maintaining patriarchal rule, or in confronting dominant discourse on issues like rape, marital rape, and domestic violence.

In the Indian subcontinent, feminist engagement with the notions of choice and consent—in both discourse and practice—were framed not only by very specific historical and political forces, but also by the class and social location of the feminist analyst herself. This essay will explore how these early frameworks were shaped, and analyse how the struggles of movements on the margins of feminism—and particularly the sex workers' movements—have challenged, expanded, and can potentially transform feminist theory and discourse around the issues of choice and consent.

Feminist Approaches to Choice and Consent: A Historical Review

Much feminist research in the '70s and '80s in India focused on gender differences in access to health care, education, training, employment, income, and political participation,[3] and of course, on control over the physical self (sexual and reproductive rights and norms) and bodily integrity (experiences of sexual and other violence).

An obvious site of feminist engagement with the consent issue was in the analysis of rape, marital rape, and conjugal rights. Rape was the dominant issue within this triad, and a huge site of mobilization, campaigns, and legal reform advocacy, especially around what came to be known as the "Mathura case", involving the rape in custody of a minor Adivasi girl.[4] Although the feminist discourse on rape was framed fundamentally around dismantling the then-prevailing construction of rape as a crime of lust, and placing it squarely as an act of power and violence, there were occasional glimpses of the consent dimension even within this. Feminists were forced to deal with the frequently used argument of rapists and their legal counsel that by virtue of their dress, conduct, or presence in a particular location at a particular time, victims had tacitly *consented* to sexual relations.[5] Indeed almost universally, consent is the standard for determining rape.

Marital rape and conjugal rights cases further complicated the feminist discourse, and gave greater scope to fundamentalist/ obscurantist backlashes against women's rights. Could there be such a thing as the need for a woman's consent to sexual relations in marriage? Could a woman actually choose not to co-habit with her husband? The discursive and activist faultlines were by now forming a pattern: the religious right and other conservative voices against women's right to autonomy and control over their bodies even within marriage, and the feminists and progressive social movements for it.

A significant part of this early work and discourse on choice was catalyzed by the contemporary debate on the "population explosion" by the obsession with India's high fertility and birth rates, and by controversial attempts by different national regimes to impose draconian population control measures that almost exclusively targeted poor women.

Feminist reaction to this was strong and unequivocal— shifting control over women's bodies from men to the state was unacceptable. High birth rates were not a result of women's choice, but a product of their social position and condition. In the lead up to the International Conference on Population and Development in Cairo in 1994, for instance, there were a plethora of studies, articles, and counter-analyses, demonstrating that not only poverty, but far deeper socio-cultural norms determined fertility by regulating women's bodies and that these would have to be addressed in order to locate the root causes of the country's population growth rate. Feminists involved in the population debate believed that not only poverty eradication, but the empowerment of women—especially by enhancing their sexual and reproductive health and rights, was the only answer.[6] The gendered nature of the population debate, and the question of male privilege and women's subjugation in the exercise of their sexuality became very clear when Sanjay Gandhi's aggressive national vasectomy campaign played a large part in bringing down an entire government.

The question of choice was brought home even more sharply, in my view, in the work of health activists in the '70s and '80s, who were witnessing at first hand the impact of women's lack of choice—especially in terms of their mobility—on their own and their daughters' health. Mirai Chatterjee's analysis[7] of the barriers that women must cross—viz., need, perception of need, permission, access, and availability—before they can obtain health services is a benchmark in feminist research of the period. The barrier she called "permission"—obtaining the consent and approval of the family members to seek medical help—sharpened the understanding of the role of choice (or lack thereof) in women's health status. Other studies served to endorse the fact that poor women in the country rarely had access to the right kind of medical care at the right time because they did not, or could not, make that choice freely; they were more likely, it was found, to ignore the problem (as in the case of urinary tract infections or uterine prolapse) or access low-cost local alternatives (such as traditional healers, religious figures, temples, etc.).[8] I have subsequently found that Chatterjee's "barriers" framework could be applied to several arenas—e.g., women's access to education, technology, public spaces, etc.—because essentially, the "permission" barrier operates in most realms for women, and goes back to the fundamental question of choice.

Consequently, feminist engagement with the question of choice in the Subcontinental context was fundamentally different from that of contemporary Western feminist articulations, which were in turn shaped by the race and class character of early Second Wave feminists. Western feminist ideologues of the time were largely white, middle-class women, who framed the debate in terms of individual women's right to make free choices around their sexuality and reproduction, whether and when to marry, and to enter male-dominated occupations and workplaces. For South Asian feminists, regardless of their class, caste or location, it was impossible to ignore the way in which poverty mediated issues of choice. It was futile to talk about women's right to choose their occupation, for instance, when caste and economic realities made such choices completely irrelevant, if not laughable. A Dalit landless labouring woman, for instance, could hardly "choose" to become a weaver or a potter, much less a doctor or engineer. She could barely, in fact, "choose" to stay in school long enough to become sustainably literate. An urban working-class or middle-class woman could not choose whether or who to marry, whether or not dowry should be exchanged in the marriage; if the marital home or husband was violent or abusive—for not bringing sufficient dowry or any other reason—she could not easily choose separation or divorce. Questions of choice thus became located more within the discourse on women's lack of "autonomy" and "decision-making" power—and the feminist movement's agenda became, therefore, to increase women's individual and collective autonomy and decision-making power within marriage, the family, household, workplace, and other public spheres.

At the same time, the phenomenon of forced marriage, dowry-related harassment, violence and death, enforced co-habitation, marital rape, divorce and maintenance, and sex-selective abortions all brought feminist attention to the lack of choice for individual women, even in contexts where poverty was not the determining or overriding factor. The apparent rise of dowry-related violence, for instance, was largely a middle-class syndrome—though it soon spread to even the poorest communities[9]—where dowry was emerging as a quick form of capitalization by the groom's family.

A whole body of case law on these contentious issues emerged in the late '70s, '80s and '90s. While many legal encounters only served to highlight the embedded patriarchal values of the legislature and judiciary, and the limits of the law as an instrument of social reform,[10] they did, overall, help push for legal reform as well as judgments to uphold the right of choice for individual women, under India's constitutional guarantee of equality and non-discrimination on the grounds of sex. For instance, there were cases filed by women being compelled to marry against their will, by women and their families facing harassment and violence for dowry, cases filed by husbands to force their more successful wives to give up their jobs or promotions in order to co-habit with them, and more recently, horrific cases of violence and murder when women choose to marry outside their caste or religion. The Mathura rape case, the Shah Bano post-divorce maintenance payment case, and the Bhanwari Devi rape case are considered hallmarks of feminist legal activism, both in terms of victories and defeats, and in unveiling the full breadth and depth of patriarchy in the region.

With the growing focus on women as victims of patriarchal traditions and gender roles, a counter-strand of action and discourse that emerged was that of *women's agency*—a little different from choice or consent, but critical to many feminist women's movements, especially at the grassroots level. Programmes like the Women's Development Programme in Rajasthan and Mahila Samakhya in several other states, focused on women's capacity to become agents in the transformation of their communities, and sought to move away from the image of victim to that of empowered and capable actors in change. The role of choice and consent within the concept of agency is worth exploring: agency assumed that women were capable, when their consciousness was raised and the right conditions created, to make choices in favour of their own empowerment and equality and reject subjugation.

Maxine Molyneux's concepts of strategic interests and practical needs were central to feminist activism and discourse in the late '80s and early '90s. The notion of *agency* converged well with these, since it implied women's capacity, when appropriately aware, mobilized and supported, to challenge their subordination and pursue their strategic interests as well as fulfil their practical needs. Empowered women, in other words, would *choose* to advance their long-term strategic interest in equality and rights—and conversely, *refuse to consent* to their oppression—as opposed to being merely content with the fulfilment of their daily needs through interventions like credit, child care, or health services.

But perhaps no event catalyzed feminist thinking and debate on choice as much as the Roop Kanwar "sati" in 1987. This teenaged widow's self-immolation in a small village in Rajasthan—one of what were then termed India's "BIMARU"[11] states—rocked the country to its deepest core, and witnessed possibly one of the most intense feminist mobilizations across the country. It also brought feminist analysis on the question of choice sharply to the fore. A range of core questions demanded engagement: Did Roop Kanwar choose to commit "sati", as her relatives and villagers claimed? Under what social and cultural conditions did she make this choice? What did choice actually mean in such a deeply patriarchal and feudal context?

Qadeer and Hasan identified three core positions in response to the "sati": that of the state, which was more concerned with establishing whether the incident met the legal conditions for being declared a real sati; that of the Hindu Right who viewed it triumphantly as a re-assertion of the highest traditional values of

Indian womanhood; and that of the "righteous intellectual", who saw it as horrific evidence of the dangers of obscurantism, and the importance of a modern, secular social agenda.[12] All three positions, they argue, betray the lack of concern with women's situation. Indeed, the Hindu Right, which was growing in stridency and support at the time, used the event to consolidate and launch its most cohesive attack thus far on Indian feminists and feminist women's movements, labelling them Westernized, elite, urban, and out of touch with the psyche of the true "Indian woman".[13]

An interesting facet of the Roop Kanwar case was that it brought back to the surface the issue of consent in feminist debates, and strengthened the link between choice and consent in the Indian feminist discourse. While fundamentalists insisted that Roop Kanwar had freely *chosen* to commit sati; feminist activists and advocates believed that she was more likely to have *consented* to the act, as a result of the enormous emotional and psychological pressure she was under from relatives, neighbours and the entire community at the time, but this could not be termed a choice. My own writing on the issue tried to unpack and bring to light the assumptions embedded within the notion of choice itself, averring that choice implies the existence of several equally viable alternatives. In the case of Roop Kanwar, or a myriad other Indian women, there is little choice in any domain of their lives, since the alternatives are *not* equally viable, given the force of tradition, cultural and social expectations and pressures, women's gendered consciousness, and the very real threat of violence or ostracism (or both) if they stray from the socially approved path.[14].

The choice-consent debate was further sharpened with the advent of pre-natal sex-determination technologies, when the issue of pre-natal sex determination and the large-scale abortion of female foetuses came to light, reinforced by the dramatic fall in sex ratios in many parts of the country. Feminist analysis and broad-based activism around the issue first began in Bombay and the state of Maharashtra, and led to the formation of the Forum Against Sex Determination and Sex Pre-Selection and their vigorous campaign against sex-selective abortions. This in turn led to the Maharashtra Regulation and Pre-Natal Diagnostic Techniques

Act in 1988, and the national Prevention and Regulation of Pre-Natal Diagnostic Techniques (PNDT) Act of 1994.[15] Here again, antagonists argued that it is women who were seeking the tests and aborting their female foetuses by choice, and any legal intervention should punish them, while proponents of the ban—especially women's groups and human rights activists—countered that criminalizing the pregnant woman served to divert attention from the factors that pushed her to make this choice in the first place: social pressures, including the rise of dowry demands, and fear of abuse or violence, desertion or divorce for bearing girl children. Feminists again argued that consenting to such a practice based on the absence of realistic alternatives did not constitute choice.

But perhaps the most complex, and for feminists, most challenging context of all was when women escaping from violent homes and marriages chose to return to them, apparently voluntarily. This phenomenon became increasingly visible by the nineties, by which time a significant number of shelters for women in distress had been set up—by feminist groups, older women's organizations, NGOs, and even the government. But not only were these woefully inadequate for the flood of women seeking to escape from violent homes and emotional and physical torment, they highlighted the enormous challenge of "rehabilitation" in an environment where living as a single woman often turned out to be even more hazardous than the circumstances they had fled. Feminists in particular had to seriously engage with what constituted sustainable rehabilitation for such women, and the cultural and class gaps that emerged between what the victims considered feasible and desirable options, and the prescriptions of their well-wishers.

A new body of research[16] and activism—including the formation of single women's grassroots organizations such as the Ekal Nari Sanghathan—focused on the genuine obstacles in the creation of safe long-term alternatives for deserted, separated, widowed, and otherwise "singled" women. The movement's inability to create long-term solutions for such women, and its limited legitimacy to prescribe politically correct feminist options for them, became increasingly clear. Flavia Agnes, feminist lawyer and one of India's most brilliant feminist minds, herself chose to return to a violent marriage at one point in her history, and her analysis of the decision remains one of the most poignant and eloquent examinations of the choice-consent problematic in the Indian context. Though middle class, she lacked marketable qualifications, and could not support her three children by living in shelters and friends' homes with any dignity or self-respect. One of her arguments was that she saw no point in merely shifting her right of choice—or rather, lack of the right to choose—from her abusive husband to the feminist movement. She refused to be converted into its anti-domestic violence symbol, or victim-survivor icon.[17]

If grappling with the complexities of domestic violence and the feminist analysis of the institutions of marriage and family was fraught with contradictions, the approach to sex work was a minefield of confusion, ambiguity and inconsistency.

Feminist Approaches to Sex Work

Critical analysis by scholars and activists has addressed the question of Indian—and international—feminism's ambivalent approach to sex work and sex workers, and the implicit lack of understanding of how choice and consent operate in this realm. But as Ratna Kapur, Chandra Mohanty, Prabha Kotiswaran, Svati Shah and others have argued, to understand the feminist dilemma one has to examine the patriarchal, colonial, and nationalist constructions of women's bodies[18], both as sacred and profane, and how the internalization of these constructions infuses feminist views as much as anyone else's. Within the Indian context, it is important to examine Hindu nationalist reconstructions of the home and family as a sanctified site of "pure" Indian-ness, and women as the progenitors and guardians of this purity.[19] Uma Chakravarti further explored the historical construction of women's chastity and bodily purity as a key element of what she eloquently terms "Brahminical patriarchy".[20] These constructions were largely untouched by the late nineteenth and early twentieth century Hindu social reform movements, which focused only on the grudging acknowledgement of women's need for education, and on campaigns against child marriage and for widow re-marriage. Constructs of Muslim identity followed similar patterns, while long-standing Christian symbolization of Eve as the temptress, and Mary Magdalene as the bad woman who found salvation through God, fit neatly into the paradigm.

These historical and social processes constructed women's bodies—and particularly, their sexual and reproductive being—as capable of maintaining or polluting caste and communal purity. Combining with tenets of Brahminical Hinduism—which permeated not only other castes through what M.N. Srinivas termed the "sanskritization" process[21], but non-Hindu communities as well—a sliding scale of chastity was prescribed: oppressed caste women had to be sexually monogamous but simultaneously available to upper caste men, while upper caste women's chastity was non-negotiable and strictly imposed through the additional measures of restricted mobility and seclusion.

Some parts of women's bodies naturally became more sacrosanct than others—the vagina, for instance. So a woman who sold the labour of her hands and feet was still a good woman, no matter how filthy or arduous the work, or even if she belonged to an untouchable caste; but one who sold sexual labour was beyond the pale. So while sex workers were part of the social landscape in every part of the country, they were symbols of the fall from grace that kept "good women" under chaste control.

This, I believe, is at the hidden heart of the matter. Emerging from societies that held women's sexual organs as the vehicle to purity and route to pollution, feminists internalized this belief and many remained—and continue to remain—unable to interrogate the patriarchal underpinnings of this paradigm. The first sign of this internalization was in the tacit hierarchy that emerged in forms of violence against women, where rape became implicitly categorized as the most heinous crime a woman could suffer. It could be argued that this was mainly because the stigma attached to the victim of rape, and the social consequences that ensued, were far heavier, while a victim of domestic violence, for instance, would at least be pitied or receive some grudging acknowledgement, if not justice. In a sense, rape was like leprosy—leading to social ostracism and isolation—while domestic violence was like tuberculosis, which, though far more contagious, elicits sympathy and support. But I submit that it was also because of the unquestioned and deeply embedded notion that violation of the most sacrosanct part of a woman's body was the ultimate, and therefore most unforgivable, expression of male dominance and control.

Sex work and sex workers, therefore, presented a unique challenge to the feminist discourse, and resulted in several positions—or divides—in feminist approaches to sex work. But at the root was the fundamental dilemma: how could they accept prostitution—essentially, the sale of sexual services—as a legitimate form of employment or livelihood? For many feminists, only two options seemed acceptable: to convert the individual prostitute into a victim, lacking any agency, further evidence of the oppressive patriarchal regime, and in need of rescue and rehabilitation; or, women of false consciousness, morally decrepit agents of the patriarchal project, whose work and existence resulted in the oppression of other women. But given that a large number of India's feminists were influenced by left ideologies, a third strand emerged, which argued that since sex work is a form of work, all labour rights and protections must be extended to sex workers. The forces catalyzing these diverse positions, and the responses to the challenge presented by sex work and the growing number of sex workers' movements within India and internationally, have been very well analysed by a number of scholars and activist-researchers.[22] But underlying the range of feminist positions was the assumption that a world without sex work would be a better place, making them unwitting political bedfellows of religious and political conservatives engaged in the campaigns against sex trafficking.

Commenting on these "theoretical and strategic tensions", Svati Shah says:

> Women's movements have been among the most vocal about prostitution for two major reasons: first, because the icon of prostitution is a female seller of sexual services, and a male buyer, and second, because prostitution was held up as evidence of the existence of a gender-based hierarchy early in the development of a contemporary feminist political and theoretical framework...the

transaction of sexual services for money has been presented by some feminists as an indication of the reduction of women's bodies to a singular, objectified image and function. The conflation of prostitution with the summary objectification of women is one way in which some women's movements have precluded the inclusion of sex workers as feminists... According to this formulation, female sex workers can only be victims of systematic patriarchal oppression, and therefore symbolic of that oppression, or participants in perpetuating that oppression on other women.[23]

In India, encounters between organized sex workers and feminist groups have been infrequent and strained. Sex workers' organizations were not invited to participate in national autonomous women's group conferences or similar feminist-controlled spaces until 2006. In fact, in the early nineties, a tentative approach by a local sex workers' group to attend a national women's conference created acute discomfort and was finally rejected on the grounds that they were not a "feminist" organization, in the sense of openly espousing the ideology and politics of feminism.[24] Sex workers are puzzled by why the dialogue with feminists is predicated upon an assumption that they must abjure—or at least, express an intention to abjure—their occupation, or reiterate the hapless victim mythology. Feminists, on their part, wonder how and why sex workers expect their support on issues like violence or police harassment or legal reform while making their occupation itself a non-negotiable.

Another curious element in feminist approaches to sex work has been the tendency to isolate their analysis of sex work from other forms of work performed by women from similar classes, skill levels, and mobility. Studies of women workers in the unorganized sector, both in India and abroad, have repeatedly brought out the high levels of exploitation, sexual harassment, poor working conditions, violence at the hands of employers or agents, a wide range of health hazards, and lack of social security and legal protection.[25] For instance, an international fact sheet on domestic work notes:

> Domestic workers are isolated and vulnerable, especially those that live in their employer's home. They are dependent on the good or bad will of their employer. As women they are subjected to gender discrimination, prejudice and stereotyping in relation to their work

which is regarded as low status, and accorded little value. They risk physical and psychological abuse and sexual exploitation, with migrant domestic workers and children being especially vulnerable.[26]

Almost all these studies, as well as activist and women's organization experiences from across the country, testify that poor women in a range of informal sector occupations routinely face sexual exploitation and violence—the supposed hallmarks of sex work—as well as a form of trafficking when they migrate in search of livelihoods. But the nature of their victimhood has somehow been viewed differently from that of women in sex work. Consequently, feminist organizing with women working in the informal sector has been imbued with the assumption that they have the agency and capacity to challenge their exploitation and mobilize for their rights within these occupations—but the only right that sex workers could mobilize around is to be rescued from sex work itself. Indeed, the only time a link is made between women workers in general and sex workers in particular, is to argue that one of the negative impacts of economic reforms at home and labour deficits abroad is the migration and entry into sex work of women from families that are impoverished or have lost their livelihoods in formerly viable industries,[27] and the "care deficit" this creates in the families and communities of origin.[28] According to Manjima Bhattacharya's perceptive analysis,

> There are three axes along which sex workers are marginalised—the criminality associated with their work, the morality that keeps them ostracised, and the informality of their labour which deprives them of bank accounts, insurance, or employment security. Recognition of their labour and economic contribution is one of the first steps in mainstreaming sex workers and according them dignity and rights.[29]

Ironically, religious and political conservatives have usurped some feminist discourse on sex work in their anti-sex trafficking crusades. Outlining a series of assumptions and positions on prostitution adopted by some feminists and anti-trafficking groups, Rao and Sluggett observe,

> A nexus of religious right, patriarchal, traditionalist and feminist individuals and groups has constituted this ideology and come together

as the anti-trafficking movement... all strive for an ideal of what is
morally "right" from their social location. In this ideal, prostitution
is inherently and morally "wrong" and therefore a "problem" for
society...

Traditionalist and conservative groups use the feminist construct that
prostitution violates women per se, but their argument has very little to
do with women's equality. Rather they feel that prostitution threatens
traditional sexual arrangements... The anti-trafficking movement has
drawn upon radical feminism, evaluating prostitution as that which
degrades all women. This is connected to a wider analysis of power
and male domination. Radical feminists would [deny] that their
arguments are based in morality; yet the moral message is evident in
their claims... an idea of female sexuality that is contaminated by sex
and all the more so when sex is separated from love and exchanged for
money. None of these understandings leave room for the female sex
worker to speak of her own subjective experience.[30]

The same authors assert that the depiction of the sex worker
as a subjugated, helpless victim, living a life of misery, needing
rescue and rehabilitation, is essential to justify the anti-trafficking
movement, but has little to do with the reality or self-image of sex
workers themselves. In fact, seizing upon stories of atrocities of
rescued sex workers, while ignoring the empowered narratives and
analysis of sex workers' organizations and movements, is a studied
and conscious process.

The rapid pace of the HIV/AIDS epidemic in the subcontinent
saw the demonization and targeting of the female sex worker in
prevention rhetoric and programmes.[31] The injustice of focusing
on sex workers as vectors, rather than male clients, brought at least
some feminist groups to support sex workers' organizations to push
for condom use and the right to reject a client they believed was
infected. Sex workers' organizations such as VAMP (Veshya AIDS
Mukabla Parishad, later renamed Veshya Anyay Mukti Parishad,
in recognition of its larger struggle against injustice), the DMSC
(Durbar Mahila Samanwaya Committee), and the Chennai-based
IFPEC (Indira Female Peer Educators Collective), through their
peer education and condom-use campaigns, also demonstrated

their superior capacity, when organized, to choose safe sex and to refuse consent to non-compliant clients, when the majority of Indian women are still struggling to do so.

Nevertheless, and through this long and rather torturous historical relationship, many feminists—like myself—have slowly come to re-examine their approach to sex work, largely because of the growing visibility, voice, and compelling analysis of sex workers movements within the country and abroad, and the open challenges these have thrown to feminist organizations and the national women's movement as a whole. This gradual awakening is thanks not only to sex workers' movements, but to movements of other marginalized and formerly invisible constituencies of women—and men; the movements of lesbian, gay, bisexual, transsexual and intersex peoples, of disabled women, of HIV/AIDS affected people, and so forth.

The turning point occurred at the National Autonomous Women's Conference held in Kolkata in 2006, after a gap of nearly nine years, where

> ...thousands of women from across the nation who had come to share their experiences of struggle, hundreds of banners with catchy slogans on women's rights, and scores of intense debates. But unlike the previous conferences, this one included groups never actively included before: women with disability, transgender people and hijras, and, most strikingly, sex workers. Over the four days of the conference, sex workers put forward their arguments forcefully and with clarity...[32]

Thus, over the past few years, a new dialogue has begun to occur and many feminist scholars, researchers and activists are beginning to listen and learn, rather than lecture or prescribe.

What Sex Workers Teach Feminism about Choice and Consent

Organized, politically aware sex workers are making their assertions within a new framework. Their argument for visibility, voice and rights goes something like this: "We may not have had a choice about whether or not to do sex work, or the other choices available to us for livelihood and survival were worse, but we now *consent* to be in this occupation, or we choose to remain in it as the most economically advantageous. We demand recognition as workers and all our rights as citizens."

What can feminists learn from this? First, the views of organized sex workers and their movements are framed within the discourse of citizenship and citizenship rights, an approach that feminist analyses of sex work have never used. At its most basic, citizenship is defined as the relationship between an individual and a particular social, political, or national community, and defines citizens as having both rights and responsibilities within those settings.[33] However, feminist critiques of citizenship theory have addressed the ways in which this kind of definition "hides the reality of unequal power on the basis of race, class, ethnicity and gender that can render women subject to double discrimination. These inequalities lead in reality to some people being excluded from the rights and responsibilities of citizenship on the basis of their difference."[34] Organized sex workers, among other politically marginalized groups, have been able to push for the recognition of this discrimination and hold the state and its machinery accountable to them.

This claiming of citizenship rights places sex workers in the same strategic and conceptual space as other marginalized and "illegalized" constituencies—the claims made, for instance, by slum- and pavement-dwellers, who are often also in a legally precarious situation, are very similar. What is striking is that in embracing the citizenship framework, both sex workers and other groups facing exclusion and stigma are seizing and shifting the debate to new ground, away from the arenas of moral probity and social sanction. This is a tactic familiar to movements of pavement- and slum-dwellers, for example, who, like sex workers, have been demonized by the state, the media, and certain class interests, because they are perceived as "illegally" squatting on public or private land, defacing the urban landscape, living in filth and squalor, and representing dens of vice and crime. By claiming citizenship rights—including the right to basic services, secure tenure, housing, health and education services, and secure employment and livelihood—they challenge their detractors to justify the deprivation of these citizenship rights.[35]

Sex workers have done the same, and in so doing, inexorably shifted the discursive, strategic, and policy focus from sex work to citizen rights. The success of SANGRAM and the VAMP collective in Sangli town and district in Southern Maharashtra exemplifies this approach—VAMP's achievements in negotiating basic services from the town municipality, in disciplining the police to protect their rights, in even stopping the screening of X-rated films in their areas, are all examples of this approach.[36] The state and local authorities have been forced to deal with these women as citizens, not as sex workers. In this context, they have demonstrated their choice of equality and refusal to consent to discrimination.

Another lesson comes from the possibilities that open up because sex work pushes people over a moral and social boundary. While in no way seeking to minimize the enormous range of problems that sex work entails, we must also recognize that for women, sex work is paradoxically liberating: they no longer have to behave within the parametres of the "good woman", or observe the cultural norms, taboos or silences around sex and the submissive sexual behaviour expected of other women. Occupying this new domain where mainstream socio-cultural norms and rules no longer operate, they are free to make choices that are not available to their "good" sisters. They can speak openly for instance, about the violence, humiliation, and duplicity of clients, police, pimps, lovers, and the larger community, in a way that poor women in the mainstream of society need years of consciousness-raising to reach.

Of course, this kind of voice and articulation requires organization. The evidence is quite clear, for instance, that up-market individual sex workers have less power to set the terms of their work than poorer but organized sex workers operating out of brothels or red light districts.[37] And like unorganized sector workers everywhere, unorganized sex workers are exploited, disempowered, and violated by the structures of the sex industry—brothel owners, pimps, procurers, police, health care providers, and the rest. At the same time, unorganized sex workers are no worse off than other unorganized workers—home-based bidi, agarbatti, pappad or garment workers, for instance, whose hours, health hazards, low wages, and lack of social security receive scant attention or redress from state machinery.

The next lesson for feminists here is that despite decades of organizing and movement building among diverse classes of women, we have not been quite as successful in catalyzing this sense of liberation in the most intimate sphere of women's lives—their relationships with their own bodies, or their sexual lives. Consequently, we have been less effective in enabling women to ensure condom use; refuse sex when they are ill, in advanced pregnancy, or simply too tired; or achieve the right to choose the terms of their sexual interaction with their partners, much less claim their right to pleasure—things that organized sex workers negotiate every day, and for the most part, successfully. Furthermore, even the limited choice that organized sex workers have in setting the terms of their trade appears more advanced than what has been accomplished through organizing among other unorganized women workers—with a few notable exceptions. It is hard to find examples of unorganized women workers' movements that are as vibrant, visible, and vocal, or made as many significant gains, as sex workers' movements have accomplished for their members in some parts of India.

Even within the domain of sexuality, sex workers' movements are pushing feminist theory by re-positioning sexual services—and hence the entire morass of choice and consent—in a fundamental way. They have taken sex out of the domain not only of morality, but of the relationship paradigm. They are saying that providing sex can be a non-emotion-based, uncomplicated physical service not dissimilar to nursing or cleaning, if only we can break out of the internalized socio-cultural box. And therefore, it can be a livelihood choice; one can freely consent to be in sex work, especially for those whose skill set and socio-economic location prevent access to work that is equivalent in both the negatives and positives. And once in it, they can, as part of organized, politically conscious movements, assert greater power and control than women in equally un-regulated sectors of the market: they can negotiate condom use, working hours, time off, housing and habitat, and health care; they can choose clients, choose the kinds of services they will and will not provide, resist and penalize violence of various kinds and by diverse actors. Condemnation of sex work, they are telling feminists, is evidence of one's co-option into the patriarchal belief system, of one's unquestioned acceptance of the mythology of the sanctity of sexual interactions. They reject concepts like "sexual slavery" and exploitation, and render it comparable to—or even slightly better than—the slavery and exploitation involved in many other occupations populated by women.

Finally, sex workers' movements are breaking through the feminist (and other progressive social movement) narratives of the poor, hapless victim. These narratives enabled supposedly progressive forces to form an ideologically acceptable connection with sex workers' interests and issues, but in reality, served to ensure their moral superiority and control of the discourse, while objectifying sex workers. Sex workers are now becoming the subjects of their own analysis by breaking free of this ideological and conceptual stranglehold. They are asserting their consent to be in sex work—whether they entered it by choice or not—and consequently challenging the victim imagery. Further, they are making shocking and uncomfortable arguments about their choice and agency in remaining within it: that it gives them a higher income, more purchasing power, better long-term economic security and independence, and far less drudgery than the other options available to them. How can members of such a dubious, stigmatized profession make such audacious, un-victim-like claims?

More importantly, not many feminist movements can claim to have parleyed their organizing into the sort of political power that many sex workers' movements have demonstrated. In Chennai, the sex workers' organization IFPEC threatened to boycott elections with the slogan of "No Status, No Vote", to push the political leaders into taking Chennai's sex industry out of the twilight zone it occupied for nearly a century, and extending all labour rights to sex workers.[38] Organizations like VAMP have had similar political success on a range of issues affecting the lives of sex workers.

If feminists could re-examine their constructs from the radically different perspectives offered by sex workers' movements, they would perhaps locate and define the notions of choice and consent very differently. They—or should I say we?—would recast choice not in the binary of "real" or "false," but as occurring along a spectrum that is defined by context. Consent would be looked at not only as a manifestation of agency within socially recognized institutions like marriage, family, state and market, or for socially acceptable alternatives, but as the right to choose a social location outside these structures. Feminists would also be forced to interrogate understandings of the complex dynamic of choice and consent, especially in gendered contexts of poverty, restricted socio-economic boundaries and mobility, and move away from the rather black-and-white analysis that our ideological conditioning has produced. But even these are just a crude sampling of the conceptual riches that lie in store for those willing to engage in a genuine process of dialogue and theorization with the organized sex worker community.

Feminists like myself have long since accepted that it is the movements we marginalized—sex workers, sexual identity, disability rights—that have, over the past decade, challenged, enriched, enlarged and renewed our theoretical and strategic frameworks, saving them from the stagnation that had set in. We have not always been willing students, or open to the intellectual creativity they bring, nor have we seriously considered the need for more sustained, structured engagements that could take us down even more exciting new paths. A long-term partnership for the production of new paradigms and strategies is the need of the day, and sex workers are a key source of learning for the future of the feminist project. The question is, do we have the humility and the courage to ask for a seat at their table, rather than invite them to ours?

Notes

1. A period generally considered to have begun in the early seventies of the last century
2. See Kate Millet, Germaine Greer, and Shulamith Firestone

3. The landmark report "Towards Equality—Report of the Committee on the Status of Women in India", released in 1974, was one of the first of its kind in the world, recording the breadth and depth of gender discrimination in the country.

4. See Kumar, Radha (1993) *The History of Doing: An Illustrated Account of Movements for Women's Rights and Feminism in India, 1800-1990*, New Delhi, Kali for Women.

5. Kumar, Radha (1993) *ibid.*, P.128.

6. Sen, Gita and Srilatha Batliwala (2000) "Empowering Women for Reproductive Rights", in Harriet Presser & Gita Sen (Eds.), *Women's Empowerment and Demographic Processes: Moving Beyond Cairo*. Oxford, Oxford University Press, pp. 15-36.

7. Chatterjee, Mirai (1988) "Women's Access to Health", Chennai, Allied Publishers.

8. Gupte, Manisha et al, (1997), "Women's Role in Decision-making in Abortion: Profiles from Rural Maharashtra", unpublished document, CEHAT (Centre for Health Advocacy and Training), Mumbai: Batliwala Srilatha, Anita Gurumurthy, B.K. Anita and Chandana Wali, 1999, *Status of Women in Rural Karnataka*, Bangalore, National Institute of Advanced Studies; Manisha Gupte, (1987) "The Social Trap", in Kamakshi Bhate, Lakshmi Menon and Manisha Gupte (eds) *In Search of Our Bodies*, Bombay: Shakti Books, pp. 6-12.

9. See Batliwala et al, (1998) "Status of Rural Women in Karnataka", Bangalore, National Institute of Advanced Studies, p.191, Fig.7, "Intergenerational Changes in Giving/Taking Dowry".

10. Agnes, Flavia (1990) "State, Gender and the Rhetoric of Law Reform", downloadable from http://www.majlisbombay.org/research_ped02.htm.

11. India's four most socio-economically backward states at that time, particularly in terms of the status of women, were Bihar, Madhya Pradesh, Rajasthan, and Uttar Pradesh, ironically termed "BIMARU"—or sick—by a noted demographer.

12. Qadeer, Imrana and Zoya Hasan (1087) "Deadly Politics of the State and its Apologists", *Economic and Political Weekly*, Vol. 22, No. 46 (Nov. 14), pp. 1946–1949.

13. Sen, Samita (2000) "Toward a Feminist Politics? The Indian Women's Movement in Historical Perspective", Washington DC: The World Bank, Development Research Group, Working Paper Series No.9, P.27.

14. Batliwala, Srilatha (1987) "For Women it is Never a Matter of Choice", in the now-defunct *Indian Post*.

15. CEHAT (Centre for Health Advocacy and Training), no date, "Call for ban on Sex Selection", http://www.cehatt.org/pndt.html: Madhu Gurung, n.d. The Disappearing Girl Child: Alarming Sex Ratio Trends, background paper, http://www.empowerpoor.org/backgrounder.asp?report_101.

16. Chen, Martha Alter (ed.) (1998) Widows in India—Social Neglect and Public Action, New Delhi/Thousand Oaks/London, Sage Publications.

17. All, personal communications of Flavis to the author in 1982.

18. Kapur, Ratna (2005) *Erotic Justice: Law and the New Politics of Postcolonialism*, Delhi: Permanent Black; and 2001, "Sexcapades and the Law", in *Seminar*, No. 505, Special Issue: Towards Equality, A Symposium on Women, Feminism, and Women's Movements; Svati Shah, 2010, Sex Work and Women's Movement, CREA Working Paper Series, forthcoming; Prabha Kotiswaran, Preparing for Civil Disobedience: Indian Sex Workers and the Law, Bangalore Alternative Law Forum, n.d.

19. See Partha Chatterjee's "The Nationalist Resolution of the Women's Question", in Kumkum Sangari and Sudesh Vaid (eds), *Recasting Women: Essays in Colonial History*, New Delhi: Kali for Women, 1989, pp. 233–247.

20. Chakravarti, Uma (1993) "Conceptualizing Brahminical patriarchy in Early India: Gender, Caste, Class and State", *Economic and Policitcal Weekly*, Vol.XXVIII, No.14; and "Social Pariahs and Domestic Drudges: Widowhood Among Nineteenth Century Poona Brahmins" in *Social Scientist*, Vol.21, 9-11, October–November 1993, pp. 130–158.

21. Srinivas, M.N. (1989) *The Cohesive Role of Sanskritization and Other Essays*, New York: Oxford University Press.

22. Rao, Sandhya and Cath Sluggett (2009) "Who Stole the Tarts? Sex Work and Human Rights", CASAM (Center for Advocacy on Stigma and Marginalization); Svati Shah, 2010, op.cit. forthcoming; Manjima Bhattacharya (2010) Moving Beyond Legislation, Infochange News and Features, http://infochangeindia.org/Women/Third-ave/Moving-beyond-legalisation.html

23. Shah, Svati (2010) *op.cit.*, p. 2-3.

24. Personal experience related to me by the leader of a sex workers' group in Bombay's red light district.

25. See, for example, the publications of WIEGO (Women in the Informal Economy Globalizing and Organizing), www.wiego.org/publications, or Shramshakti, report of the National Commission on

Self Employed Women and Women in the Informal Sector, 1988, or www.sewaresearch.org.
26. WIEGO factsheet on domestic workers, 2009, www.wiego.org/publications.
27. Parrenas, Rhacel Salazar (2001) "Servants of Globalization: Women, Migration and Domestic Work", Stanford, CA: Stanford University Press.
28. Ehrenreich, Barbara and Arlie Russell Hochshild (Eds), (2004) "Global Woman: nannies, maids and sex workers in the new economy", New York: Macmillan/Henry Holt & Co.
29. Bhattacharya, Manjima (2008) "Sex Workers as economic agents", In Infochange News and Views, October 2008.
30. Rao, Sandhya and Cath Sluggett (2009) *op.cit.*, p.
31. Seshu, Meena (2010) "Sex workers continue to be treated as vectors of disease", Infochange, http://infochangeindia.org/200801106826/Agenda/HIV/AIDS-Big-Questions/Sex-workers-continue-to-be-treated-as-vectors-of-disease.html.
32. Bhattacharya, Manjima (2008) *op.cit.*
33. http://en.wikipedia.org/wiki/Citizenship.
34. Meer, Shamim with Charlie Sever (2004) "Gender and Citizenship—Overview Report", Bridge pack on development and gender, Sussex: Institute of Development Studies, p. 2.
35. See the articulations, for instance, of the National Slum Dwellers Federation and Mahila Milan in India, and of the transnational Slum/Shack Dwellers International—at www.sparcindia.org, and www.sdinet.org.
36. Personal communication of Meena Seshu.
37. Rao and Sluggett, *op.cit.*
38. See *Times of India*, Chennai edition, April 19, 2009, "Sex workers warn of poll boycott".

Sex Work, Trafficking and Human Rights[1]

SANDHYA RAO AND CATH SLUGGETT

There has been much reflection on the problem of human rights from a cultural perspective; discussions have included arguments about cultural relativism and legal rights having more leverage than human rights.[2] In this essay, we focus on the trouble that "human rights" is causing on the ground; how, for example, it is used in anti-trafficking measures, as a position to justify rescue operations and the rehabilitation of sex workers against their will; how censorious judgements issued by law-implementing agencies are made through moral prejudice, and in the name of human rights. We do not deny that the notion of "human rights for all" has been an extremely useful idea, instrumental in delivering justice to those struggling against oppression, and in bringing world attention to massive violations. Indeed, we recognize that the language of rights combined with collective power is a powerful instrument, offering socially marginalized groups, including sex workers, a level of authority to negotiate in hostile situations. Clearly, though, human rights must go beyond the rhetorical if they are to be truly transformative. Otherwise, there is the danger that rights could further disadvantage the already vulnerable. Women's organizations, for instance, state that when women complain of domestic violence and try to assert their rights, there is often increased violence.[3]

The "trouble" being caused by human rights increases exponentially when we begin to talk about sex workers. Indeed, "rescue" from sex work is deemed to be the beginning of the assertion of sex workers' human rights, reiterating the deep-rooted belief that human rights exist only when one lives in conditions of socially accepted morality. Today, the world over, there are organizations working for the rights *of* sex workers, but few engage with the right *to* sex work. Accounts of sex work in the "developing" countries are bound to images of misery, and being seen as "violence" and a lack of choice. Indeed, an overriding representation of the female sex worker in India is as "trafficked". Trafficking in women means young women and girls being transported and forced into prostitution, usually by fraud. The United Nations definition of trafficking is: "The recruitment, transportation, transfer, harbouring or receipt of persons, by means of the threat or use of force or other forms of coercion, of abduction, of fraud, of deception, of the abuse of power or of a position of vulnerability or of the giving or receiving of payments or benefits to achieve the consent of a person having control over another person, for the purpose of exploitation".

We critique the paradigm of sex work and trafficking and examine how and why this construct of the "suffering" sex worker operates through the untenable links being made between sex work, coercion and trafficking. The alarming words that describe a female sex worker's "condition" in the "third world'—such as "indescribable physical and mental torture"; "institutionalized sexual slavery"; "victims of the evil devadasi custom"—become social "truths", thwarting a more encompassed understanding of sex workers as people, not dissimilar from ourselves. We examine the conceptual schema that underlie the project of anti-trafficking, unpacking how these "fit" with what the powerful consider to be "problems". Rescued from awful conditions, her dignity is restored and self-esteem supposedly regained through learning the craft of basket weaving or tailoring. Such seemingly straightforward "facts" about sex workers in India are extremely compelling—especially so because they fit in with colonial assumptions about poverty, the "east", gender oppression etc.—but these make us lose sight of other, very important, facts. The fact, for instance, that often sex work is not a pitiable situation or even a survival strategy, but a *better livelihood option* than other forms of unskilled and low-paid labour to many women and men, often with additional problems of sexual harassment. Some of the women in sex work have spoken about the advantages of sex work over other forms of labour: that the hours are more flexible, enabling childcare, and allowing for taking up other kinds of work. They claim that sex is a "given" in marriage and not always desired by women. Being paid for sex, they argue, provides a greater level of independence as compared with other women—free from controlling husbands or boyfriends—and other workers who necessarily work under command. However, these facts are ignored.

Another unseen "fact" is that some women do sex work because it gives them purchasing power. Sex workers are no different from most people in that they want the security of owning a home, have aspirations for their children, and desire things that make life more convenient and comfortable. Without ignoring the difficulties that are involved in sex work, these are truths too. Does a sense of moral indignation drive the refusal to see sex work as a valid job option? Why does the same logic of morality not apply when we are talking about women working in fish factories? Why, when a woman says she chooses to do sex work, is that choice read as fictitious, preferring the conviction that there is no "real" choice in sex work? And in this respect, what is a "real" choice as compared with an "unreal" choice?

The Panacea of "Rights"

Human rights have emerged as "the tool" to address all issues of suffering, wrongs and injustice. Since December 10, 1948, when the United Nations adopted the Universal Declaration of Human Rights, the latter has morphed many times into CEDAW (Convention on the Elimination of Discrimination Against Women), CRC (Convention on the Rights of the Child) etc., with more and more rights claimed as "human" and therefore universal. However, we see the limitations of human rights in addressing many of the "injustices" around us. For example, social and familial injustices often remain un-addressed within the human rights framework. The proliferation of international human rights instruments, organizations and rhetoric has meant that almost all issues are framed as human rights issues, be they for workers, women, children, people with disabilities, and so on.

However, sex workers—both male and female—seldom exercise rights that are deemed to be "fundamental" to human existence. Of course, it can be argued that there are flaws and inefficiencies in the implementation of rights. However, here we focus upon on problems with the human rights framework.

Access to and the exercise of rights has led to a transformation of society. After all, rights are framed and institutionalized to put right what is wrong and often as an answer to a specific problem. Discrimination against women is a case in point. Women's rights have been added to, from time to time, as more issues have been raised by the women's movement. However, the underlying assumption is that accessing rights should bring about equality by challenging and transforming unequal social dynamics.

There have been several critiques of human rights from a variety of sectors. It is useful to consider the viewpoints and ideologies behind these.

Rights Critics

From an anti-rights position, it is argued that "progressive" individuals and social movements have been deceived by the promise of rights. It is claimed that rights advocates have been unable to show how to implement a practical politics of rights and that rights merely confront the powerful with their abuses.[4] From Marxist, critical and feminist perspectives, rights are said to be individualistic, abstract and disempowering. Rights struggles are either examples of depoliticized culture or invocations of dangerous discourse.[5] A prime example of this is the women's struggle in India. By and large, this has ceased to be a political struggle on the ground, and has moved into de-politicized work such as credit and savings, and self-help groups.[6] This has come about partly through overuse of rights rhetoric. Because rights are confrontational, the dialogue becomes very scattered and skewed.

Some writers on the Left have warned that a politics of rights led by new social movements threatens to shift social struggle away from the structural conditions at the root of inequality. Fudge and Glasbeek warn of the danger of the legalization of politics.[7] They contend that in attempting to achieve changes that go to the heart of social relations, social movements are thwarted by elements within legal discourse itself. The problem of the rights discourse includes hegemonic concepts such as the public/private distinction, individualism and commoditization. The view that women should have sex only within marital relations is one example of a problem of struggle that involves the state.

Even cases that have been regarded as "victories" of the legal battle by progressive forces are not considered transformative since, at a deeper level, the dependency of rights claims upon legal processes leaves unchallenged the myriad factors external to law, which drive the politics of litigation. One example is when there is domestic violence. Women do not want to access courts of law because of the adverse impact that it has on their reputation. Again, the Supreme Court of India has declared sexual harassment at the workplace a human rights violation. However, many women or men don't complain about harassment because their character, behaviour, morality, ethics, etc., will be torn to bits. Apart from structural and systemic lacunae, it is often these kinds of cultural forces that prevent women from accessing the courts and institutions of justice.

Marxists believe that rights place too much power in the hands of the state, and that the struggle against the state should eventually lead to its dissolution of "withering away". In recent years, feminist scholars have detailed a particular critique of the gendered character of international law and the human rights framework. They argue that modern international law has incorporated a number of assumptions from Western legal thinking, particularly in relation to the place of law in society. These include essentially patriarchal legal institutions, wherein the assumptions are that law is objective, gender-neutral and universally applicable, and society is divided into public and private spheres.[8] The patriarchal order is deeply internalized by the people, be they men or women in state institutions. The assumption that law is gender-neutral often has a juridogenic[9] effect on women. The human rights instruments and the legal institutions have failed to ameliorate the oppression and discrimination of women. Carol Smart suggests that rights discourse "has become more of a weapon against, than in favour of women." She argues that the rights discourse reduces intricate power relations in a simplistic way and that the promise of rights is impeded in practice by inequalities of political and economic power. The balancing of competing rights, she claims, often results in a reduction of the power of women and the appropriation of rights by more powerful groups.[10]

There have been numerous debates—in which cultural relativists have been very vocal—about the universality of human rights. These have revolved around whether rights are culture-specific or universal. One argument is that the intersection of strong systems of collectivism, i.e., tribe, caste, family and religion make for different cultural specificity than the assertion of universality claimed by the political North. Though the scope of this essay doesn't permit us to discuss this here, we maintain that irrespective of human rights being universal, their assertion is culture specific.

We now turn to examine how rights, particularly those of sex workers, are operationalized. Are their rights violated in the name of human rights? Are morality and sexual morality thinly disguised as rights? Whose rights are being protected in the name of human rights? And how does this impact the lives of sex workers?

The human rights framework is overly state-centric where the state both confers and violates rights. Human rights are constructed as the right of the individual vis-à-vis the state, but the logic of the state is anything but in the spirit of human rights. Take, for example, the amendment to the Immoral Traffic Prevention Act 2006 (ITPA). The object of this law is not to victimize or punish the women doing sex work but to tackle their exploitation. However, the state, in this case, violates the rights of women to work by criminalizing the client as well as the sex worker who works independently, and potentially even her family members.[11]

It would seem, then, that we are a long way from seeing the effective deployment of rights by sex workers. In actual terms, rights remain at the level of being a rhetorical tool, or as Amartya Sen puts it, merely "heart-warming sentiment".[12] Does this make human rights quite meaningless and are rights not rights at all for sex workers? According to another critical viewpoint, it does not necessarily follow that laws made in the name of human rights result in more justice. In fact, they can have a retrograde effect. Ratna Kapur suggests, "the proliferation of laws in the name of human rights serves at times to remind us how our good intentions, passions and progressive "swords" may have turned into boomerangs."[13]

Even if sex workers do try and articulate their struggles in the rights framework, it is more than likely that they would be further disadvantaged. Invoking rights necessarily means making visible the fact that they are sex workers. Visibility has its own problems of stigma. When actions are taken by or for already stigmatised groups, there seems to be more violence.[14] Moreover, visibility does not seem to have resolved the problem of non-acceptance.[15] The strategy of finding sensitive political allies is perhaps a better one.

Stigma is a social issue and cannot, perhaps, be dealt with by the human rights framework alone. Sex workers face stigma in almost all areas of their lives. Landlords often refuse to rent space to them. On the streets they are called "whore" and other pejorative terms are used as well. Their children find it difficult to get into schools, and so education is denied to them. In police stations and hospitals they are humiliated. The list could go on. Though rights are promised as a tool to better lives, this leaves untouched the question of stigma and how to deal with it. Sex workers who are visible either by choice or accident, or through "sting" operations, face this on a daily basis and it seriously impacts their lives.

Wendy Brown elaborates upon this. She says that subordinated people cannot access rights to resolve injury, and the process of invoking and attempting to access rights often makes their condition or "injury" worse,

> Thus rights for the systematically subordinated tend to rewrite injuries, inequalities, and impediments to freedom that are consequent to social stratification as matters of individual violations and rarely articulate or address the conditions producing or fermenting that violation.[16]

This is particularly true of social stigma. Members of sex worker collectives say that in dealings with police or any other violent or oppressive forces, the collective provides the courage, support and often the tools to overcome the violence, which takes the shape of wrongful arrest and abuse by the police. To attempt to deal with this individually would rewrite their injury.

The Problem of Conflating Sex Work with Trafficking

When we look "beyond" rights at other possible pathways to justice for sex workers, we need to question the current paradigm, where prostitution is read *through* the discourse of trafficking. This paradigm inhibits a comprehensive understanding of the issues at hand. A blurring of the categories of migration and trafficking further confuses the overall picture. The collapsing of sex work and trafficking, in a country like India, results in an overriding conception of sex work as "violence" and a lack of choice. A theoretical shift is required.

We believe the links made between sex work, coercion and trafficking are untenable. They often do not reflect what is taking place on the ground. The belief that all women in prostitution are trafficked, and that trafficking exists because of the sex work industry, is a "truth" that has gained worldwide attention. This renders sex workers in the third world as victims, and if they wilfully move across borders, it criminalizes them as well. Because of the asymmetry of power between anti-trafficking organizations and those who work from streets, homes and brothels—where sex work is part of life—the truth claims of the powerful are listened to and others are not. When listened to, these increasingly attain the status of common sense.

Anti-trafficking initiatives have been largely responsible for the "commonsense" notion that sex work and trafficking are the same. The conflation of the two issues has the effect of circumscribing what is known about sex workers. It is virtually impossible to see beyond the misery that seems to epitomise the "lot" of a sex worker. This partial understanding blocks perceiving the sex worker as a person who is happy *and* sad, and it does not allow people to imagine aspects of their lives apart from the experience of sex work. The following excerpt is but one example:

> The popular perception that women in prostitution are criminals continues to be perpetuated by the state's insensitivity. Courts and

policy-makers now well understand that prostitute women and children are merely the victims of that violence and not criminals and even the NCW now refers to these women as Commercially Sexually Exploited (CSEs). The state is also aware that prostitution is a crime only in that it is a form of violence on the prostituted women, therefore these women deserve compassion and access to proper rehabilitation. [17]

Is it possible that such descriptions can describe an ordinary woman? An important step towards addressing this one-sided depiction of sex workers is to use reflexivity as a resource. We unpack some of the conceptual schemes that make this knowledge plausible. In this essay, we look at how conceptual schemes are shaped to fit what the powerful consider to be "problems". Here, we are referring to the powerful as non-sex worker, middle-class, feminist or human rights activist or academic. Some women in sex work have spoken about how they actually prefer work situations that are not so free because they offer more protection or is more economical.[18] When advocates of human rights operationalize meanings of "freedom", "exploitation", or "oppression" to secure rights for women, this is often done without consulting women on what *they* experience as freedom, exploitation or oppressive conditions. In securing abstract notions of human rights, there is a tendency to ignore the diversity of lived experience. This could lead to causing more harm to the people one is claiming to "help". Raiding the homes of sex workers and forcibly rehabilitating them is an example. Can there be a more paradoxical situation than human rights suspending people's human rights? One of the questions that need engaging with is of what is achieved through considering sex work a social problem and who benefits from this problematising.

The Impact of Conflating Sex Work with Trafficking

The emphasis of knowledge that constructs sex workers as victims functions to bolster righteous interventions. In our view, action taken on partial knowledge can have serious consequences. These are often far more disastrous to the sex worker than the conditions themselves.[19] Much has been documented of how anti-trafficking interventions severely impact the mobility, livelihood and the basic safety and security of sex workers, migrant and immigrant women.[20] Conflating sex work with trafficking also impacts sex workers' lives in many tangible ways. Below we discuss the effects on women's material conditions.

A US-funded Christian NGO regularly initiates police raids on a powerful collective of sex workers in Sangli. Many of the women are devadasis and extremely articulate about their rights. Clearly, the aim of the raids is two-fold: to silence and quell the political mobilization of these women and to eradicate the customary practise of the devadasi. The raids do not distinguish between those who sell sex and those who do not. Since they are planned and executed under the auspices of rescuing "minors", any young woman who is found in the house of a sex worker is presumed to have been trafficked. In these raids, women are arrested despite most being above the legal age of consent. Taken from their homes, they are then detained in police cells, forced to take a bone density test to ascertain age, and sent to remand homes or rehabilitation centres. At each stage of the intervention, women experience gross human rights violations. Their right to livelihood and their right to reside wherever they want is suspended; their right to privacy and their right to liberty and equality before the law is taken away because they are being "taken care of". Some sex workers sustain injuries in trying to escape being "rescued".

These methods of rescue are violent and extremely disruptive to the daily lives of women and further, they impact on actual earnings. With more raids, there is an increase in fear on the streets and hence fewer clients. This does not mean that sex work stops, but working conditions become aggravated and this can only mean women take greater risks to secure daily income. In the moment of "rescue", the idea that sex work may offer women a better option than other forms of unskilled or low-paid labour is entirely disregarded.

Secondly, collapsing trafficking and sex work has the effect of clouding understanding about the sites and forms of violence that women in sex work experience. The majority of sex workers speak of violence perpetrated by the state, not by clients or traffickers.

The police ask for free sex, rape and beat them and demand bribes to drop cases. Earlier, fearing greater violence, women in VAMP would plead guilty to soliciting or "prostitution" despite this not even being a crime. With knowledge of the law and the strength of the collective, they now plead not guilty. However, state violence continues as they are taken to court, where they face the scorn of judges. This is despite the fact that the Indian Constitution guarantees equality before the law. Anti-trafficking discourse overlooks these sites and forms of violence because of the emphasis on the violence of the trafficking experience—and on the allegedly violent relationship between the trafficker and the women.

Sex work, like many other types of work, has its hazards. However, the inseparability of sex work as a category from trafficking policy tends to increase these hazards. The suggested amendment to the ITPA that criminalizes clients in the name of curbing trafficking is but one example of how women will face greater hazards in their work.

Inserting the "Self" into Knowledge Production

We invest in the belief that one's standpoint—in other words, where one is positioned in the socio-cultural hierarchy—influences one's judgments.[21] It is important to explain the relevance of this, rooted as it is in the ethics of sociological inquiry and an interrogation of knowledge production. Examining the conceptual schemes of sex work and trafficking is important because these constitute our social location. In other words, how does a social location influence the way a person frames certain kinds of questions and projects? What are the assumptions being made about women and their sexuality, or about the relationship between sex and work, for instance? These assumptions will have a significant impact on the knowledge produced and, more importantly, on the effects this knowledge has on targeted populations. In short, there is no "objective" knowledge production about social problems.

What are we talking about when we say there are conceptual schemes underlying the move to conflate sex work and trafficking? Essentially, we mean not accepting uncritically what is presented as the definitive "reality" of sex workers (i.e. they are "injured" by sex work), and asking questions about how this seeming reality has been put together. We ask: why does the anti-trafficking discourse not target men or transgender people in sex work? Why do the anti-traffickers not target women in Global North nations? Why are sex workers who work from five-star hotels not deemed "vulnerable" to sexual exploitation and subsequently rehabilitated? Is anti-trafficking really about protecting women's interests?

A Moral Crusade Against Women

The tensions within the debates on sex work and trafficking are to do with women's, and not men's, participation in the sex industry and the movement of women across national borders. This points to a conceptual scheme of the anti-trafficking discourse that is heterosexist and typically gendered—where the domains of sexual exploitation and sex work are marked out according to archetypal constructs of gender and sexuality. Fixed beliefs about men and women's behaviour or characteristics are projected. The implicit assumption here is that women and men should be monogamous, and have sex freely only in "loving" relationships.

Hence, when women have multiple sexual relationships or are involved in trading sex for money, moral indignation surfaces. When men are sex workers, or procure sexual services from women, society judges them in very different ways, if at all. The exclusion of male sex work from the anti-trafficking debates is blatant and yet barely commented upon. We suggest the omission functions to keep women, and the contention of their sexuality, at the centre. However, through this, only a partial account of what is actually happening on the ground is presented.

Research and experience points to the fact that there are as many men in sex work as there are women; that men can be exploited in the sex industry and that trafficking of men and boys into sexual service occurs. These issues get discussed within a context of containing HIV or preventing child sexual abuse but rarely within debates on trafficking. Neither male sex work nor trafficking of boys and men seems to incite the moral outrage that is witnessed over women.

Studies conducted in India have shown a high prevalence of men selling and buying sex from each other.[22] The focus of the research has been on sexual behaviours of MSM (men who have sex with men) for HIV prevention. A lacuna remains in knowing how men encounter sex work. For example, whether they experience sex work as exploitative; the social and economic contexts that lead them to sex work; the sites, types and incidence of violence they experience; and the relationship between male sex work and migration to trafficking networks are issues that are hardly known. A study conducted in 2007 on male sex work and *launda* dancing reveals that young men[23] are "trafficked" by "peer pimps" to rural Bihar and Utter Pradesh.[24] The obscuring of these experiences within trafficking debates serves to underscore the "problem" of sex trafficking as a "gender" (read "women's") issue.

Further, the anti-trafficking discourse completely overlooks the prevalence of women procuring paid sex from men. Research shows this does not give a true picture. A situational analysis of prostitution amongst boys[25] in the city of Hyderabad, for example found that the majority of the boys' clients (76 per cent) were women.[26] Disregarding the possibility that women can be "sexual exploiters" and procurers of paid sex not only discounts the male sex worker's experiences but shores up the fiction that women can only occupy a victim position in a matrix of power between men and women.

Hence, archetypal constructs put a boundary around what is considered a legitimate scope of inquiry so that certain things can be said in debates on trafficking. (i.e., sex trafficking is a women's issue). Indian law and international standards on preventing trafficking state that *anyone*, be they male or female (and presumably transgender), can be trafficked. They also assume that trafficking in persons is primarily for the purpose of prostitution.[27] And yet, in actuality anti-trafficking measures target neither men and boys as "victims" of sex trafficking nor women as sexual exploiters. If commercial sexual exploitation is the issue at stake, surely there should be no apparent reason why men and boys are not likewise targeted by anti-trafficking initiatives and rescued and rehabilitated from sex work. Most feminists and social activists uphold the importance of targeting women as victims of sex trafficking, justifying it with a causal argument: the social and historical oppression of women has led to increased risk of being trafficked and sexually exploited. However, for two reasons, neither point can be empirically demonstrated. Firstly, as we have shown here, without the hard evidence to suggest otherwise, we cannot assume that men in sex work experience less exploitation and are not trafficked for sex work. Secondly, the imprecise definitions of trafficking and its conflation with migration mean that the statistics delivered on victims of trafficking are equal to those who have migrated voluntarily. As Kapur notes, "the absence of women or girls is routinely considered tantamount to 'missing persons', and therefore trafficked".[28]

One can only conclude that the huge investments being made in the area of sex trafficking and sexual exploitation have less to do with these phenomena and more to do with controlling women's mobility and their sexuality. The real problem is women saying they want to be in multiple-partner partnerships in a commercial environment. When women go against the archetypal stereotype of a "good" woman, they are considered the "problem". It is they who are regulated, rather than trafficking.

Constructed "Differences" of Global South and North

When women are poor, from the Global South (henceforth referred to as South and the Global North as North) nations and do sex work or migrate, there is an increased sense of moral outrage. Underlying the "concern" for such women, another conceptual schema is operating: the belief that the experiences of women from the South are radically "different" from those in the North. The "difference" between realities is constructed thus: women's lives are limited by gender power relations in the South, while in the North they are emancipated from gender inequality and experience more "freedom" and therefore more "choice". The primary referent here is the notion of freedom. There are deeply racist assumptions operating from this referent and a moral civilizing mission at its core. It is from here that the impulse to "liberate" springs: the Afghani women must be liberated from the burqa, the devadasi from barbaric customs, and women in general from the "shadowy syndicates of trafficking".[29] Women in the North, conversely, are perceived as no longer oppressed by their gender; as less in need of protection; as in control, politically equal, economically autonomous and sexually "liberated". When making the decision to do sex work, they are not considered to be doing so under duress or because of their subjugated gender position in society. In fact, in the North, sex workers are increasingly posited as markers of a sexually progressive society—as part of the rainbow of diverse sexualities to be proudly claimed, albeit with "political correctness" as the undergrid. Chandra Mohanty maintains that this "difference" has been advanced by western feminist discourse on women in the "Third World". She charges feminism with portraying the "Third World Woman" as a singular monolithic subject and views this in effect as colonization of the subject. In her words, this constitutes "a discursive or political suppression of the heterogeneity of the subject(s) in question".[30] In our view, the debates that collapse sex work with trafficking "read" the female sex worker in Third World settings in precisely this way; *through a discursive and political suppression of her lived reality.* Mohanty argues that Western feminism has projected its own class-culture as the norm through repeated and erroneous description of Third World women as "ignorant, poor, uneducated, tradition-bound, religious, domesticated, family-oriented, victimized."[31] Sex workers in the South are portrayed similarly, their multiple layers of experience subjected to a singular representation of suffering.

Feminist knowledge is an important resource for social change agents, informing social programming. The radical feminist argument posits sex work as unequal power relations between men and women, and as an extreme form of violence against women. The feminist analysis is appealing to social change agents because women are categorized as homogenous, sharing the commonality of gender oppression as the most violent of all forms of oppression. By default, the category of "woman" becomes equated with powerlessness in relation to men. The problem with feminism, as with some political discourses, is that it attempts to find a variety of cases to prove the point that women as a category are powerless. Feminism's political agenda ends up being at the cost of focusing upon the specificities that create powerlessness in a particular context.[32] Irrespective of how women in sex work actually experience powerlessness, they are presumed powerless in the act of selling sex because sex work is deemed unequivocally a relation of exploitation. Though sex work has been a divided debate for feminists, it is plain to see that this understanding of sex work in the South has been extremely influential.

Class as a Conceptual Scheme

When women in prostitution in the North are no longer read as violated by sex work or as "victims" and there is a growing "politically correct" outlook towards them, why are Indian sex workers not similarly read? Partially, the shift in perception is to do with the way that sex work is represented in the public domain. Media significantly influences public opinion. As one recent study found, Indian print media routinely projects the sex worker "victim" image in news stories, which would account for why the "victim" holds public sway so powerfully.[33] Shifting material and economic conditions also influence the way sex work is read. For example, the business of sex work has been revolutionized by information technology. Many women now independently conduct business through mobile phones and the internet. Autonomy means increased economic power for women; in real terms, the sex worker no longer symbolizes the victim. She is often wealthy, independent, savvy, and enviable. As the lives of American and European sex workers have been changed by technology, so have those of Indian sex workers, including those from poorer backgrounds. Many of the VAMP women, for example, conduct business without pimps, earning relationally the same as a western sex worker. Far from exemplifying "exploited" women, they are role models for other women who come from villages, moving up the social ladder through gaining more economic power.[34]

This is reflected in buying land, owning homes, driving and owning vehicles, and sending their children to private schools. And yet, an equivalent shift in understanding about these lives has not taken place. The image of the affluent, commanding and techno-savvy sex worker is reserved for the North or "high-class" sex worker. At best, there is doubt, and at worst, complete disbelief that a working-class sex worker can be equally empowered. This class distinction is embedded in the assumptions that power anti-trafficking interventions. It is the working class and poor sex workers who are beleaguered by the victim rhetoric, and it is their agency that is denied. In a privileged position of determining the problems, the middle class preserve a state of immunity by maintaining the focus on the poor.

Myths About Sex Work and Trafficking

Since it is impossible to justify "saving" empowered, confident, and happy women, the picture of misery and victimization surrounding sex workers in the Third World is a necessary myth to maintain. This provides justification for anti-trafficking organizations to promote rescue and rehabilitation. We subscribe to the view that the image of misery that surrounds the Third World sex worker has captured the popular imagination *not* because it defines actual social conditions. Rather, it reflects a series of claims *about* social conditions being made by anti-trafficking organizations. These claims include but are not limited to the following:

1. Prostitution, by definition, is evil and therefore a human rights abuse.
2. Prostitution is universally and categorically a form of violence because the sex acts that take place within prostitution are degrading and involve violence and coercion.
3. Sex workers lack agency and there are no elements of choice in taking up sex work.
4. Prostitution is both the cause and effect of sex trafficking, and so most women who are in sex work have been trafficked.

5. The magnitude of both sex work and trafficking has greatly increased on a global scale.
6. Legalizing prostitution would have the effect of increasing sex trafficking.
7. Clients and traffickers are evil.

Each of the above claims works to support another, and together they produce the effect that prostitution is a global "social problem" that is growing in seriousness and magnitude through trafficking. One understanding is that these claims constitute the ideology and institutionalization of a moral crusade.[35] The ideology is that prostitution is immoral.

A nexus of religious right, patriarchal and traditionalist, and feminist individuals and groups has constituted this ideology and come together as the anti-trafficking movement. Agreement, and a working relationship, is formed between them, because all strive for an ideal of what is morally "right" from their social location. In this ideal, prostitution is inherently and morally "wrong" and therefore a "problem" for society. Subscribing to beliefs of any one of these groups, political leaders are lobbied by anti-trafficking organizations to execute international and state policy on sex work and trafficking. These claims then become extolled in policy, gradually convincing wider public opinion of their truth-value. The interests of each of these groups are diverse. The religious right's rationale for making these claims is based on a patriarchal norm of controlling women's sexuality, articulated as an ethic of sexual integrity. Many religious traditions believe that prostitution is evil because it violates the relationship between love, sex, and reproduction. However, the grounds for this belief are located in the fact that while in sex work, women are not under male control within the family. Traditionalist and conservative groups use the feminist construct that prostitution violates women per se, but their argument has very little to do with women's equality. Rather, they feel that prostitution threatens traditional sexual arrangements. Feminists have clashed over prostitution, liberal and radical viewpoints being the most divergent. The anti-trafficking movement has drawn upon radical feminism, evaluating prostitution as that which degrades all women. This is connected to a wider analysis of power and male domination. Radical feminists would deny that their arguments are based in morality; yet the moral message is evident in the claims. This assumes an idea of female sexuality that is contaminated by sex and all the more so when sex is separated from love and exchanged for money. None of these understandings leave room for the female sex worker to speak of her own subjective experience.

Moral crusades, as Weitzer suggests, rely on research executed by activists who subscribe to a particular ideology. Research provides the ground for authenticating social problems. It provokes public concern and a wider reaction of moral panic. Despite it being noted that there can be no proper counting of trafficked sex workers because of imprecise definitions, and the extremely enigmatic issues of will, choice and coercion, there is nevertheless a plethora of research conducted "on" trafficked women in the South.[36] Often such research—despite narrating dubious statistics—earns legitimacy because it is commissioned by prestigious organizations. One tactic to endorse findings is the repeating of instances of atrocity, used to indicate how the "problem" of sex trafficking is escalating. Research on sex trafficking has been known to rely heavily on convenient and non-random samples. Violating research ethics, results are generalized onto a wider population.[37] By claiming a universal reality based on the worst-case scenario, the diverse experiences of sex workers and migrants are erased. For many sex workers and migrating women, the choice is often between different levels of exploitation, since their social location and experience does not provide them immunity from exploitation. Thus, a certain amount of exploitation may be acceptable towards a perceived better future, a more profitable destination. Yet, research studies on sex work and trafficking do not accommodate these facts.

Though research is one way of convincing the public of the need for a "better" life for sex workers, the urge to improve others' lives operates at an individual level too. It is often a dedication to helping others that is the force behind a moral crusade. This becomes an identity and much time is spent in thinking about how people ought to live and how to achieve that vision.[38] While we do not attempt here a psychological analysis, it is important to ask the question why there is no self-reflection in social agents. The conviction that sex workers are only victims—and acceptance of this as social fact and not a social construct—must be challenged.

Re-looking at Interpretations of Violence and Ourselves

Thinking outside of traditional constructs of violence may bring us closer to understanding why many sex workers want the protection of a pimp. Secondly, there is a problem when women are not seen as *anything but* sex workers. Their other identities—as productive wage earners, contributors to local economies, carers of families, mothers, sisters, wives or autonomous and extremely capable women—are wholly overlooked in lieu of a singular view of them as either fragile and in need of protection, or as a threat to a notional idea of decency. Neither reading offers a possibility to shift thinking about sex work—in fact both subdue the freedom to think.[39] Without acknowledging the interlocking connections that sex workers have with many people, the complexity of their relationships is often reduced to a flat view, seeing them only in relation to pimps, clients, or brothel owners.

What is needed is a greater engagement with prostitution. This engagement should involve, as Martha Nussbaum suggests, greater care over scrutinizing "all our views about money making and alleged 'commoditization'" and to be "on guard against two types of irrationality: aristocratic class prejudice and fear of the body and its passions."[40]

In sum, our contention is that all those working on preventing trafficking must be concerned with the *method* of knowledge production in order to conceptually de-link sex work from trafficking. This involves not only evaluating how much the process of inquiry on trafficking has been from a social location of the interventionists—who have the means to be heard—but crucially, creating opportunities for hearing from persons who have traditionally been excluded from knowledge production. We argue that the latter know something that the former do not. Because the powerful always think they know better, the road ahead will be difficult and problematic, but it is crucial and it will be exciting.

Concluding Thoughts

As long as sex workers continue to fall victim to the over-represented and misleading correlations between sex work and trafficking, human rights, as a tool for changing sex workers' lives, will remain inadequate. But if human rights do not live up to the promises made, what is the alternative? Do we then abandon the framework of rights all together?

The language of rights, with its emphasis on entitlement and duty bearers, etc., is a powerful one and could have backlashes that are unexpected and often violent. This could have an adverse impact on the lives of the sex workers as a group or individually.

A possible answer could be developing tools for negotiation. One of the most potent tools for negotiation is collectivization. It is evident that rights can work when there is collectivization. The collective has the capacity to deal with the backlash if and when it happens. In addition, the collective could strategize ways of using the rights framework for the betterment of their lives. However, the process of building the collective is a long and arduous one. Clearly then, the rights framework cannot be abandoned, but needs to be modified to fit the struggles and needs of different disadvantaged groups. The collective will be in the best position to decide how and when to engage with and deploy the rights framework.

All the tools of negotiation are strengthened by collectivization. The collective helps in myriad ways. It seems to be a pre-condition to negotiation and compromise. Firstly, it adds to collective bargaining power. This, as is well known, is a compelling force in negotiating for anything. Secondly, when the collective has evolved, it needs the vigor of politicization. It is only through this that workable and sustainable strategies can be ironed out. The politicization makes it possible to frame the issues in political ways that are most beneficial to the group.

Thirdly, it is evident that the collective needs to have a mass base. It is only with the help of numbers that negotiation has the potential to be successful. It is obviously difficult to make a large impact with a small collective. Further, the combination of collective strength and information and knowledge of the law is a forceful tool. For instance, women in the VAMP collective are able to negotiate with the police, who harass them and threaten arrest. The women are able to tell the policeman that they are not soliciting and therefore breaking no law, albeit the negotiation is in small ways and not at the level of policy change. However, it is in these small ways that women find answers to their practical concerns. This may not be the answer for their strategic interests, that is, their long term and all encompassing needs. From these small ways, though it is a quantum leap, sex worker collectives could develop negotiating tools for policy change, changing attitudes, lessening stigma.

Notes

1. This chapter has been adapted from "Who Stole the Tarts? Sex work and Human Rights", Sangram, 2009, by the same authors.
2. For a detailed analysis see Chapter 10 of Amartya Sen's *Development As Freedom*, 1999.
3. Organizations like Vimochana, Bangalore and Hengasara Hakkina Sangha, Bangalore.
4. Fudge & H Glasbeek, "The Politics of Rights: A Politics with Little Class", *Social and Legal Studies* Vol 1 1992: 45-50.
5. D Herman, "Beyond the Rights Debate", *Social and Legal Studies* Vol 2 1993: 25.
6. For more on this see Batliwala and Dhanraj's article "Gender Myths that Instrumentalize Women: A view from the Indian frontline" in *"Feminisms in Development: Contradictions, Contestations and Challenges"* (eds.) Cornwall, Harrison & Whitehead. 2007.
7. Fudge & Glasbeek.
8. H Charlesworth, C Chinkin & S Wright, "Feminist Approaches to International Law", *American Journal of International Law* Vol 85 1991: 613-644.
9. Impact of judicial intervention like the iatrogenic effects of medicines, The juridogenic effect is the adverse effect that the law and judicial process have on women.
10. Smart, *Feminism and the Power of Law* Routledge, London:1989.

11. ITPA Amendment 2006 Section 2 (f) : definition of prostitution extends to include individual instances of sex work; Section 5c: punishment of those found visiting or in a brothel; Section 4: punishment of those living off earnings of a sex worker.
12. Sen, *Development as Freedom* p. 228.
13. Kapur, "Human Rights in the 21st Century: Take a Walk on the Dark side" Vol 28:4 *Sydney Law Review* 665-687
14. The VAMP collective designed a system of red cards for sex workers so that they could access the public health system. This however, identified them as sex workers and had an adverse impact. The idea was abandoned.
15. In the western context irrespective of a whole host of rights for lesbian and gay people, most do not profess their sexual orientation publicly due to fear of non acceptance.
16. *Suffering the Paradoxes of Rights* in Left Legalism/Left Critique (2002) ed. Wendy Brown and Janet Halley. Duke University Press London: 2002.
17. Desouza. "Razing Baina, Goa: In Whose Interest?" *EPW*, July 24, 2004.
18. Agustin, *Sex at the Margins:Migration, Labor Markets and the Rescue Industry.* 2007: p. 33.
19. Ronald Weitzer, "The Social Construction of Sex Trafficking: Ideology and Institutionalization of a Moral Crusade". *Politics & Society* Vol. 35 No. 3 September 2007: 447– 475.
20. See Kapur, 2005; Schreter & Jewers, 2005; Murray, 1998; Doezema, 1998.
21. Sandra Harding. "Rethinking standpoint epistemologies", in L. Alcoff and E. Potter (ed.) *Feminist Epistemologies.* Routledge, New York: 1992.
22. See Khan, 2001; Dandona, 2005; Asthana, & Oostvogels, 2001
23. The majority of the sample (69% n=400) was between the ages of 20 and 26 years.
24. Lahiri & Kar, " *Dancing Boys: Traditional Prostitution of Young Boys in India*" 2007.
25. The study follows the CRC as its definition of child. However, data reveals that 63% (n=30) of the study's sample of "boys selling sex" was 18 years of age which means that they were "adult".
26. Akula, S L. "*A Situational Analysis Report of Prostitution of Boys in India (Hyderabad)*" . ECPAT International, 2006:38.
27. UN *Convention for the Suppression of the Traffic in Persons and of the Exploitation of the Prostitution of Others—Article 1.* The Parties to the

present Convention agree to punish any person who, to gratify the passions of another: (1) Procures, entices or leads away, for purposes of prostitution, another person, even with the consent of that person. *ITPA section 5a*—Where any person recruits, transports, transfers, harbours or receives a person for the purposes of prostitution. *US Protocol 2000 Article 3:* Trafficking in persons shall mean... Exploitation shall include, at a minimum, the exploitation of the prostitution of others or other forms of sexual exploitation.

28. Kapur, *Erotic Justice* 2005:145 . See also Kapur and Sanghera (2000) on the questionable evidence of trafficking statistics.
29. Doezema, "Ouch! Western feminists" "wounded attachment" to the "third world prostitute". 2001.
30. Mohanty, Chandra Talpade. "Under Western Eyes: Feminist Scholarship and Colonial Discourse" Feminist Review, 30 1988:61.
31. Ibid: 65.
32. Ibid: 66.
33. See "Beyond Vice and Victimhood: Content Analysis of Media Coverage on the Issues of Sex Workers." SANGRAM, 2008:9.
34. We learnt this from a sex worker in VAMP.
35. Weitzer, 2007.
36. See Agustin: 2007:38.
37. Wahab and Sloan, "Ethical dilemmas in sex work research" 2004:3.
38. Agustin. 2007: 4.
39. Sen. *Identity and Violence: The Illusion of Destiny.* 2006: 174.
40. Nussbaum, "Taking Money for Bodily Service" in *Sex and Social Justice* 1999: 280.

References

Akula, Sree Lakshmi (2006) "A Situational Analysis Report of Prostitution of Boys in India (Hyderabad)", ECPAT International, Bangkok: 2006. Available at: http://www.humantrafficking.org/uploads/publications/India_Hyderabad.pdf

Agustin, Laura Maria (2007) *Sex at the Margins: Migration, Labour Markets and the Rescue Industry*London: Zed Books

Asthana, Sheena and Robert Oostvogels (2001) "The social construction of male "homosexuality" in India: implications for HIV transmission and prevention", *Social Science and Medicine* Vol 52: 707-721

Batliwala, Srilatha (2007) "When Rights Go Wrong" *Seminar* Issue No. 569 January: 2007

Available at: http://www.india-seminar.com/2007/569/569_srilatha_
batliwala.htm
——— (2006) "Sexuality and Women's Empowerment—The Funda-
mental Connection" in *Plain Speak*. TARSHI New Delhi: 2
——— & Deepa Dhanraj (2007) "Gender Myths that Instrumentalize
Women: A view from the Indian frontline" in Cornwall, Andrea,
Elizabeth Harrison & AnneWhitehead, eds. *Feminisms in Development:
Contradictions, Contestations and Challenges* London: Zed Books
Brown, Wendy (1995) *States of Injury: Power and Freedom in Late Modernity*
New Jersey: Princeton University Press
Brown, Wendy (2002) "Suffering the Paradoxes of Rights" in Brown,
Wendy and Janet Halley (eds) *Left Legalism/Left Critique* London:
Duke University Press
Carroll, Lewis (1995) *Alice's Adventures in Wonderland*. Wordsworth
Classics, Hertfordshire
Chambers, Robert (2008) "Participation, Pluralism and Perception of
Poverty", in N. Kakwani and J. Silber, (eds.) *The Many Dimensions of
Poverty*. London: Palgrave-Macmillan: pp. 140–164
Charlesworth, H. Chinkin, C & Wright, S "Feminist Approaches to
International Law", *American Journal of International Law* Vol 85.
1991: 613–644
Dandona, Lalit, et al (2005) "Sex Behavior of men who have sex with
men and risk of HIV in Andhra Pradesh, India", *AIDS* Vol 19:
611–619
Desouza, Shaila (2004) "Razing Baina, Goa: In Whose Interest?"
Economic and Political Weekly, July 24.
Doezema, Jo (2001) "Ouch! Western feminists" "wounded attachment"
to the "third world prostitute"" *Feminist Review*, No. 67, Spring:
16–38
——— (1998) "Forced To Choose: Beyond the Voluntary v Forced
Prostitution Dichotomy" in Kempadoo, Kamala and Jo Doezema
(eds) *Global Sex Workers: Rights, Resistance and Redefinition* (eds)
London: Routledge.
Fudge, J & H Glasbeek (1992) "The Politics of Rights: A Politics with
Little Class", *Social and Legal Studies* Vol 1. :45–50.
Harding, Sandra (1992) "Rethinking standpoint epistemologies", in
L. Alcoff and E. Potter (eds.) *Feminist Epistemologies* New York:
Routledge.
Herman, D. (1993) "Beyond the Rights Debate", *Social and Legal Studies*
Vol 2 : 25

Kapur, Ratna (2006) "Human Rights in the 21st Century: Taking a Walk on the Dark Side", *Sydney Law Review* Vol 28:4 : 665-687

———— (2006) *Erotic Justice: Law and the New Politics of Postcolonialism* New Delhi: Permanent Black.

Khan, Shivananda (2001) "Culture, Sexualities, and Identities: Men Who Have Sex with Men in India" *Journal of Homosexuality*. Vol 40: 99-115.

Lahiri & Kar (2007) "Dancing Boys: Traditional Prostitution of Young Boys in India", A Study Report on Launda Dancers 2007. Available at: http://www.unodc.org/pdf/india/publications/htvs_miniweb/dancing_boys.pdf

Lin Lean Lim (ed) (1995) *The Sex Sector: The Economic and Social Bases of Prostitution in Southeast Asia* Geneva: International Labour Office

Mohanty, Chandra Talpade (1988) "Under Western Eyes: Feminist Scholarship and Colonial Discourse" *Feminist Review,* Vol 30: 61

Murray, Alison (1998) "Debt-Bondage and Trafficking: Don't Believe the Hype" in Kempadoo, Kamala and Jo Doezema (eds) *Global Sex Workers: Rights, Resistance and Redefinition* London:Routledge

Nussbaum, Martha (1999) *Sex and Social Justice*. New York:Oxford University Press

Ramanathan, Sheela. "Worst jail jitters trap women". *Combat Law* Vol 7 Issue 2. March-April: 2002. Available at: http://www.combatlaw.org/information.php?article_id=1105&issue_id=39

Sahni, Rohini, V. Kalyan Shankar, Hemant Apte (eds.) (2008) *Prostitution and Beyond: An Analysis of Sex Work In India*New Delhi: Sage Publications

Sanghera, Jyoti and Ratna Kapur (2000) "An Assessment of Laws and Policies for the Prevention and Control of Trafficking in Nepal", The Asia Foundation & The Population Council

Schreter, Lisa Diane & Mariellen Malloy Jewers (2007) "The danger of conflating trafficking and sex work: a position paper of the sex workers project at the urban justice centre", Sex Workers Project at the Urban Justice Center, New York: 2007

Sen, Amartya (1999) *Development as Freedom* Oxford: Oxford University Press

———— (2006) *Identity and Violence: The Illusion of Destiny* London: Penguin Books

Smart, Carol (1989) *Feminism and the Power of Law* London: Routledge

Wahab and Sloan (2004) "Ethical dilemmas in sex work research", in *Research for Sex work* Vol 7, June

Weitzer, Ronald (2007) "The Social Construction of Sex Trafficking: Ideology and Institutionalization of a Moral Crusade", *Politics & Society* Vol. 35 No. 3 September : 447– 475

Other Resources:

SANGRAM (2008)"*Beyond Vice and Victimhood: Content Analysis of Media Coverage on the Issues of Sex Workers.*": 9

SANGRAM-VAMP and Point of View The Struggle to be Human: A Training Manual.

SANGRAM (2006) Of Veshyas, Vamps, Whores and Women. http://www.pdhre.org/rights/work.html

The Politics of Prostitution in Brazil
Between "State Neutrality" and "Feminist Troubles"

SONIA CORRÊA AND JOSÉ MIGUEL NIETO OLIVAR[1]

The Early Debates

As in many other places around the world, discussions about prostitution[2] in Brazil intersected with political debates regarding the abolition of slavery in 1888.[3] Christina Pereira (2005) observes that when European medical doctors began visiting Brazil around 1840 and began studying prostitution with their local partners, a large majority of the prostitutes were black slaves. Venereal diseases and syphilis in particular were associated with prostitution and both were interpreted as symptoms of social degradation resulting from slavery.

During this time, state proposals regarding prostitution were inevitably mired in the complex political spirals of the growing anti-slavery struggles. The call for abolition of slavery and prostitution was deployed as a modernizing and civilizing proposition: to abolish slavery and prostitution was to promote social and political progress. For instance, in the 1870s when anti-slavery sentiments were at a peak, Miguel Tavares, a police sheriff in Rio de Janeiro, "liberated" around 200 slaves who were engaged in prostitution. Though this episode is remarkable, state intervention did not shift towards the abolition of prostitution, nor was the so-called French model of regulation adopted. This model prescribed the definition of restricted zones for the exercise of commercial sex (red light districts) and systematic public health intervention to prevent venereal diseases among prostitutes as a way to protect spouses and families.

A number of factors explain the reluctance of the Brazilian elites to accept the French model, which would project the image of the state becoming a "master" of the prostitutes. Such a move would have been politically unacceptable in light of the calls for abolition of slavery (Pereira 2005). Liberal repudiation of state regulation of private life might have also played a role in this unusual policy restraint. However, since prostitution was seen as a "necessary evil" in the eyes of the male elites, its abolition, it was felt, would have a negative impact on male sexual behaviour and family structure.

Even after slavery was abolished in 1888 and the Republic established a year later, the Brazilian state neither adopted the French model—as happened in Argentina, Uruguay and Colombia—nor did it assume a strong abolitionist position with regard to prostitution. This was despite the fact that pressures on the state to abolish prostitution increased as the country became a recognized destination of trafficking of "white slaves". By the early 20th century, in addition to slaves and poor Brazilian white women who offered sexual services, many foreigners, in particular Jewish women from Eastern Europe transported to Brazil by the so-called Jewish mafias, began to inhabit the sex markets in Rio and São Paulo.

This unresolved debate left a lasting imprint on Brazilian state response to prostitution. The current legal frame borrows from the abolitionist frame of criminalization of those who exploit prostitution, but does not go as far as to criminalize soliciting or the practice per se. Since the 20th century, and most particularly after 1920, the state invested heavily in the control of venereal diseases, but did not implement well-defined zones or health identity cards for prostitutes. This choice of a middle ground hygiene policy is not trivial because according to Carrara (1996) the discourse and state interventions regarding the "growing and appalling incidence of syphilis" constituted a core element of public health concern until the 1940s.[4] At the same time,, this ambivalence triggered conflicts between the police, judicial authorities and prostitutes. Though these were not based on written rules, they affected the lives of sex workers negatively.

But there are other angles to prostitution in the late 19th and early 20th century which also should be highlighted. Rago (1985) and Kushnir (1996) analyse how prostitution and prostitutes played a significant role in the early period of Brazil's modernization and urbanization. Rago (1985) examines how strict sexual morality was connected with women's incorporation in the proletariat during the first waves of Brazilian industrialization. Later (1990) she examines how male elites who until then had remained very "provincial" were impacted on by the sophistication of European prostitutes working in São Paulo. Both authors recapture the history of a self-supporting association created by prostitutes of Jewish origin in Rio de Janeiro, which constructed a cemetery for the community and ensured a "pension" for the prostitutes who could no longer work.

All told, Brazilian policies with relation to prostitution between the late 19th and late 20th centuries contradictorily combined moral "tolerance", police intervention, judicial regulation and strong concerns for hygiene. This "model" did not inhibit prostitution, but left the space open for calls for the eradication of sex work to capture the social imagination and for state and societal violence against sex workers to remain unquestioned and unpunished. It kept alive the latent 19th century notion of prostitution as a necessary evil, while allowing for prostitution to be portrayed as a realm of seduction, pleasure and freedom in literature, cinema and on television. It is not, therefore, surprising that contemporary politics regarding prostitution erupted into an open rebellion against police abuse. It later expanded and gained increasing social legitimacy as part of wider citizenship struggles around the state response to the HIV/AIDS epidemic.

Contemporary trends: 1970–1990[5]

In 1979, protests against police repression of streetwalkers in São Paulo ushered in the era of the contemporary politics of prostitution in Brazil. The Amnesty Law was also approved in the same year. This represented a turning point in the Brazilian democratization process (Leite 2009)[6]. The violations perpetrated by the police in São Paulo triggered a reaction from the prostitutes themselves and mobilized the support of artists, intellectuals and also of the emerging gay movement (Grupo Somos) as well as a few feminists. Given the prevailing censorship, the impact of the protest and its political visibility were remarkable. Notably, it opened the space for prostitution to be included in the agenda of Brazilian democratization.

Efforts aimed at fighting discrimination, stigma, police violence and calling for respect with regard to prostitutes' work gained support not just among artists and intellectuals, but also among progressive religious groups, mainly the Protestants.[7] While progressive Protestant sectors were the main supporters of the newly emerging prostitutes' movement, the Catholic Pastoral of Marginalized Women was also created during the same period. Although under the influence of the Liberation Theology, the Pastoral was mainly devoted to "rescuing" women from degradation, some of its branches shifted focus from the moral condemnation of prostitutes to a critique of prostitution as an effect of the capitalist system.

By the early 1980s the politicization of prostitution had become a full-fledged reality. Gabriela Leite, who had emerged as a key voice, appeared in the national media and also participated in seminars and other public events. Soon, leadership from among sex workers emerged in many other cities around the country. The Brazilian Network of Prostitutes was created during the first National Meeting of Prostitutes in 1987, the focus of which was on "violence". In 1988, the newsletter *Beijo da Rua* (Street Kiss) was launched with the headline "Prostitution is not a police matter". Right after the establishment of the National HIV/AIDS Programme (1988), the second annual National Meeting of Prostitutes revolved around prevention programmes among sex workers. Between 1990 and 1993 a number of local associations of prostitutes were created and local and state level meetings organized (Olivares, 2010). In 1994, the third National Meeting of Prostitutes discussed health and sexual fantasies. Five years later, the Brazilian Network of Prostitutes became a member of the Latin

American and Caribbean Network of Sex Workers (REDTRASEX), which was founded in 1997.

It is worth looking more closely into the connections that developed between the prostitutes' movement and the state in relation to HIV/AIDS. In 1989, the National HIV/AIDS Programme called upon Gabriela Leite and other leading actors to discuss the Previna Project, a prevention strategy to be implemented among female and male sex workers, gay men, drug users and prisoners.[8] These connections expanded after 1994, when a loan by the World Bank was approved to support the Brazilian national programme, as both the state and the Bank recognized that NGOs were better equipped to reach out to the most vulnerable groups. Resources were earmarked to fund prevention projects, which NGOs and community associations could access through periodical calls for application.

By the early 1990s *travestis*[9] who too were engaged in commercial sex started mobilizing around HIV/AIDS prevention and care. The first National Meeting of Transvestites Liberated for HIV/AIDS took place in 1993 and in 1996 the National Programme on HIV/AIDS established the umbrella project SOMOS (the "We Are" Project) to fund prevention and support activities specifically amongst *travestis* and MSM engaged in commercial sex. In the late 1990s, the national strategy for NGO financing began to emphasize on supporting networks, instead of exclusively focussing on individual organizations, a feature that clearly prevailed in the 2000s.

The trajectory of the feminist movement in the decade of the '70s to the '90s was also intense. Between the first national feminist meeting in 1979 and 2000, 12 meetings took place and three major regional Latin American Feminist gatherings were held in Brazil. After 1987, the composition of national feminist encounters became more diverse, with gatherings specifically for black women, rural women and lesbians. Throughout these years the struggle against gender-based violence and the call for women's health—or reproductive rights after 1984—were central in the Brazilian feminist agenda.

As elsewhere in the world, a key feature of this long and winding road was the establishing and legitimizing of feminist NGOs and women's studies (later gender studies). Most importantly, with democratization, the feminist movement was able to positively impact at the legal and policy levels, as illustrated by the creation of the National Council for Women's Rights in 1985 and the full enshrinement of the principles of gender equality in the 1988 Brazilian Constitution. In the next decade, feminists were challenged by the growing incidence of HIV/AIDS among the female population.

The role played by the Brazilian feminist movement in regional and global debates during the 1990s is widely recognized, particularly with regard to the UN conferences in the 1990s. A less discussed feature of this internationalization process is the gradual incorporation of the anti-trafficking agenda in the work being done by Brazilian feminists. The first initiatives addressing sex tourism and trafficking were established in the northeast of Brazil in the first half of the 1990s.[10]

A few other policy streams must also be included in this picture. The first is the emergence and maturation of the LGBT rights movements. Advocates for the rights of homosexuals (Grupo Somos) were already visible in the first battle for prostitutes' rights in 1979. Since then—and in part due to the need to respond to rights and non-discrimination claims triggered by HIV/AIDS—the Brazilian LGBT movement expanded and emerged as one of the most vocal movements south of the Equator in the 2000s.

Another relevant strand concerns the realm of children and adolescents' rights. In 1990, a year after the UN Convention on Children's Rights (CRC) was adopted, the Statute of Children and Adolescent Rights (ECA) was approved in Brazil. Sexual abuse and exploitation of children and adolescents is a core component of the ECA and much investment has been made in this area of work, which involves a wide web of civil society organizations. As in other countries, police interventions and policy initiatives which have potentially restrictive (or even abusive) impacts on sex work are justified as measures to protect children and adolescents (Ho 1995).

Lastly, the 2000s witnessed an increasing visibility of debates and proposals related to trafficking in persons, in particular for sexual purposes. Brazil had signed all previous conventions on the trafficking of women for prostitution and the country also had a criminal law related to this. However, the 1999 Palermo Protocol to the UN Convention against Organized Crime related to Prevention, Repression and Punishment of the Trafficking in Persons, in particular Women and Children, ratified by the Brazilian Congress in 2004, had a deeper institutional impact. The political climate in relation to trafficking and prostitution was also influenced by the guidelines adopted by the Bush administration through the Trafficking and Violence Protection Acts,[11] as specific USDAID funds were channelled for this area of work at the country level.

Prostitutes and Feminists: Past Intersections

Even a superficial mapping of interactions (or their absence) between the feminist and the prostitutes' movements indicates that gaps and tensions have always existed in Brazil. Recalling the 1979 prostitutes' rebellion in São Paulo, Jacira Mello says that feminist participation in the protest was minimal and confined to youth:

> The violence of police action was brutal and performed in daylight. Prostitutes were chased and detained by policemen, thrown into cars like animals (...) A few prostitutes even threw themselves from high floors to avoid being caught. Progressive sectors, which were also fighting the dictatorship, were outraged. A protest was organized which involved among others the gay Grupo Somos and a small number of feminist lesbians. My colleagues and I were very young. We were also quite close to the feminist movement and started calling on feminists to join the protest. But to our disappointment our call did not get a response. In some quarters, I should say, reactions were in fact negative, even aggressive.

Mello's description cannot, however, be used to describe all the interactions between feminists and the emerging prostitutes' movement in the late 1970s and 1980s. For instance, Gabriela Leite attended many seminars and public events where feminists were also present and this led to very productive debates. It was also not uncommon for feminist collectives to engage with emerging prostitutes' leaderships at local forums. In feminist circles, prostitution provoked much intellectual curiosity and, quite often, feminists equated prostitution with marriage as a strategy to critically analyse traditional gender relations.[12] Prostitution became the subject of social science research, including women's and gay studies (Gaspar 1985; Perlongher 1987; Rago 1985, 1990 among other works). During the 1980s, a few documentaries and videos on prostitution were produced and directed by acknowledged feminists.[13] In the 1990s, when research mainly shifted towards epidemiological and behavioural studies of HIV/AIDS and condom use amongst sex workers, feminist researchers were also involved (Chacham et al, 2007; Guimarães 2001, 2002; Pasini, 2000).

However, Jacira Mello is right in pointing out that these virtuous liaisons presented another angle. Brazilian feminist thinking and action was deeply inspired by Marxist critiques of society and the state. While few groups openly aligned themselves with Engels' critique of bourgeois morality with regard to prostitution, large sectors of the feminist movement tended to view prostitution as the culmination of male capitalist exploitation of the female body.[14] Additionally, as both the feminist and the prostitutes' movements became more institutionalized, the synergy and mutual curiosities of the early days of Brazil's democratization somehow died down. By the late 1990s dialogues involving the two movements were scarce, which is in fact intriguing given that at that point in time, the growing feminization of HIV/AIDS would have opened many windows of opportunities for more exchanges across the two movements.

The Shifting Terrain of the 2000s

The landscape in the 2000s was quite distinctive, in particular because other policy trends became more vigorous. Advocacy for children and adolescents' rights and related laws and policies gained strength after the ratification of the Optional Protocol to the Convention on the Rights of the Child on the Sale of Children, Child Prostitution and Child Pornography,[15] in 2003. A similar trend was observed in relation to national legal and policy initiatives concerning trafficking in persons, which have also become more solid after the ratification of the Palermo Protocol in 2004, as well as by the International Labour Organization's Convention concerning the Prohibition and Immediate Action for the Elimination of the Worst Forms of Child Labour ('Worst Forms of Child Labour Convention' No.182 of June 17, 1999). In January 2004, the Palermo Protocol was ratified and in March the same year a presidential decree formally adopted its definitions as guidelines for domestic policies. In 2006 another decree was approved under which the government created an inter-ministerial group to draft the corresponding National Plan, which was approved in January 2008. This comprises of an ambitious four-pronged approach: production of evidence-based information; prevention programmes aimed at addressing root causes and protecting the most vulnerable groups; protection of victims (non-discrimination, access to justice and consular services and re-integration); and repression (surveillance, control and investigation).[16]

These new trends impacted public debates around prostitution and state policies and led to relevant legal reforms. One illustration of this shift in public debate and policy orientation is the national study (Pesquisa sobre o Tráfico de Mulheres, Crianças e Adolescentes, PESTRAF) examining the trafficking of women, children and adolescents (CECRIA 2002). PESTRAF was the Brazilian component of a broader inter-American initiative supported by a consortium of donors,[17] which engaged in a wide and diverse group of constituencies: children's rights groups (both state bodies and civil society organizations), human rights NGOs, gender studies units, feminist organizations and religious institutions.[18] The national coordination of the study was done by CECRIA (a research centre on children's rights), ANDI (a news agency on children's rights) and the Catholic Pastoral and Service for Marginalized Women.[19]

After the publication of PESTRAF's findings in 2002, initiatives relating to sexual abuse and exploitation of children and trafficking intensified at the Congressional level. In 2003, a Parliamentary Inquiry Commission to Investigate Sexual Abuse and Exploitation of Children and Adolescents was created, and two years later, Law Provision No. 11.106 was approved to amend various aspects of the

Penal Code relating to sexuality, including the section originally titled "Traffic in Women". Two main changes were introduced. First, a gender neutral language of "Trafficking in Persons" was adopted, even though the content of the law continued to be restricted to trafficking for the purpose of sexual exploitation. Second, a new section on "Internal Trafficking" was added to the text.[20] These policy and legal changes also implied channelling of international and domestic resources to fund civil society activities in anti-trafficking work and the prevention/eradication of sexual exploitation of minors.[21]

Moving to the realm of feminist politics and gender equality, important policy changes took place in the first half of the 2000s. In 2003 the Special Secretariat for Women's Policies was created to enhance a series of participatory processes for informing policy design in the domain of gender equality. Two national conferences were held in 2004 and 2007 in which 20,000 women participated. Also in 2006, Law No. 11.340 (Lei Maria da Penha) to prevent and punish gender-based violence was enacted. This was a provision which had been debated since 2004 and had become the flagship programme of the Lula administration. However, it is worth noting that the policy guidelines that emerged from the two conferences include measures to prevent and eradicate trafficking in women and girls under the general chapter on gender-based violence.[22]

Concurrently, politics related to sex work was also very fruitful as the Brazilian Network of Prostitutes intensively mobilized around the agenda of labour rights. Having Germany's and New Zealand's legal reforms as references, the Network called for the recognition of prostitution as an occupation by the National Census Bureau and the Ministry of Labour, a demand which was positively responded to in 2002. In 2003 a draft bill, which aimed at regulating labour relations in the realm of commercial sex work, was presented by Representative Fernando Gabeira to the Congress. Among other legal changes, the provision proposed the deletion of Article 231 of the Penal Code which addresses trafficking of women for sexual purposes.[23] In a 2004 meeting, the Brazilian Network of Prostitutes strategically decided to refuse any partnership or collaboration with groups engaged in anti-trafficking projects.

At the same time, researchers also started questioning existing data on trafficking, which they maintained lacked empirical consistency. For instance, Piscitelli (2005) and Grupo DAVIDA (2005) criticized the methods, sources and findings of PESTRAF and of other investigations of sexual trafficking, arguing that a majority of these studies were based on press reviews and lacked stringent research methodologies. Their analyses strongly suggest that most studies tend to inflate figures and conflate trafficking with prostitution, sexual exploitation of minors and migration (Piscitelli 2009; Piscitelli 2008).

These were the political conditions in 2005 when the Brazilian government decided to suspend the USAID agreement for HIV prevention, because neither officials nor NGOs were willing to accept the imposition of the "prostitution oath" attached to PEPFAR funds. Soon after this landmark decision, DAVIDA, the NGO directed by Gabriela Leite, decided to launch a fashion brand inspired by clothes worn by prostitutes. The new brand was cleverly called DASPU, an acronym for *Das Putas* (of whores), a name inspired by an upper-class fashion shop located in São Paulo called DASLU, which was then under investigation for tax evasion. The project mainly aimed at raising financial resources to support DAVIDA's activities. However, what it managed to also do successfully was de-stabilize moral standards and the social imagination with regard to prostitution.[24]

These trends have been interpreted nationally and internationally as signals that a new policy and legal frame would recognize the rights of prostitutes as labour rights and adopt a more rational and less ideological approach to trafficking. However, as seen earlier, structural policy conditions and trends were more complex and contradictory. Under the surface, national policy frames and laws were rapidly aligning with global norms concerning sexual trafficking and exploitation of children and adolescents. In addition, the country experienced growing conservative religious influence, both Catholic and Evangelical, on policy and legislative debates, which also substantively impacted the climate regarding the politics of prostitution.

It is also worth mentioning here that throughout the 2000s law enforcement operations multiplied in areas connected with prostitution. In most cases these were fuelled by a growing moral panic related to the trafficking and sexual abuse of minors; after 2005 this was an effect of legal reforms with relation to the definition of trafficking, which now includes national dislocation of persons. For instance, Olivar (2010) reports abuses in law enforcement operations since the early 1990s in Porto Alegre, which intensified in the 2000s. Most relevant yet, less than a month after the suspension of the USAID agreement in May 2005 the Federal Police raided a boat party at the Rio Marina after receiving a tip that drugs and minors providing sexual services were aboard.

Twenty-nine American male tourists, most of them black, and 40 sex workers were apprehended. The police immediately realized that neither minors nor drugs were involved and, consequently, the women were freed. Despite formal complaints by the American consulate, the tourists' passports were confiscated. The Federal Police publicly announced that the men were accused of the (non-existent) crime of "sexual tourism" and would therefore be deported. The case was extensively publicized by anti-trafficking organizations as a major policy "victory". Other episodes can also be identified across the country in the same period, which simply involved the mobility of prostitutes, but were depicted as "trafficking" and subjected to investigations (Grupo DAVIDA 2005).

Last, aspects relating to urban cleansing must also be highlighted here. In 2009, the Help complex (bar, restaurant and disco) on Copacabana beach in Rio, which had historically been a key location for sex tourism and prostitution, was closed down because the state government decided to convert it into an Image and Sound Museum (Silva and Blanchette 2005). State actors responsible for the project deny that Help's closure was guided by anti-prostitution or anti-sex tourism sentiments, but it is evident that the project is part of the overarching plan of "urban cleansing" in preparation for the 2014 World Cup and the 2016 Olympics, and it should not be disconnected from the general policy climate with relation to sex work. By closing a space where women had personal autonomy as providers of sexual services, the state is essentially pushing sex workers towards much more coercive conditions of confined prostitution, pimp control and exploitation (Silva and Blanchette 2009; DAVIDA 2010).

The Late 2000s: Encounters, Fractures, Suspended Conversations

There were feminists calling for the abolition of prostitution in Brazil even earlier but their voices were not heard till the 2000s. A turning point in reshaping Brazilian feminist views about sex work seems to be connected with the establishment of the Brazilian chapter of the World March of Women in 2000, which manifested a clear position against prostitution, informed by a critique of capitalist exploitation, gender-based violence and marketization of women's bodies.

As the decade unfolded, the views of the Women's March on sex work gained a foothold in the larger women's movement and among relevant feminist organizations and networks, in particular among groups working with gender-based violence and also among other larger organizations. One example of this is the creation of the Articulation of Brazilian Women (AMB), in preparation for the Beijing Conference, which comprises of a diverse range of organizations. AMB has never made a public and formal anti-prostitution statement, but it includes organizations engaged with anti-trafficking activities and projects aimed at eradicating the sexual exploitation of minors. Not surprisingly, AMB quite often expresses abolitionist views in academic and activist events as well as in policy dialogues with state authorities.

The Pastoral of Marginalized Women has also expanded its activities and scope of work. In the early 2000s it created the Service for Marginalized Women which is more directly engaged with anti-trafficking and media-related activities. Later on a new ramification of the Pastoral was established: the GMEL (Group for Women, Ethics and Liberation) which, significantly enough, is headed by an ex-sex worker. It is also worth noting that today the

Women's March works in strategic partnership with the Pastoral of Marginalized Women in both the political mobilizing of grassroots efforts and policy advocacy work.

It is, therefore, not surprising that changes in discourse and practice also occurred in the realm of sex work activism itself. As noted earlier, by the late 2000s voices from the Brazilian *travesti* movement had started criticizing the notion of "agency" that tends to inform positions favourable to prostitution rights. However, unlike the feminist positions, which spoke about and for others, the *travesti* critique was articulated from within and mainly contested the confinement of transsexuals and transvestites in the "restrictive realm of sex work".[25]

The prostitutes' movement could not remain immune to the effects of the changing policy and funding climate. In 2004, the national meeting of the Brazilian Network of Prostitutes (BNP) formally decided not to compromise with the anti-trafficking agenda; a decision was also taken to more systematically focus the advocacy agenda on prostitutes' labour rights.

In contrast, novel spaces for interaction among feminist activists and those working for prostitutes' rights have opened up. These must be seen in the context of the two major national conferences on women's policies, and also the realm of HIV/AIDS. Since the 1990s, when epidemiological data suggested that the number of HIV infections among women had substantively increased, the need to systematically invest in the containment of the epidemic in the female population was felt. This agenda gained momentum after 2006 when the feminization of HIV, gender inequality and violence achieved greater legitimacy at the international level, a trend which coincided with the consolidation of the Special Secretariat for Women's Policies and the adoption of the new law against gender-based violence.

In 2007, the Health Ministry, in partnership with the Special Secretariat of Policies for Women, approved the National Comprehensive Plan to Address the Feminization of STD/ AIDS Epidemics, which also includes prevention and treatment guidelines to respond to the needs of sex workers and transsexual women. When the draft plan was discussed with civil society groups, a number of feminist organizations contested the inclusion of transsexual women, but the inclusion of prostitutes was not disputed. The plan was openly welcomed by sex workers' organizations because according to Gabriela Leite: "When the government and the women's movements include prostitutes in a global plan to address AIDS we have taken another major step to overcome the stigma against prostitution."[26]

In addition, a series of debates also took place in which the subjects of prostitution and trafficking were openly discussed. However, the results were not always positive. Between 2006 and 2007 the Brazilian government, in partnership with UNAIDS and UNFPA, hosted two international consultations on HIV and sex work in Rio de Janeiro (2006) and Lima (2007). In Rio, the composition of the meeting did not facilitate any sort of consensus. It ranged from the Coalition Against Trafficking to a large number of networks engaged with sex work and prostitution such as the Network of Sex Work Projects, the Latin Sex Workers Network (RETRASEX), and the Asian and Pacific Network of Sex Workers, as well as representatives of European and Caribbean organizations working with sex workers. Among governmental officials the spectrum went from representatives of the PEPFAR office to the very progressive officers from the Brazilian HIV/AIDS programme. The final document, prepared by UNAIDS and released in April 2007, was harshly criticized by sex workers' networks because it did not make the necessary distinction between trafficking and prostitution, which led to the creation of a working group to revise the text in 2009.[27] In contrast, the 2007 Latin American consultation was a success probably because it involved female and transsex workers as well as governmental agencies which allowed for greater consensus on difficult subjects. In Lima, RETRSEX and the BNP formally assumed advocacy on sexual rights as part of the human rights agenda of sex workers.

In 2008, the Department of AIDS and STDs convened a similar national consultation, which also involved various state agencies, the BNP, the Federation of Brazilian Prostitutes, the National Association of Travestis (ANTRA), NGOs working in the field of HIV and Congressman Fernando Gabeira. The working group that prepared the consultation agreed that the terminology to be used in conversations and in the final report would be "persons engaged in prostitution" to encompass the various categories and denominations applied to sex workers.[28] But in the course of the debates the Brazilian Federation of Prostitutes proposed the terminology "persons living in situations of prostitution", a term widely used by abolitionist groups. In addition, a few leaders of the transvestite movement expressed the view that prostitution is a coercive and restrictive condition. Gabriela Leite, representing the BNP reacted strongly to these arguments. All this led to a stalemate, which greatly delayed the dissemination of the final report.[29]

A few months later, the Special Secretariat for Women's Policies sponsored a workshop aimed at preparing a national seminar on sex work. Both the BNP and the National Federation of Prostitutes were invited, but the BNP decided not to participate because in their view the results of the HIV/AIDS consultation had not been very productive. The Brazilian Federation of Prostitutes was represented both by their leader and a member of the Service for Marginalized Women (a branch of the Catholic Pastoral).

In this workshop, participants representing academia and various ministries like health, labour and women's policies, reaffirmed that prostitution was not illegal in Brazil and should be addressed through a human rights framework. The representative from the Ministry of Justice constantly called attention to problems related to trafficking in persons and the sexual exploitation of minors, but she did not come up with any legal or rights-based position about prostitution. In contrast, the representative from the Pastoral called for public policies and appealed to professionals to help women wishing to leave prostitution. The National Federation of Prostitutes expressed the view that the regulation of prostitution— as any other labour activity—would aggravate the problem of trafficking and sexual exploitation of minors. Representatives from the World March of Women and from the Articulation of Brazilian Women proposed that the Brazilian government should call for the drafting of an international convention aimed at abolishing prostitution (Special Secretariat of Public Policies for

Women 2008). This led to another deadlock, this time at the heart of a feminist-informed state policy arena.

Since then, troubling signs have been detected which suggest that these tensions may be negatively affecting funding for *organized* prostitutes claiming their rights. To cite an example, in 2008 the BNP submitted a work proposal in response to a call for applications by the Department of STD/AIDS, but was not selected. According to Gabriela Leite, the reason was that the selection committee felt that the project excessively emphasized on the promotion of labour rights at the expense of HIV/AIDS prevention. In 2009, another call for applications was launched and officials from the HIV/AIDS Department persuaded the BNP to once again apply, but the group was not able to fulfil the newly adopted bureaucratic requirements. In this second round, however, the proposal submitted by the Association of Prostitutes of Ceará (APROCE) as the legal representative of the Brazilian Federation of Prostitutes was selected. [30] This meant that for the first time since the 1980s the BNP was not funded by the national HIV/AIDS policy.

At the same time a series of state-civil society consultations took place to come up with the design, implementation and monitoring of the 2006 National Policy and 2008 National Plan to Address Trafficking in Persons. Civil society participants in these events not only overlap, but they also differ from the groups present at the HIV/AIDS consultation and National Secretariat on Women's Policy Workshop. The documents reviewed indicate that anti-trafficking work currently underway involves the participation of the Brazilian chapter of the Global Alliance Against Trafficking in Women (GAATW), which is known for not aligning itself with stark abolitionist positions. But the wider civil society platform there engaged includes feminist organizations that have publicly expressed anti-prostitution positions. [31] Policy documents on trafficking suggest that the government hoped that these multiple and parallel debates would interconnect and eventually pave the way towards a broader policy consensus on prostitution, trafficking in persons and sexual exploitation of minors. But the tensions and deadlocks that had to be dealt with in this process have hampered this convergence.

These episodes, though worrisome, did not lead to the conclusion that Brazilian policies were inexorably shifting towards an open abolitionist and criminalization of prostitution position. The state could be eventually criticized in some quarters for dialoguing with both groups expressing radical views against prostitution and those supporting sex workers' rights and the labour regulation of the sex industry. But one can also argue that dialoguing across different positions is one basic rule of democratic deliberations. More importantly, in these debates key state actors have managed to be reasonably neutral to a large extent while navigating the radically opposed positions at play.

It is also worth noting that, in global arenas, the Brazilian government has openly spoken against the criminalization of sex work. This first happened in the 2005 session of the UN Commission on the Status of Women when a US sponsored resolution on trafficking was being discussed (Collet 2007). Then the position was taken up in the two consultations on HIV and sex work mentioned earlier and again in June 2010 when Brazil strongly supported the report presented by Anand Grover, Special Rapporteur on the Right to Health to the UN Human Rights Council, which calls for the decriminalization of same-sex relations, HIV transmission and sex work.

However, during 2010, a number of signs could be detected, which suggest that the balance may be shifting towards the abolitionist side more rapidly than predicted. During the general elections, religious conservative forces exerted enormous pressure over candidates on moral issues. When leaving a meeting of pastors, the then candidate Dilma Roussef, an Evangelical leader, informed the public that the group had demanded from her a firm position against abortion, same-sex marriage and the criminalization of prostitution and urged aggravated punishment for drug use. In December, at the Congress level, the Rapporteur of the Gabeira law provision—calling for legalization of sex labour—finally issued its report. The text has been totally altered and now the provision aims at criminalizing clients of sex work; in other words it proposes the adoption of the Swedish model.[32]

At the societal level, although tensions are on the rise, interactions between feminist activists, researchers and the prostitutes' movement remain alive. In addition to the main policy conferences and other related events, the Fazendo Gênero Symposium (Doing Gender Symposium)—a gathering of more than 3,000 people which has been taking place every two years since 1994—for the first time included two working groups on prostitution in its meeting in 2008. A quick search on the web-based library "Scielo" which comprises a majority of Brazilian public health and social science journals identifies 52 papers in which the topic of prostitution is addressed. While child and adolescent prostitution and HIV/AIDS are privileged themes, a large number of published works examine other dimensions of sex. Prostitutes' voices that call for human rights and their critique of the easy collapsing of trafficking and prostitution and the victimization discourse are still audible in public debate and relevant policy arenas.

In November 2010, an International Seminar on Sexualities, Feminisms and Lesbian Experiences in Belo Horizonte included a panel to discuss "Dissident Pleasures and Sexual Rights". Speaking on this panel, Gabriela Leite pressed for the rights of sex workers and called for a more systematic dialogue with feminists on policies regarding trafficking, which is predicted to escalate as the 2014 World Cup and 2016 Olympics draw near. While there have been tensions, the dialogue did take place and Gabriela's positions were supported by the majority of the audience. This was the first time in a long time that feminists and the sex workers movement leadership engaged in a public dialogue about prostitution.

Hence, while it would be excessive to say that Brazil is experiencing a full-fledged abolitionist wave, there are strong signs indicating that the political and policy landscape is different from what it was 10 to 15 years ago. Abolitionist positions, both extreme and mild, are circulating widely and episodes of moral panic with relation to sexual exploitation of minors, trafficking of women and girls and sex tourism are pervasive and directly involve state actors, particularly at the local levels. Most importantly in the last few months of 2010, positions calling for the criminalization of prostitution or that of their clients, have for the first time been manifested at high levels of the policy machinery and there are reasons to predict that this trend will continue in the years to come. On the other hand an important step has been made to start re-weaving the conversations between feminists, lesbians and sex workers. The views of feminists, lesbian and sex work activists with whom we dialogued must be situated and interpreted in relation to this complex, shifting and paradoxical background.

Visions, Positions, Perceptions

Sex workers' perspectives

The right of a prostitute should be seen as a woman's right to choose. I am proud of my life; I have the right to choose. What I do should not to be seen as an imposition simply because I have no house, I have no leisure, I have no health. The federation is composed of women over 20 years of age, because adolescents must be in school learning skills. Prostitution implies many dangers. We discuss public policies mainly thinking about the sexual exploitation of children and adolescents. We do so because after legalization major problems arose because of trafficking and exploitation.

Rosarina Sampaio[33]

I understand prostitution as a core question to be discussed when we discuss sexual rights (...) I understand prostitution as the right to sell sexual fantasies. Beyond desire and a sexual right, prostitution is work. As work, it implies rights and duties. Today prostitutes have no labour rights. If labour relations are forbidden, everything is forbidden and this is the gap in which criminal mobs get in. This is what produces exploitation. Exploitation exists, because prostitution is a "waste land".

Gabriela Leite

We do work but do not have any labour or legal support, even when there is a huge demand for sex work in society. The vision that people have of prostitution is that it is very bad, that those persons engaged in it do not have a say. But it is not like that. There are people who would like to be wealthy entrepreneurs but cannot and so they become cleaners. This is not bad or wrong in itself. It is simply a means of survival. I think prostitution is a means of survival. Some people do it because they lack other opportunities. Others do it to just to supplement their incomes. But there are also those who engage in it as a hobby, in the same manner as people who work during the week and go painting during the weekends. (...) What needs to be struggled against is not prostitution per se, but exploitation, as we fight against exploitation in other labour areas. This is really needed because there are many people who exploit the labour of women, transvestites and boys engaged in the sex trade.

Janaina Lima

Feminist Perspectives

The longstanding lobbyists who advocate for the legalization of prostitution, or rather the legalizing of the "pimp profession" are back on the scene, bringing up their cheap and easy discourse about the freedom of the body, as well as lies about the positive impacts it will have on the lives of women in prostitution. Nobody can argue against the rights of women in prostitution, especially the right to live without violence, but the question is much deeper: Will we accept this to be their choice? What world is this in which poor women are condemned to the marketization of their bodies, of their sex? We must elaborate further on what we have seen since we have re-launched our offensive against the marketization of women's bodies and expanded our operations with regard to the discussion on prostitution.

Newsletter of the World March of Women, June 1, 2010

The feminist movement must address prostitution through the frame of sexual division of labour and feminization of poverty. The term "autonomous prostitution" deserves a broader debate because we must ask: What exactly is economic autonomy in Brazil? In Brazil what exactly does it mean to freely choose an occupation?

Ticiana Studart [34]

Prostitution... is the right of all women to do with their body what they want to. They have the right do to with their body what they think is best for their own lives. I had the privilege to get to know many prostitutes quite closely. I could find in them the same dignity, the same entrepreneurship that I see in rural women, female workers and domestic workers. In the perception of a majority of those I have met they were performing a type of work with their bodies. This was very clear to them. In reality most of them have a precise working time, there is time to work and time not to work. There is always decision-making at play. Therefore as I see it, this is an option.

Jacira Mello

In my view, prostitution, like any other relation in society, is a relation that involves exploitation and that implies domination. Since I believe in social transformation, since I have a utopian vision, I would like these types of relationships to be overcome (…) I am critical of all forms of commoditization of human relations, I criticize the encroachment of market relations into all spheres of life. But on the other hand, when I think of prostitution from the point of view of a social question, I do think that today we have to also commit ourselves to the struggle of female prostitutes. I do think they must organize themselves. I think they must have access to rights and to safety. I always address the question through these two angles.

Betânia Ávila

To be frank, I do not know what my position is today. On the one hand, I do think there is one dimension that is related to the exercise of freedom, meaning sex work should also be thought of in terms of women's autonomy. This is quite easy for me to say. And because of this, I say that we should also frame sex work in terms of rights. But on the other hand, what can we do about the exploitation of prostitutes? (…) This is where I identify the obstacles and problems.

Valeria Pandjiarjian

Prostitution is a job and must be recognized as such. I take as reference my own experience as a researcher in anthropology. What is the difference between my work and work in prostitution? Both domains of work have rules and agreements. If I say this is a form of work I do not mean to be naïve. I can fully see the exploitation it implies, and the type of exploitation is the same. There is always exploitation and it is necessary to define what exploitation we are taking about more clearly. For example, think of a soccer player. He may have his leg injured, but will have to play because he is the advertising face of a certain beer company. His may be in a highly paid job. But it is also highly exploitative.

Elisiane Pasini

It is a profession, which could imply other conditions of work, other qualities of life if it was not so stigmatized. There's always a sad story behind the experience of a prostitute (…) Also if there was not so much guilt in the experience of those engaged in the profession it would be much better. I do think it is really great when women decide to be prostitutes and become good professionals.

Rosângela Castro

I belong to the group which says that I have the right to my body, to my sexuality, to my motherhood. If this body is mine, and in capitalism all work has a value, I have to define a price for sex work. Why not precisely define the price of a blowjob?

Claudette Costa

Sex Workers' Comments on Feminist Views of Prostitution

A "feminist position" on prostitution has not been fully articulated. They have never gone deep into the debate. Everything that feminists say about prostitution is common sense. Before feminism, common sense said that the women who engaged in prostitution were a bunch of shameless women who did not like to work, who did not want to have a husband, who were sex addicts. Then with "modernity" came the arguments of poverty as a driver of prostitution and the view of women as victims was crafted. Feminists have adopted this vision, without understanding that it is mere naturalization. It is a view of prostitution that is used by everybody, not just by feminists. Therefore, this cannot be considered a feminist position on prostitution. With very few exceptions feminists always use the same mantra: male exploitation of women, the dominator versus subordinated relations (…) On the other hand I must also say that there are some nuances. I divide feminists into "orthodox" and "modern". But I should say that the "modern" ones are few… very few.

Gabriela Leite

I cannot say if feminists are for or against prostitution because they never come here to talk with us. But if they think that prostitution is a very strong form of machismo, I say no. It is a very strong form of survival.

Laura

The feminists should learn a bit more about our world. They should really understand how a prostitute lives, what the life of a sex worker is like. They put us in the band wagon of marginality, while we're trying to get out of the wagon (...) They cannot understand this is a job. Either they cannot, or they do not want to. Now tell me: Who in this world is working for free? In any profession people work for money! You provide services for money, we do the same. Today, in the 21st century, we set the rules, we define what to do and how to do it. Did you know that? Things have changed. The old "macho" ways of men determining what they wanted simply because they were paying are gone. Today they do not even raise the issue. I teach men a lot. I tell them to be good to their wives, counsel them on how to solve problems with their children. Today being a prostitute is not simply about sex.

Nilce Machado

I vaguely know of the feminist position. It is about the exploitation of the body, it is about machismo exploiting femaleness, isn't it? Well I do think there is confusion in the feminist position because sometimes they say I can make my own decisions about my body, and then at other times they say I have no power to decide. How come? I wonder if this position would be the same if women demanded sex work from men in large quantities. Or what arguments they would resort to if a majority of those paying for sex, even with other women or transvestites were women.

Janaina Lima.

Encounters and Mismatches

In 1979, we were at the demonstration in Boca do Lixo. Some feminists had come there just to "watch", they did not come close to the demonstration, they kept apart, walking on the sidewalk. Later on, because I had been involved with the demonstration, the group engaged with the alternative feminist paper, Nós Mulheres, invited me to participate in the production of a video that was titled The Women of the Boca *(...)*

Then in 1986, I also directed a more mature video on the subject, which expressed my own views on prostitution, which was called Kissing on the mouth *and after that I directed* Girls, *because I realized that the two universes, one of older women and one of girls who were just starting to engage in prostitution when they were 12, 13, 14 years old, were very different.*

Jacira Mello

My views on prostitution come from having met and interacted with members of the prostitutes' movement. But I should say that I have always been fascinated by the image of the harlot. My father was a civil servant, and sometimes we had to go downtown to a place called Praça Tiradentes. I was very young, but I saw those women street walking and could not take my eyes off them. My father kept saying, "do not look at them, do not look!" Then when I was a teenager, I studied in a nun's school and a colleague told me that her cousin had become pregnant, had had an abortion, was evicted from her home and was living in the Mangue red light district. So five of us went there. We entered Pinto de Azevedo street, which was the main point of the district, but the prostitutes quickly evicted us from the place because we were wearing our school uniforms. They even said that they would call the police. That was an amazing experience.[35]

Rosangela Castro

On the night of March 8, 2010 there was a ceremony for International Women's Day at the government palace (...) When I arrived, there was a lot of confusion because two women from the Recife Association of Prostitutes were struggling with the doormen, who had allowed one of them in, but not the other, alleging that she could not enter because she was wearing a mini skirt. Quite evidently, the real issue was not the mini skirt, but her whole appearance and it was very clear that she was being stigmatized. There was a big controversy because the ceremonial staff said, "We can do nothing because this is protocol." We, the feminists, reacted and said: "If this is the rule, it is not anymore, because today the rule will change, and she will join us inside. If she cannot come in, we will not enter either." Finally she got in despite wearing a mini skirt.

Betânia Ávila

I started studying female prostitution in 1998, when I was a fellow of the Fundação Carlos Chagas.[36] I often got a negative reaction from my programme mentors. They said that I was being too romantic in relation to prostitution. I was not romantic, I simply described the life of prostitutes as I was observing it and I thought this should be respected (...) I suffered great pressure from my mentors who said: "You are not showing the violence that exists in that place." There was enormous pressure on me to say that I had seen violence in prostitution and that the world of sex work was very bad. I did not agree to say that it was just bad.

Elisiane Pasini

The State of the Debate

Feminist positions today are very similar to the positions voiced in the 1970s and 1980s. At that time, several women who had not thought seriously about prostitution, women who had neither discussed nor read about it but had a strong anti-capitalist, Marxist vision always interpreted prostitution as an evil, as a male capitalist invention. The same vision affirmed that after socialism prostitution would disappear (...) Feminism has not dared to think of prostitution with the same investment and curiosity it has devoted to other topics such as domestic violence. Feminism talks extensively about women and work, women and violence (...) But when it comes to prostitution, it speaks of the "prostitute" as an illustration of the worst possible human condition. And it somehow preserves the romantic vision that a revolution will get rid of this "scourge of humanity".

Jacira Mello

We are opening a path by way of force. Today it is not possible to simply say that we are victims. We have built a movement and we are consistent in terms of the arguments and questions we raise. We have a worldwide movement that is intervening at all levels of the debate. So people have to stop and think: These women exist politically, they are out there, they are women. During my 30 years of activism I have always said: Above all I am a woman. But people forget that a prostitute is also a woman (...) This is a major problem (...) But I should also say that today there are more spaces for dialogue. Today we can already talk a little bit with the feminists (...) A little bit more.

Gabriela Leite

This is certainly a controversial issue within the feminist movement. I think we have not given enough thought to the subject. Moreover, positions are not made explicit (...) I think Brazilian feminism has great difficulty in dealing with the issue. I cannot say clearly what the blind spots are in the position expressed by the prostitutes' movement? Maybe what is problematic is its excessive pragmatism. It recognizes the reality as it is but stays there, without a perspective of transformation.

Betânia Ávila

In the feminist field, I do not see any debate, or at least I myself have not participated in any debate. Not even at the level of CLADEM have we been able to discuss this issue in depth. There is no deeper discussion or argument which may allow us to go a little further (...) When trafficking, violence and prostitution are joined to one another, everything gets confused: the subjects, the situations, the conditions, the treatment required for each type of problem and the need to recognize different approaches and specific needs. This confusion makes it difficult to provide adequate answers, or worse yet, it leads to incorrect answers which end up resulting in the further violation of rights.

Valeria Pandjiarjian

The debate on prostitution is veiled (...) Within feminism we have moved forward on a whole range of themes (...) But when prostitution is at stake, we face a sort of missing piece, or if you want, a piece that does not fit well into the puzzle. This "piece" is related to the freedom of the body, a topic on which we never speak. I do think that the feminists still have a big taboo in relation to sexuality, to the blossoming of women's sexuality. We still think that "fucking" is bad and dirty, and that "fucking for money" is worse. But the problem is not confined to feminist movements. It is also difficult to engage with the prostitutes' movement and its leadership. One main political knot is that the movement leaders do not use a feminist lens. They do not consider themselves feminists and therefore do not join forces with us with relation to other issues.

Elisiane Pasini

Feminism is in favour of prostitutes organizing themselves as professionals. Is this not the case? I know of a group of feminists who think that sex workers must be professionalized and have their work ruled by formal labour contracts. But there is no consistent debate on this matter. As far as I can see there is no debate at all. And, when there is some debate it is always very fallacious.

Heliana Hemetério

Unfortunately within the transvestite movement the position that prostitution is exploitation and must be abolished also exists. The reason behind such a notion is that society sees prostitution as something dirty, so some people in the movement also think that to be socially accepted, transvestites too have to fight against prostitution. I am one of the few people in the movement who still speaks openly and positively about prostitution. But the internal debate is totally paralyzed (...) It is important to open this debate. Yes we must talk with the prostitutes' movement. But before that we must discuss among ourselves: How can we engage in a discussion on prostitution in Brazil, without firstly learning about it ourselves? Moreover, the debate brings to the forefront the rivalry on the street. The rivalry that exists in the daily life of the sex trade is transported to the movements. Then when Gabriela calls for the regulation of prostitution, there are those who say: "Who is she to say that? What does she know?" (...) On the other hand, we also need to have discussions with those feminists who are critical of prostitution, and contest their vision. Because as I see it, their problem with prostitution is not simply women getting paid to have sex, their problem is that women are getting paid to have sex with men. I am convinced we need a much broader discussion about prostitution.

Janaina Lima

These differing perceptions and visions about prostitution are evidence of the diversity of views and approaches, and the need to continue discussions between the various voices—feminists, prostitutes, transvestites.

Notes

1. A key partner in this exercise was Adriana Piscitelli, an Argentinean anthropologist who lives in Brazil and teaches at the Federal University of Campinas and is recognized as one of the leading

researchers on matters related to sex tourism, prostitution and trafficking in Brazil. We also thank all women who graciously made time in their busy agendas to be interviewed. In the feminist and lesbian communities: Betânia Ávila (SOS Corpo), Claudette Costa (Liga Brasileira de Lésbicas), Elisiane Pasini (THEMIS), Jacira Mello (Instituto Patrícia Galvão), Heliana Hemetério (Grupo Arco Iris), Rosângela Castro (Grupo Felipa de Souza), Valéria Pandjiarjian (CLADEM, Brasil). In the sex work community: Friederick Strack (Advisor to the Brazilian Network of Prostitutes); Gabriela Leite (DAVIDA and Brazilian Network of Prostitutes), Janaína Lima (Grupo Identidade), Nilce Machado (Núcleo de Estudos da Prostituição), "Laura" prostitute who works in the central area of Porto Alegre.

2. The terms "prostitution" and "sex work", "prostitute" and "sex worker" have been used interchangeably in this chapter, though the term "prostitute" is more widely used in Brazil.

3. Full abolition was preceded by a series of partial measures such as the suspension of slave trade (1850) and the granting of freedom to children of slaves born in Brazil, the so-called Free-Womb Law (1870).

4. The syphilis "moral panic" expanded since the 1850s. The figures on incidence were constantly magnified and the disease was associated with the degrading effects of slavery, with the "natural and uncontrollable sexual impulses of enslaved Africans, but also the pre-colonial indigenous population" ,(19th century) and later on with racial miscegenation and the detrimental impacts of urbanization and modernizing (20th century).

5. This jump from the early 20th century to the 1970s democratizing period does not imply that nothing happened in between. Though this is clearly a period that has not been extensively researched, strong evidence can be identified in literature, urban chronicles and personal memoirs, which suggest that prostitution was a vital component of Brazilian social life in the 1930s, 1940s, 1950s and 1960s.

6. This extreme repression had, however, antecedents in São Paulo. Rago (1985) analyses how in the 1950s when rural-urban migration accelerated and unemployment levels were very high, the number of brothels increased. When the São Paulo state government closed the brothels in reaction street prostitution increased, which was systematic subject to occasional but brutal police operations.

7. For instance, Superior Institute of Religious Studies (Instituto Superior dos Estudos da Religião, IESR) in Rio, operated as an

umbrella organization for prostitutes' activism by housing the first initiatives launched by Gabriela Leite. The Lutheran Church was at the origin of NEP in Porto Alegre.

8. The other persons were Lourdes Barreto (from the Association of Prostitutes of Belém) and Roberto Chateaubriand and Laura Celeste (from the Gapa Network).

9. A category in Brazil equivalent to *hijra* or transgender, the term *travesti* has now been politicized.

10. The Women's Life Collective (Coletivo Mulher Vida) was established in Olinda, Pernambuco in the early 1990s with a clear focus on sex tourism. Later there was the Grupo Chame in Bahia, which was already addressing trafficking for European countries. While we have not collected specific data, it would not be wrong to say that these initiatives were already supported by anti-trafficking funds.

11. The Trafficking and Violence Protection Act of 2000 (P.L. 106-386), the Trafficking Victims Protection Reauthorization Act of 2003 (H.R. 2620) and the Trafficking Victims Protection Reauthorization Act of 2005 (H.R. 972).

12. For instance, in an early Northeast Regional Feminist Meeting in 1980 in Olinda Pernambuco, a public panel was held in which Eleonora Menicucci, to the shock of the audience, equated the monetized relation between husband and wife to sex work as a critique of sexual morality stigmatizing prostitution.

13. Jacira Mello directed *Beijo Na Boca* was launched in 1982 and *Meninas* (Girls) was finalized a bit later. Eunice Gutman directed *Amores da Rua* (Street Love), which was launched in the late 1980s but which still had much political relevance in the 2000s when the agenda of prostitutes' rights as labour rights gained visibility and legitimacy.

14. This ideological dominance was emphasized by Jacira Mello, who recalled that in São Paulo in the early 1980s, a closed feminist meeting was called to discuss major controversies emerging in the wider women's movement, among which were abortion and prostitution.

15. The Optional Protocol was adopted by the UN in May 2000 and it entered into force in 2002. The fact that it was ratified by Brazil in 2003 shows the high level of interest and political commitment to this policy agenda on the part of both Brazilian state and society.

16. The three Executive Decrees defining the integration of Palermo into national guidelines were No. 5.107 (March 2004), No. 5.948 (January 2006) and No. 6.347 (January 2008). The drafting of the National Plan to Combat Trafficking in Persons was coordinated by the National Secretary of Justice, the National Secretary for Human

Rights and the National Secretary for Women's Policies. The other state institutions which were involved included the Office of Public Prosecutors and a wide range of civil society organizations. This list, however, did not include the National Network of Prostitutes.

17. The international coordination of the research was composed of the Women's Commission of the Organization of American States, the Inter-American Institute on the Child and the International Institute on Human Rights Law (De Paul University) and the Brazilian project was supported by ILO, USDAID (through POMMAR and Partners of America), Save the Children (Sweden) and the CWF Institute (which though based in Brazil, is funded by the Swedish Crown). The Brazilian government support was channeled through the National Secretary on Human Rights.

18. Four feminist NGOs and one academic gender study unit were involved in the research: Rede Acreana de Homens e Mulheres (Rio Branco), Núcleo de Pesquisa em Sexualidade e Gênero (UFAC-Acre), Casa Renascer (Natal), SOS Corpo (Recife) e Geledés (São Paulo) (State of Acre Network of Men and Women (Acre), the Center for Gender and Sexuality Studies of the Federal University of Acre, Re-birth Home (Natal), SOS Corpo (Recife) and Geledés (São Paulo).

19. Information available on the Pastoral website makes it evident that the Pastoral may not have fully adhered to a strong abolitionist position in the 1980s, but by the 1990s this alignment was strongly established, as its list of activities mentions a meeting with the International Abolitionist Federation. The trajectory described in the webpage also indicates that the Pastoral, which in the 1980s was relatively marginal and experienced tensions with the hierarchy, has received increasing support since the 1990s from high level bodies of the Catholic Church.

20. Another related trend is that in 2008 a Parliamentary Inquiry Commission on Pedophilia was established, which proposed and approved amendments to the ECA and the Penal Code. It was triggered by national and global debates on child pornography on the Internet. For instance, in 2008 when the International Conference on Sexual Abuse of Children and Adolescents sponsored by ECPACT was hosted in Rio, child pornography featured high on the agenda and achieved great media coverage. While the Conference was underway in Rio, the Congress approved a reform of the ECA proposed by the Commission aimed at redefining the crime of child pornography. This change was incorporated in the Penal Code in August 2009,

when an amendment was also adopted increasing the penalty of
agents involved in the exploitation of adolescents between 14 and 18
years of age.

21. The main agencies involved in anti-trafficking related activities in
Brazil include ILO, UNODOC, UNICEF, OIM, the Swedish Embassy,
Cordaid, Save the Children, Oak Foundation and USAID. While
the flow of international resources is one key aspect of the policy
scenario being described it has not been possible to map it properly.
One figure we have been able to collect is that that USAID granted
$800,000 for "trafficking prevention" line of work between 2003
and 2008. Another key aspect with relation to funding is that these
flows reached Brazil exactly when resources to fund sexual and
reproductive rights and HIV/AIDS prevention work started becoming
increasingly less.

22. The law has positively created a strong and broad social consensus
with respect to the repudiation of all forms of gender-based violence.
However, it does not seem excessive to suggest that in some
quarters, particularly among grassroots women's organizations, this
strong sentiment of repudiation may have fuelled the classical and
easy correlation that reads: *gender violence equals trafficking which equals
gender-based violence.*

23. The provision is inspired by the 2002 German legislation. It proposes
the deletion of three articles of the Penal Code: 228 (facilitation of
prostitution), 229 (the ownership of brothels) and 231 (on trafficking,
since it exclusively referred to women trafficked for sexual services).
The proposed text reads as:

> The National Congress decrees: Art. 1 Payment for sexual services
> can be demanded. Paragraph 1 - Payment for services of a sexual
> nature is demandable for the time during which the person remained
> available for those services, no matter whether or not this person was
> requested to provide the services. Paragraph 2 - The payment for
> sexual services can only be demanded by the person who provided
> the service or remained available for providing it. Art. 2 Articles
> 228, 229, and 231 of the Penal Code are revoked. Art. 3 This law
> shall come into force on the date of its publication. The provision is
> paralyzed at the Congress level as it has been systematically blocked
> by Catholic and Evangelic groups of parliamentarians.

24. Right after DASPU was launched DASLU reacted threatening DAVIDA
and Gabriela Leite with a lawsuit for "defamatory attack on a good
name". DASPU publicly stated that it was not going to change the

name and DASLU gave up pursuing legal action after realizing that it had no legal basis. This episode resulted in debates in the print media and on television, making DASPU rapidly known to a very diverse audience. Since 2005, DASPU has hosted a number of fashion shows in Brazil and abroad including the 2008 International AIDS Conference in Mexico and the 2010 International AIDS Conference in Vienna.

25. The position manifested in the Brazilian movement echoes the analyses and stances developed by Argentinean groups such as ALLIT. Lohana Berkins, who is a member of the group, refuses to recognize prostitution as work and prefers to use the terminology of "persons living in prostitution" because she sees prostitution as a transitional situation that can be experienced by any person in the course of her life. She also believes that it is necessary to offer people ways out of prostitution. In her view, prostitution exists because the activity is legitimized in society and also because states, either socialist or capitalist, benefit from the income resulting from the sex market. However, persons in situation of prostitution do not benefit from these same colossal earnings (SPW 2009). Available at: http://www. sxpolitics.org/?p=2975

26. The implementation of the plan faced a series of obstacles and the strategy and guidelines were revised in mid-2009. An evaluation is currently underway.

27. Gabriela Leite participates in the UNAIDS working group as one of NSWP representatives.

28. This terminology was a sort of umbrella term encompassing other names and categories circulating in political debates on the subject such as prostitutes, sex workers, sex professionals, escort girls and a plethora of popular denominations. The language consensus was an important pre-condition for ensuring productive engagement of all the sectors involved because an ongoing debate started in the 1990s when Gabriel Leite and the Brazilian Network of Prostitutes started contesting the terms sex workers and sex professionals, because in their view this language aimed at sanitizing the "bad words" prostitutes and prostitution. This was a clear choice to politically re-signify the term, which determined the name of the network itself; it also inspired the title of Gabriela Leite's autobiography published in 2009: *Daughter, mother, grandmother and prostitute.* But not everybody agreed with this option, because among other reasons prostitutes are a female category that does not apply to men transexuals and transvestites engaged in sex work.

29. The report was not posted on the web, but it was included in the same CD-ROM that contains the last version (2009) of the National Plan to address the feminization of HIV/AIDS and STDs.

30. The project comprises partnership with a range of organizations whose work can be characterized as abolitionist, as is the case with Pastoral for Marginalized Women.

31. In 2008, SODIREITOS (partner to GAADW) published the results of a research on trafficking on women from Dominican Republic and Brazil to Suriname (Hazeu 2008). Although the 2008 report criticizes the methodology and findings of the PESTRAF, the general tone of these documents is not very different from what prevails in anti-prostitution literature, as by and large the main focus is still on trafficking for sexual purposes and there is a strong emphasis on victimization. The GAADW Brazilian chapter was also involved in the production of the monitoring report of the National Plan to Address Trafficking in Persons (ASBRADE et al. 2009) and ASBRADE is directly involved in prevention work and reception of deported and trafficked persons at the airport of Guarulhos. Their performance is considered excellent by Adriana Piscitelli (personal communication).

32. The Evangelical group emerging from the 2010 elections runs across all political parties and now constitutes the third biggest group at the House, counting in addition with two strong representatives at Senate level.

33. Rosarina Sampaio is the president of the National Network of Sex Workers. She was not interviewed. This quote was identified in the report on the Workshop on Female Prostitution organized by the National Secretary for Women's Policy in 2008.

34. Taciana Studart was not interviewed. She represented the World March of Women in the Workshop on Female Prostitution organized by the Special Secretary for Women's Policy in 2008. This citation was also identified in the workshop report.

35. Rosangela Castro in her testimony refers to two main prostitution areas in downtown Rio. One of them, the Mangue, does not exist anymore.

36. The Fundação has for many years run a Ford Foundation supported grant programme for gender studies.

References

ASBRAD, CARITAS, CEDECA- EMAUS, CHAME, Coletivo Leila Diniz, IBISS/CO, SODIREITOS, Consórcio Projeto Trama (2009) *Relatório de Monitoramento do Plano Nacional de Enfrentamento do Tráfico de Pessoas.* Available at http://www.google.com/search?hl=pt-PT&client=firefox-a&hs=vUa&rls=org.mozilla:ptPT:official&&sa=X&ei=Xa8oTO_2FMiEuAfQsdmsAg&ved=0CC8QBSgA&q=Relat%C3%B3rio+de+Monitoramento+do+PNETP&spell=1

Carrara, Sérgio (1997) *Tributo a Vênus: A luta contra a sífilis no Brasil, da passagem do século aos anos 40.* Rio de Janeiro: FIOCRUZ

CECRIA (Leal, Maria e Leal M (org)) (2002) *Pesquisa sobre tráfico de mulheres, crianças e adolescentes para fins de exploração sexual comercial no Brasil: relatório nacional.* Brasília: CECRIA

——. *Plano Nacional de Enfrentamento da Violência Sexual contra Crianças e Adolescentes (2000)* Brasília: CECRIA

Chacham, A. S. S.G.Dinz, M.B.Maia, A.F.Galati, L.A. Mirim (2007) "Sexual and Reproductive Health Needs of Sex Workers: Two Feminist Projects in Brazil" *Reproductive Health Matters*, v. 15, p. 1-11

Collet, A. (2007) *Interrogating "Sexualities" at Beijing+10*, SPW Working Paper 3, Available at http://www.sxpolitics.org/?cat=49

DAVIDA (2010) *Human Rights and Female Prostitution.* Available at http://www.sxpolitics.org/?cat=54&search=we-recommend

Fonseca, Claudia (2003b) "Familia y profesión : la doble carrera de la mujer prostituta". *La antropología brasileña contemporánea : contribuciones para un diálogo latinoamericano* Buenos Aires: Prometeo, 95-135

Gaspar, Maria Dulce (1985) *Garotas de programa: prostituição em Copacabana e identidade social.* Rio de Janeiro: Jorge Zahar

Girard, F. (2004) *Global Implications of U.S. Domestic and International Policies on Sexuality*, Sexuality Policy Watch. Available online at http://www.sxpolitics.org/?cat=49

Grupo DAVIDA (2005) "Prostitutas, "traficadas" e pânicos morais: uma análise da produção de fatos em pesquisas sobre o "tráfico de seres humanos"". *Cadernos PAGU* (25), 153-185

Guimarães, K and MERCHAN-HAMANN, E. (2005) "Comercializando fantasias: a representação social da prostituição, dilemas da profissão e a construção da cidadania" . Rev. Estud. Fem. [online]. vol.13, n.3 pp. 525-544 . Available from: <http://www.scielo.br/scielo.php?script=sci_arttext&pid=S0104-026X200500

0300004&lng=en&nrm=iso>. ISSN 0104-026X. doi: 10.1590/ S0104-026X2005000300004.

Hazeu, M. (2008) *Pesquisa Tri-nacional sobre Tráfico de Mulheres do Brasil e da República Dominicana para o Suriname: uma intervenção em rede*. Available at http://www.sodireitos.org.br/site/interna. php?idn=4&con=m

Kushnir, B. (1996) *Baile de máscaras*. Rio de Janeiro: Imago

Leite, Gabriela (2009) *Filha, mãe, avó e puta: história de uma mulher que decidiu ser prostituta*. Rio de Janeiro: Objetivo

Olivar, José Miguel (2010) *Guerras, trânsito e apropriações: políticas da prostituição de rua a partir das experiências de quatro mulheres militantes em Porto Alegre, Brasil*. Doctoral Dissertation. PhD Social Anthropology, Universidade Federal do Rio Grande do Sul, Porto Alegre: PPGAS/ UFRGS

Pasini, Elisiane (2000) "O uso do preservativo no cotidiano de prostitutas em ruas centrais de Porto Alegre". Fábregas-Martínez e Benedetti (org). *Na Batalha: sexualidade, identidade e poder no Universo da Prostituição*. Porto Alegre: Decasa/Palmarinca/GAPA-RS, 31-46.

Pelúcio, Larissa e Miskolci, Richard (2009) "A prevenção do desvio: o dispositivo da aids e a repatologização das sexualidades dissidentes". *Sexualidad, Salud y sociedad. Revista latinoamericana.* CLAM/IMS no 1, 125-157

Pereira, Cristina (2005) "Lavar, passar e receber visitas: debates sobre a regulamentação da prostituição e experiências de trabalho sexual em Buenos Aires e no Rio de Janeiro, fim do século XIX". In *Cadernos Pagu* (25), julho-dezembro: 25-54.

Perlongher, Néstor (1087) *O negócio do michê: prostituição viril em São Paulo*. São Paulo: Brasiliense

Piscitelli, Adriana (2005) "Apresentação: gênero no mercado do sexo". *Cadernos Pagu* (25). Campinas, 7-23.

———— (2007)Prostituição e trabalho. In: *Transformando a relação trabalho e cidadania: produção, reprodução e sexualidade*. Organizadoras: COSTA, Albertina; SOARES, Vera Lúcia et al. São Paulo: 183-195.

———— (2008) "Entre as "máfias" e a "ajuda": a construção de conhecimento sobre tráfico de pessoas". *Cadernos PAGU* (31), julho-dezembro: 29-64.

Rago, Margareth (1985) *Do cabaré ao lar: a utopia da cidade disciplinar, Brasil 1890-1930*. Rio de Janeiro: Paz e terra

———— (1990) *Os prazeres da noite: prostituição e códigos da sexualidade feminina em São Paulo (1890-1930)*. São Paulo: Paz e Terra

Red de Trabajadoras Sexuales de Latinoamérica y el caribe (1990) *10 años de acción: la experiencia de organización de la Red de Trabajadoras Sexuales de Latinoamérica y el Caribe.* Buenos Aires: Redtrasex

Rodriguez, Marlene (2003) *Polícia e prostituição feminina em Brasília—Um caso de estudo-.* Tese de Doutorado. Departamento de Sociologia da UnB. Brasília, dezembro

Secretaria Especial de Políticas para as Mulheres. *Relatório do Workshop sobre prostituição feminina, 23-24 de abril de 2008.* Brasília: SPM, 2008.

Silva, A.P. and Blanchette, T 2009. *Amor um real por minuto. Overview paper presented at the SPW Latin American Dialogue on Sexuality and Geopolitics. Available at http://www.sxpolitics.org/pt/?p=1186*

UNICEF Innocenti Research Center .2009. Handbook on the Optional Protocol on the Sale of Children, Child Prostitution and Child Pornography. Florence

A Walk Through the Labyrinths of Sex Work Law

RAKESH SHUKLA

Lawyers by definition spend much of their time engaging closely with laws and their complex provisions. I am no exception: something of a "good boy" lawyer, a moralist and impacted by a particular strand of feminism, I had never, until recently, handled cases of sex workers. I had never had a sex worker as a "client". Conversely and for much the same reasons, I never encountered a sex worker as a customer-client. I was struck however, by the similarity in the terminology—of "soliciting", "servicing" and "clients'—that applied to both law practitioners and sex workers. But of course the similarity did not extend to other areas—for one profession was considered "respectable" and therefore completely different from the other "lowly" and stigmatized one.

My encounters with the laws relating to sex work began when I was approached by the Veshya Anyay Mukti Parishad (VAMP, a collective of women in sex work) to put down the provisions of the law in simple easily readable language in a booklet[1] meant to be used by sex workers. In addition to compiling legal provisions on paper and earlier judgments in the shape of case law, this assignment involved analysing the actual working of the law as it impacted the lives of sex workers.

One of the most enduring stereotypes in Indian society relates to sex workers, who are generally assumed to be either brazenly sexual or helpless and pathetic victims. This dichotomous image of a prostitute, perpetuated by dozens of Hindi films churned out by the Bombay film industry, looms large in the popular psyche, as it did in mine. No sooner had I begun my research, however, that the stereotype began to crumble: the women I met were strong and independent, many had showed extraordinary courage in braving social stigma, in daring to challenge the law, asserting their right to equality, and to practising their profession and living as full fledged citizens of this country. In the case study below, I look at one of the earliest challenges to the patriarchal law on sex work. The story unfolds in the 1950s in newly-independent India.

Shama Bai and SITA

Shama Bai, a courageous 24 year-old, petitioned the Allahabad High Court in 1958 seeking that the recently enacted Suppression of Immoral Traffic Act (SITA) in 1956 be declared unconstitutional and invalid.[2]

In an unparalleled defiance of social norms and stigmatization, Shama Bai declared that she was a prostitute and a singer in Allahabad, a conservative town in the state of Uttar Pradesh. Her petition affirmed that prostitution was the hereditary trade and means of livelihood for her and her cousin. She had two younger brothers who were her dependents and who lived only on her earnings through prostitution. She contended that SITA prohibited her from carrying on her trade and profession, a fundamental right guaranteed under the Constitution of India.[3] She held that the chances of her being rehabilitated as a "good" housewife in society were nil and that she knew no other trade or profession, and the enforcement of SITA would therefore lead to her starvation.

Shama Bai asked the Court to issue a writ commanding the state not to interfere with the carrying on of her trade of prostitution or from interfering with customers visiting her house. She also prayed that the landlord and Chief Tenant of the building be restricted from evicting her from the premises where she was living and carrying on the profession of a prostitute.

What the Court Said

The outcome was mixed. The judgment conceded that prostitution is a profession, trade or occupation within the meaning of Article 19(1)(g) of the Constitution and has existed in all civilized societies from the earliest times. The Court mentioned the external causes which induce women to turn to prostitution along with the difficulty of finding employment, excessively laborious and ill-paid work and maltreatment of girls at home. In a clear demonstration of the biases of the judges, the court listed "promiscuous and indecent mode of living among the overcrowded poor", "the aggregation of people together in large communities and factories, whereby the young are brought into constant contact with demoralized companions"; "demoralizing literature and amusements" and "the arts of profligate men and their agents" as other causes of prostitution.

The Court noted that the Constitution allows reasonable restrictions to be imposed in the interests of the general public on the right to carry on any trade, profession or occupation.[4] It observed that where the effect of a restrictive legislation is to totally prevent a citizen from carrying on a trade, profession or occupation, such a restriction is unreasonable and void. Examining the provisions of SITA the Court held that the legislation imposed restrictions, but could not be said to prohibit the carrying on of the trade or profession of a prostitute.

The subjective aspects of the legal process can be noted in the Court's intermixing of opinion with fact. While examining the reasonableness of the restrictions imposed on the profession of a prostitute, the Court brought in the whole baggage of value-loaded morality and observed that prostitution was "a slur on human dignity, a shame to human civilization", commenting that its eradication was the ultimate aim of all civilized nations. Conflating prostitution and trafficking, the judgment referred to the Constitutional prohibition of traffic in human beings and *begar* (bonded labour) and other forms of forced labour[5] while determining the reasonableness of the restrictions imposed by the legislation. Examining the sections of SITA with this perspective, almost all the provisions were held to be "reasonable restrictions" on the fundamental right to carry on the trade or profession of prostitution.[6] The Court expressed the opinion that Section 20 of the Act, which gave power to the Magistrate to order the removal of a prostitute from an area was an unreasonable restriction on the fundamental right. Similarly the presumption under section 4(2) that a person living with or habitually in the company of a prostitute would be deemed to be living off the earnings of prostitution and punished was opined to be unreasonable and unconstitutional.

In a surprise move, even after expressing the opinion that these two sections could be severed and the rest of the Act upheld, the Court did not pass any order declaring the two sections as invalid on the grounds that as no adverse order had been passed against Shama Bai, she had no right to approach the Court for declaration of the legislation as invalid and rejected the petition.

Thus, one of the first challenges to SITA was smothered by a patriarchal judiciary.

Moral Mindset

Recently there was a move to amend the law in India with regard to sex work, in order to make provisions for the punishment of clients. The seemingly pro-woman amendment to the Immoral Traffic (Prevention) Act, 1956 (ITPA) to prosecute persons who visit brothels[7] initiated by the women and child department of the government seems to be in response to the often-voiced remark: "Why should men who buy sex go scot-free?" The proposed amendment has been strongly endorsed by the National Commission for Women, a statutory body. However, this apparently pro-sex worker proposal, aimed at removing discrimination by prosecuting male clients, has been perceived by sex workers—the women directly impacted by the amendment—as nothing less than an attack on their right to livelihood. The National Network of Sex Workers held a press conference opposing the amendment and pointed out that the move would drive prostitution underground, make HIV prevention work more difficult and would lead to more risky and hazardous working conditions.[8]

Needless to say, the amendment was formulated without consulting anyone actually involved in sex work. The lack of discussion does not come as a surprise, because even though India is a society with a large number of oppressed categories, sex workers are considered to be at the bottom of the heap. Almost everyone takes the high moral ground when it comes to sex work and there is a general unwillingness, and often a refusal, to listen to the workers themselves on desirable changes in the law and their working conditions.[9] The proposed amendment clearly showed that morality was the dominant prism through which sex work was viewed and the impact of this had been evident from the very beginning, when the law was made, and in all the later changes that had taken place in it.

British colonialism and Victorian morality influenced the law as well as the social and cultural norms in India with regard to prostitution. An exploration of the status of women providing sexual entertainment in traditions such as *ganikas*[10] mentioned in the *Arthshastra*, the 3rd century BC treatise by Kautilya, or *devadasis* or *tawaifs*[11] is outside the scope of the present work. Victorian notions of respectable women having no sexual desire, and the lustful male with an insatiable need for sex impacted the general attitude toward sex work. This resulted in the enactment of the Contagious Diseases Act, 1868, which made testing for venereal diseases (among sex workers) mandatory and required government licensing of sex workers.[12] This served the purpose of supplying "disease free" to British troops. However, concerns in late 19th century England about young women being led astray into immorality, and allegations that the state was supporting "vice" led to the repeal of the legislation.[13]. A law for licensing and testing of sex workers, it was believed, would provide a rationale for the legitimization of an "immoral" activity. Repeal of the law was looked upon as closing an avenue which could be used to lure innocent girls into prostitution. The binary of "good" women on the one hand and sex workers ("bad" women) and/or helpless victims forced into sex work and in need of rescue on the other continues to impact the law in India.

Statutory Framework

The Immoral Traffic (Prevention) Act, the law pertaining to prostitution/sex work enacted in 1956, was originally called the Suppression of Immoral Traffic Act (SITA[14]). The SITA reigned for three decades until 1986 when the name itself was changed to

Immoral Traffic (Prevention) Act or ITPA.[15] The origins as well as the title of the legislation reflect the conception of sex work as being synonymous with trafficking and its stigmatisation. The legislation was enacted in pursuance of the 1950 ratification by the Government of India of the International Convention for the Suppression of Traffic in Persons and of the Exploitation of the Prostitution of Others.[16] The Convention on trafficking was impacted by earlier International Agreements. These predecessor agreements were framed exclusively to engage with the issue and fears of white slave trafficking as indicated by their nomenclature: International Agreement of 18th May, 1904 for the Suppression of the White Slave Traffic[17] and International Convention of 4th May, 1910 for the Suppression of the White Slave Traffic. Trafficking would be generally understood to mean transporting a person by means of the use of threats, force, coercion, abduction, fraud or deception.[18] However, the legislation enacted in pursuance of the Convention on Trafficking—SITA—did not even have a definition of trafficking from the inception, leave aside provisions to check it. Indeed, a provision defining and creating the offence of trafficking is sought to be added by the Immoral Traffic (Prevention) Amendment Bill, 2006.[19]Yet so deep is the association of prostitution with trafficking that the law with regard to sex work is called prevention of "immoral traffic".

The legislation (ITPA) penalises acts like keeping a brothel,[20] soliciting in a public place,[21] living off the earnings of prostitution and living with or habitually being in the company of a prostitute.[22] In a departure from criminal jurisprudence, which clearly indicates the stigmatisation of sex workers, the ITPA has paradoxical offences like detaining a person[23] "with or without his consent" in premises where sex work is carried on[24] or taking a person, "with or without his consent" for the purpose of prostitution.[25] Again, the provisions dealing with raid and rescue make no distinction between "adults" and "minors".[26] Ordinarily, in the case of adults, consent or the lack of it is a crucial factor in offences like abduction or illegal confinement which determines whether or not an act is to be dubbed criminal. The legislation gives power to a Magistrate to order the removal of a prostitute living within the local limits of his jurisdiction from the area.[27]

Consent and Choice

Viewed from the constitutional perspective of fundamental rights and the principles of criminal jurisprudence, the single most important feature of the legislation as well as the judgments by courts which stands out is the denial of choice to an adult individual who is a sex worker. The courts seem in total denial with regard to petitions by women in sex work asserting their right to pursue their profession. Thus, provisions clearly in violation of fundamental rights authorizing the "rescue" of adult women in sex work against their will from brothels have been upheld by courts. Even if the legislation as well as courts proceed on the assumption of initial entry of a person as coercive and unwilling, an adult could well choose to remain in sex work. It is a violation of the right to life and liberty, the right to move freely and the right to reside in a place of choice to pick up and detain an individual against their will in the name of "rescue".

Vignettes

The complex issue of consent and choice is best illustrated by the perceptions of women in sex work, recounted in a fact finding[28] into raid and rescue operations at GB Road, the red light area of Delhi by the Andhra Pradesh police on January 8, 2008:

A: Anita (name changed), almost 30 years old, was deserted by her husband, who later fell ill and died in Andhra Pradesh. She had a one-year-old son and a two-year-old daughter at that time. For three years, she did manual labour in the village—lifting weights, construction work—and barely managed to survive. Then she came to Delhi and took up sex work. Her children are both studying in Andhra Pradesh and she goes to meet them once in every two months.

B: *"If we could've earned a livelihood in our villages, why would we have to come here? We are supporting and managing our families."*

C: *"They (the police and the NGOs) earn rewards and we are harassed."*

D: *"For a lot of women there, sex work is a khandani pesha (traditional occupation). For others its majboori (compulsion) since there is no other support."*

E. *"All the women were crying when they were pushed into the police van. They were crying because their children and families in their village would now come to know what they were doing in Delhi. No one was asked even once whether they were trafficked, or had been forced into this work, or if they were minors."*

F: The daughter of F, one of the arrested women, was about to get married in a month and the women sex workers at GB Road were agitated over the fact that the police taking her back to the village would cause extreme humiliation and that the marriage was most likely to be cancelled.

Law in Action—Raid and Rescue

The age-old strategy of "raid and rescue", authorized by law and popular with the state, appears to have been ineffective, besides being violative from a rights perspective.[29] The "raid and rescue" approach has to be seen in the context of anti-trafficking measures.[30] The strategies employed have to be examined from the point of view of the human rights, dignity, privacy and confidentiality of persons who have been trafficked.[31] Invariably, the girls/women "rescued" feel they have been "arrested", and have been in fact kept in confinement and imprisoned. The issue of trafficking also needs to be seen in the context of the rights of migrant workers[32] and the right to work and choice of employment.[33] In fact, for the purpose of "reform", certain provisions authorise the detention of "rescued" individuals not accused of any crime for periods longer than the punishment prescribed for some of the acts categorized as offences.[34]

"Raid and Rescue" in Delhi

The Andhra Pradesh police arrived in Delhi armed with an order from a Magistrate in Kadri (located in Anantapur district of Andhra Pradesh) with authority to raid one specific brothel in Delhi, arrest six persons and rescue twelve women identified as "victims". The police conducted raids in brothels throughout G.B. Road, the red light area of Delhi, on a cold winter's night in early January, 2008. In the course of the raids the women were abused, dragged by the hair and beaten. The police were on the lookout to "rescue" women from Andhra Pradesh and based on their stereotypes of the appearance of women from the southern state, picked up 150 women and took them to the police station. Seventy-five of the women were released after questioning and ascertaining that they were not from Andhra Pradesh. The other seventy-five were detained in the police station.

In a raid meant to prevent trafficking of women the lack of arrest of even one man speaks of the way the law, ostensibly for the welfare of "victim", operates in practice. As the criminal case necessarily needed some accused, twenty-four of the women—possibly the slightly older ones—were arbitrarily shown as accused and the rest of fifty-one women were shown as "rescued". All the women detained and arrested were adults and had been staying in Delhi for years. The "rescued" were not allowed to meet anyone and treated as "dangerous" constantly accompanied by police at the time of production in court and not allowed to talk to anyone. The authorities refused the attempts of friends and colleagues to hand over blankets, warm clothing and a few personal belongings to the "rescued" women. Without being given an opportunity to express their wishes about whether they wanted to stay in Delhi, the women were put in a train and sent against their will to Hyderabad and then to Kadri. In Delhi, extensive press and television coverage had been arranged by the police of the raid and rescue from sex work of 150 women from Andhra Pradesh. In Kadri, the police once again paraded all the women before the press. The media covered the spectacle in a predictably sensational manner, violating the privacy of the women and the requirements of anonymity in such cases.[35]

Voices of the "rescued"

Legal provisions and arguments in courts justifying rescue and raids apart, it is testimonies from witnesses to the raid and rescue operations in Delhi by the Andhra Pradesh police on 7 January, 2008 which offer a real picture of the law in action:

A cook in the brothel: *"Even as they grabbed and caught the women, and chased out all the clients, many of the men who work here, including me, ran out with them... they were using abusive, sexist language while attacking the women."*

A witness: *"The women were beaten up and violently dragged away from here. They were also not allowed to pick up anything or wear slippers or take some clothes with them... it was horrible."*

Sex worker 1: *"The police did not ask us anything, not even our names. They just started slapping, beating and manhandling us. The SHO of Kadri Police Station, Munawwar Husain, also the Investigating Officer on the case, molested us. He yanked us by our hair and pulled at our breasts. He had come during the previous year's raid as well. He pushed many of us on the floor and tried to drag us out."*

Sex worker 2: *"They separated us according to the region we belonged to and started dragging women from the South down the stairs. They really manhandled us... we begged them to stop, but they wouldn't."*

Sex worker 3: *"They broke the locks of my make-up box, searched cupboards and picked up my mobile phones, generator keys, papers and money. No panchnama (written record) was made for them, so I can't even make a formal complaint... how can I hope to get my things back? They don't have the right to do this... because technically, I have not even been arrested and am not part of the case. This is out and out badmashi (misconduct)!".*

Sex worker 4: *"We were all hit and abused by the male police. The female police didn't hit anyone. The police also threatened to rape us."*

Sex worker 5: *"One woman's hair was pulled so hard that her neck got twisted badly... they just dragged her away."*

Sex worker 6: *"Our mobile phones were taken away."*

Sex worker 7: *"We will come down ourselves with our dignity in place... don't drag, abuse or beat us."*

Reform and Rehabilitation

A person accused of an offence under the ITPA is entitled to apply for release on bail while the criminal case proceeds. Similarly, the punishment for various offences under the law is specified by the statute. For example, the maximum sentence for the offence of prostitution in the vicinity of a public place is three months imprisonment.[36] However, in case of a female offender found guilty of prostitution in the vicinity of a public place, the law authorizes the detention of the person in a corrective institution for a minimum of two years and maximum of seven years for the purposes of reform, if the Court concludes that the offender will benefit from instruction and discipline in the corrective detention.[37]

A person rescued in a raid from a brothel does not have the right to be released on bail if she is not accused of any offence. Ironically, because the person is not charged with an offence there is no specified period of punishment. The law authorizes a magistrate to order detention of persons removed and/or rescued, and not accused of an offence, to detention of a minimum of one year and a maximum of three years in a protective home.[38]

The provisions are meant in the nature of social welfare legislation with the object of reform and rehabilitation of the individuals concerned. However, for the persons detained, it is the same as being in jail with their liberty curtailed, even though they have not accused of any crime. The apparently laudable objectives of reform and rehabilitation remain on paper, with dismal living conditions and no worthwhile skill being taught to earn a living on release from the "protective" home.

The Truth about Rehabilitation

An excerpt from the official view and the words of two rescued women in sex work, now back in the profession, speak volumes.

> OFFICIAL SPEAK: "The AP government has many schemes to rehabilitate those victims of the sex trade who express interest for the same. Apart from ₹10,000 in cash that is given to each victim, housing and employment is also provided to them. Moreover, NGOs are also authorized to provide them with necessary items like clothing, and even assist them in getting reintegrated with their families...

The Andhra Pradesh government runs an effective rehabilitation programme for women rescued from brothels".

RESCUED SEX WORKER 1: "I was very young when I got into the profession... so some years ago I was "rescued". But at the rehabilitation home, we were never given any money, much less vocational training. The officials in the Home talked to us really badly, made us do menial chores like "jhadu-pocha" (sweeping-swabbing of the floors). The moment I was out of there, I came running back to GB Road—why would I go anywhere else?"

RESCUED SEX WORKER 2: "Often the corrupt officials make us sign blank forms so that they can pocket the money."

This incident of "rescue" is similar to the numerous "raid and rescue" operations that take place across the country in the name of the public good.

Rights of Women in Sex Work versus the Public Interest

In the Anglo-Saxon jurisprudence followed in India, only the persons whose fundamental rights were violated had *locus* and could approach courts for redress. The concept of Public Interest Litigations (PILs) arose in the late seventies and relaxed the rigid notion of *locus standi*—and the principle evolved that "public-spirited" individuals could approach the courts on behalf of the exploited sections of society to make fundamental rights a reality for the marginalized classes. PILs filed in courts ostensibly for the welfare of prostitutes bring out the embedded notions of morality and respectability reflected in attitudes towards women in sex work. The cases were filed by apparently "public-spirited" individuals concerned about society and the welfare of prostitutes, and without any consultation with the sex worker community. The judges proceeded with the matter without inquiring into the basis of the petitioner's case asking for wide-ranging directions from the courts with regard to women in sex work. The nature of relief asked for in the prayers of the petition makes it fairly clear that the cases were filed based on stereotypical notions about prostitutes formed on the basis of celluloid and media representations.

The courts too made no effort to ascertain the wishes of the community whose interests were centrally involved and impacted by judgments in such litigations. In fact, the courts themselves have used the "amorphous" public interest, clearly excluding women in sex work as part of the "public" and denying them the rights of equality as full-fledged citizens of the Indian Republic, to dismiss petitions by women in sex work challenging provisions of the law which clearly violate their fundamental rights. These rights violations deeply impact the lives of women in sex work .

Segregation of Children

Gaurav Jain, an advocate,[39] in 1988 after reading a report in the magazine *India Today* filed a writ petition in the Supreme Court of India under Article 32 of the Constitution as a public interest litigation. Jain sought to forcibly take away children from their sex worker mothers in order to rescue them from falling into an immoral and depraved way of life. The petition asked for directions from the court to provide separate schools with vocational training, hostels, with medical check-up facilities in each state and union territory for children of prostitutes up to the age of 16 years.

The court proceeded with the matter without even considering the basic and preliminary issue of the rights of the sex worker mothers to have their children stay with them. The crucial question of ascertaining the wishes of the mother and the child before adjudicating upon the issue of mandatory removal of the child from mother was totally ignored by the court. Submissions on the lines of "prostitutes do not want to have children and ordinarily when children are born to them it is in spite of their desire not to rear children" were presented on behalf of the petitioner. No rational basis or factual data like surveys ascertaining the wishes of sex worker mothers were produced in support of submissions of this nature. In a society valorizing motherhood, the extreme stigmatization and prejudice with regard to women in sex work is manifested in looking at them as something akin to a separate species, devoid of ordinary human emotions.

The court order which included phrases like "the children of prostitutes should not be permitted to live in an inferno" shows how the court too subscribe to the stereotype that such children grow up without maternal love. The court took the view that segregating prostitutes' children by putting them in separate schools and providing separate hostels would not be in the interest of such children. However, it held that accommodation in hostels and reformatory homes should be adequately available to "help segregation of these children from their mothers living in prostitutes' homes as soon as they are identified."[40] It appointed a committee to consider the problems faced by the children of prostitutes. The committee submitted its report and made various recommendations for the rehabilitation of the children of prostitutes and setting up of juvenile homes. The two judges agreed with the directions for rehabilitation of the children. However, one of the judges gave general directions for the eradication of prostitution. This issue has now been referred to a larger bench for consideration and is, at the time of writing, still pending.

"Rescuing" a Community

Vishal Jeet, another advocate, filed a writ petition in 1989 under Article 32 of the Constitution of India by way of a Public Interest Litigation asking the Supreme Court of India to direct the Central Bureau of Investigation to:

1. Institute an enquiry against those police officers under whose jurisdiction red light areas as well Devadasi and Jogin traditions are flourishing and to take necessary action against such erring police officers and law breakers;
2. Bring all the inmates of the red light areas and also those who are engaged in "flesh trade" to protective homes of the respective states, and to provide them with proper medical aid, shelter, education and training in various disciplines of life so as to enable them to choose a more dignified way of life, and
3. Bring the children of those prostitutes and other children found begging in streets and also the girls pushed into "flesh trade" to protective homes and then to rehabilitate them.

According to the court order, "the petitioner has filed 9 affidavits said to be sworn by 9 girls who claim to be living in the brothel houses pleading for rescue and a list of 9 girls who are morally afraid to swear the affidavits." The averments made by the petitioners are of victims confined in tiny claustrophobic rooms for several days without food until they succumb to the vicious desires of the brothel keeper. The phrases used are on the lines of the victims "submitting their bodies to all dirty customers including even sexagenarians with plastic smiles." However, no other facts or material indicating the ascertaining of the wishes of the sex worker community for the sweeping reliefs asked for from the court like bringing all inmates of red light areas to protective homes was produced for adjudication of the matter.

The Supreme Court looked upon prostitution as an evil and the judgment is replete with phrases like "prostitution always remains as a running sore in the body of civilization and destroys all moral values" and "this malignity is daily and hourly threatening the community at large."[41] Referring to sex work as "cancerous growth", the judgment observes that "this malignity cannot be eradicated by either banishing, branding, scourging or inflicting severe punishment on these helpless and hapless victims… weeping or wailing throughout."

The conception of sex work as the destroyer of all moral values seems quite out of proportion in the context of the realities and societal ills of the world, and is indicative of the extreme anxiety associated with sex work. The need for all "prostitutes" to fit the stereotype of "total victims" who are "weeping and wailing throughout" is in sharp contrast to the reality that many women in sex work are strong, independent women. Similarly, the imagery conjured up the use of words such as branding, scourging, banishing to describe "appropriate" punishments for sex workers, shows clearly how the legal system, which may describe them as victims, actually stigmatizes them. The judgment then makes the jump from sex work to the constitutional prohibition of "traffic in human beings" and to provisions of the Indian Penal Code which specify procuring a minor girl,[42] selling of minors for prostitution[43] and buying of minors for prostitution[44] as offences.

Sex, Gender and Law

In a first, the Election Commission of India in February 2010 along with "Male" and "Female", introduced a third column of "Others" in voter enrolment and registration forms. The category is meant to cover intersex and transsexual persons. In October 2010, the Unique Identification Authority of India (UIDAI), emulating the Election Commission introduced a third column along with M and F, labeled "T" for transgender in the enrolment form for the identity. While these are welcome beginnings of the need to recognize that binaries of gender are insufficient, the law predominantly slots individuals under two labels—male and female.

Criminal Law

The starkest effect of forcing persons into the two categories of Male and Female is reflected in the working of the criminal justice system. Jails and police lock-ups have only the two sections of Male and Female. This results in intersex, transsexuals, hijras and kothis [45]being interred in the Male section of the detention places resulting in widespread harassment, torture and rape by other inmates as well as police and prison authorities. The problem becomes worse when the individuals happen to be in sex work.

To cite a prominent example, Kokila, a "hijra" (transgender) sex worker was raped, beaten and brutalised by a group of men in Bangalore. She went to the police station to get a criminal case registered against the perpetrators. Instead of lodging a first information report (FIR), the police chained her naked in the lock-up and tortured, humiliated and sexually abused her. Today, rape of men and transgender persons in general and particularly in custodial settings like prisons, police lock-ups, juvenile homes for neglected and delinquent children remains invisible. At the time of writing, the definition of rape under the Indian Penal Code covers the rape of a woman by a man and the act of penetration is necessary to constitute the offence of rape.[46] There is no law with regard to acts of male rape and of child sexual abuse in India. The police prosecute persons for these acts under a provision titled "Unnatural Offences" which punishes "carnal intercourse against the order of nature with any man, woman or animal" with up to ten years imprisonment.[47] The act of penetration is required to constitute "carnal intercourse". The provision criminalizes homosexuality and only recently, in a landmark ruling by the Delhi High Court in 2009 on a petition by NAZ Foundation, has been interpreted to exclude acts between consenting adults.[48] The main grounds for excluding acts among same sex adult partners from the ambit of Section 377 is discrimination and violation of the fundamental right to equality. The matter is presently pending in appeal in the Supreme Court of India.

The law regarding rape has long been critiqued by feminists as inadequate in dealing with a range of violent acts against women which do not involve penile-vaginal penetration. Similarly, activists working in the field have felt that Section 377 is inadequate in dealing with a number of acts perpetrated against children and have long been demanding a specific legislation covering child sexual abuse. Efforts to amend the provisions of existing laws and enact new legislation dealing with sexual assault have been ongoing for over two decades.

Sexual Assault Bill

In response to sustained efforts by civil society and women's rights groups, the government brought in the Criminal Law (Amendment) Bill, 2010 which makes changes in the Indian Penal Code and the Criminal Procedure Code. Besides including gendered crimes such as acid attacks in its ambit, the Bill proposes to define the offence of "sexual assault" in place of the present offence of "rape". The definition of sexual assault covers a wider range of offences rather than penile-vaginal penetration, and includes insertion of other body parts and objects into the vagina, anus, urethra or mouth of a woman. The proposed definition of sexual assault does not make the offence gender-neutral and retains the framework of "man" as the perpetrator with the "woman" as the victim/survivor. The Bill does not propose to introduce any provision covering the rape of an adult male. The lacuna of the absence of a provision to cover acts of adult male rape would remain even after the proposed amendments come into force. The Amendment Bill proposes to introduce a new provision with regard to "sexual abuse of minors". A minor has been defined as a person under 18 years of age. The definition of sexual abuse of minors follows the ambit of the proposed offence of "sexual assault". The proposed provision with regard to child sexual abuse is gender neutral and by use of the word "person" ensures that acts perpetrated on boys, girls, inter-sex and transgender individuals would fall within the ambit of the new offence.

There has been a demand by a section that the rape law be made gender-neutral; that the term "person" be substituted wherever "Man" and "Woman" has been used in the rape law. Feminists and a number of women groups have opposed the demand looking upon it as a dilution of the law and leaving room open for harassment by making women "accused" of rape if the provision is made gender-neutral. Similarly, a strand of the queer rights movement took the view that given that homosexuality itself was criminalized, the first step should be to decriminalize it rather than make the definition of rape gender-neutral.

Immoral Traffic (Prevention) Act

The government of India ratified the International Convention for the Suppression of Traffic in Persons and of the Exploitation of the Prostitution of Others in 1950 and enacted the Suppression of Immoral Traffic Act or SITA in 1956. The legislation was premised on the assumption that all sex workers were women and therefore the law left out males, intersex or transgenders in sex work. Given the increasing visibility of male, intersex and transgender people in sex work, the Government took limited cognizance of the reality, and in 1986 along with changing the name from SITA to ITPA brought in an amendment to substitute the word "person" for "woman" in ITPA.[49] However, the legislation in practice continues to treat women as victims, and the aim of checking trafficking has in reality been used against women in sex work; prosecution of male pimps and brothel owners has been rare. There has been no study to find out whether the change to the term "person" from "woman", thus covering others in sex work, has affected the working and implementation of the law.

Transgender Hijra and Kothis in Sex Work

Violence by police toward vulnerable sections of society is endemic in India. However, the combination of being a sex worker and a transgender individual seems to provoke the police to perpetrate the worst kind of violence and humiliation. Compounding matters is the fact that a predominant feature of the transgender sex worker's life is verbal, physical and sexual violence by non-state actors with little redress. The transgender *hijra* and *kothi* in sex work do not fit into the neat binary of "man" and "woman" and seem to invite particularly vicious violations of a sexual nature by local goondas and hoodlums in the place of business, usually public parks. The hoodlums demand *hafta* (weekly protection money) as well as free sex which must be without condoms. Refusal results in terrible violence. The sex workers have little recourse to the criminal justice system. Refusal by the police to lodge a first information report (FIR in common parlance) is the norm. Demand for protection money and free sex by the police is also common. In addition to beatings, the highly visible non-conforming sexuality of the *hijra* and the *kothi* becomes the focus of verbal humiliation as well as the infliction of physical assault on the intimate and sexual parts of the person. The threat of violence and actual violence by state and non-state actors is the all-pervasive reality of the lived existence of a *hijra* or *kothi* sex worker. In addition to the stigma associated with sex work, the "deviant" transgender identity and sexuality of the *hijra* and *kothi* individual seems to threaten the conventional social order and provoke anger, rage and violence from the police as well as in the general public. In the present definition of rape, as well as in the proposed introduction of the offence of "sexual assault" in the penal code, the act of the rape of an adult male or transgender person remains outside the ambit of the offence.

Vignettes

Jhuma's story

The story of Jhuma (name changed) as recounted in mid-November 2010[50] poignantly brings out the interface of law in action and transgender persons in sex work.

Jhuma is a dark, attractive transgender sex worker who identifies herself as a *kinner*—a *hijra* she explains. She is 20 years old and has been in this "line" since she was eight. She tells me how, about five years ago, the local hoodlums where she does business in Delhi demanded *hafta* (protection money) in the range of ₹20,000 per week. In addition they wanted sex without using condoms. When she refused they knifed her in the stomach. She pulls up her shirt to reveal deep, extensive scarred tissue as a result of the severe stabbing. The police refused to record her statement. Her family members were scared and told the police that she fell from the roof. No case was filed against the perpetrators. Jhuma recounts that just a week prior to the interview, about five hoodlums again slashed her arms with blades over the demand for *hafta* and free sex. She pulls up the sleeve of her long shirt to show cut marks by blades on the underside of the forearm.

She adds that the police are equally violent—beating and demanding *hafta* and free sex and using extremely abusive language. She has had three criminal cases of theft, soliciting in a public place and blackmail foisted on her by the police for refusing to comply with their demand for free sex. At the time of production in court, she was asked by the judge about her appearance, the public prosecutor used abusive language to describe her. Jhuma protested, she explained to the judge that she was a *kinner* and gay but she does not do any *galat kaam* (wrong thing). The judge sent her to jail for three months.

She was initially put in the women's section of the jail, but soon transferred to the men's section. She had a terrible time in the male section of the jail. She was repeatedly stripped and people would jump into her bed when she was sleeping or bathing and rape her. Inside the jail, she was also forcibly injected with an unknown drug and then sexually abused. Her complaint to the authorities elicited the response that it was not possible to get injections and drugs inside the jail.

The police would come with torches and search for us in the park. They used to take 500-1000 rupees from the customers. The local goons used to rob the chains and purses of the customers. The goons used to tell us to get boys to the area so that they could be robbed— "We will give you half"—but we never agreed. Some of the customers lodged FIRs about being robbed but the police would blame us and say "It is due to you hijras".

Savita's account

Main 18 saal kee hun (I am 18 years old—the "I" is feminine). I consider myself gay. I have been in this "line" for eight years. The police come to the park with torches. If they catch us, they box and kick us, they rob our money and they also rape us, that too without condoms. The boys (hoodlums) also come and demand sex for free. Five-six of them come almost every day. They also rob us of money. I hide the money. They use sexually abusive terms to address us: *"Gandmare", "Haluye", "Dalle", "Randi", "Bhonsdi ke"*.

Mahua's account

I am 18 years old. I have been in this "line" for six-seven months. I was in a car with four boys (customers). The police caught us— they threatened the boys and took money from them. The police gave me my money. The said, "Tell us where it happens".

Sachin's Story

My name is Sachin and I am 23 years old. I am the fifth child in a family of four elder sisters. As a child I always enjoyed putting on make-up like vibhuti or kum kum (usually worn by females) and my parents always saw me as a girl. I am male but I have only female feelings… Then one day my parents asked me to leave the village to avoid the shame. "Go work somewhere else", they said. I don't know how to read or write, I never went to school, how would I ever get a job?

But sex work was not easy. The police would just come in the night, see me walking in "satla" (drag) and would just hit me with a lathi. I became scared of even walking on the streets.

Smita's Story

For the past three years, Smita has been living with her husband Tejasvi. On the night of 18 March 2002, at around 9 p.m., she and her husband were standing in front of a commercial complex on St. Marks Road (opposite Bishop Cotton Girls High School gate, in front of Richie Rich Ice Cream Parlour). Four policemen in a Hoysala van (no. 1) dragged her by her hair and pushed her and her husband into the van by force, snatching away her mobile phone.

In the police station, she was pushed into a room with her husband. Some fifteen or twenty policemen stripped her naked in the presence of a senior police officer (Circle Inspector Munirathnam Naidu). Smita describes him as being around 50 years old, wheatish skin colour, 5'4" in height and very fat. All the 15-20 police men stood around her, sexually abusing her by touching her all over her naked body. They humiliated her further by forcing her to spread her thighs and touching her sexual organs.

Many of them hit her with lathis on her head, hands, thighs, shoulders etc. They also attempted to shave off her hair. She continuously begged them to let her go and even fell at their feet. They verbally abused her by repeatedly referring to her as *gandu* (a male who has anal sex), bastard, son of a bitch and used the foulest language as they continued to beat her, making vile comments like: "Did you come here to get fucked anally? Whose cocks did you come here to suck?"; "People get AIDS from you, one day you will die of AIDS, *chakka* (feminine looking male who plays the passive partner during sex), I will fuck your mother."

Morality and Discrimination

The role of morality is not confined to the statute and the working of the law with regard to sex work (ITPA) but impacts other crucial areas including the fundamental rights to life, liberty, equality, free movement, residence and shelter of persons in sex work. In the monsoon season of 2004, the rains that bring joy to millions of people in India brought only grief to the residents of Baina beach in Goa. Carrying out an order of the Goa bench of the Bombay High Court, for the identification and demolition of 250 huts being used by women in sex work, the state government set about bulldozing hundreds of hutments right in the midst of heavy rains lashing the area. The object of the demolition was the restoration of an "unspoilt Goa" by cleansing it of the "sin" of sex work. The hutments were the homes of women who had been living there for the past 40 years. They had valid ration cards, voter identity cards, electricity bills and tax receipts as proof of their being bona fide residents of Baina. Many of their children attended schools in the area. In fact, many children born in Baina were vote-casting citizens of the area. However, despite the production of these documents clearly establishing legal residence, the women in sex work were denied domicile and their houses demolished with impunity.[52] Their very citizenship was swept aside in a tide of moral outrage. Few civil society groups protested.

The criminal justice delivery system is the other major area in which morality plays a vital role in denying access to justice for crimes committed against prostitutes/persons in sex work. The law with regard to assault, grievous hurt, rape and kidnapping makes no distinction and is uniformly applicable regardless of the identity or profession of the victim/survivor. However, in reality, non-persons like sex workers seem to be routinely subjected to beatings and rape without any consequences for the perpetrator.

Endnote

Total legal prohibition of sex work is a demand that enjoys considerable support in society. International women's organizations/coalitions as well as a number of NGOs work in this area with the perspective of the total outlawing of sex work. Regulation refers to state control of women in sex work through licensing, which is prevalent in Germany and Netherlands and has been suggested in Kolkata as a possible route to take. Decriminalization refers to repeal of laws against sexual activity in a commercial context and is an alternative strongly advocated for, especially by some collectives and associations of people in sex work. Proponents of this option point out that state control or regulation would decrease the autonomy and increase the vulnerability of people in sex work in a kind of "licence raj", leading to extortion by inspectors and sundry state authorities. Regardless of the view followed, there is a consensus with regard to trafficking, and on the entry of minors in the profession. The difference perhaps lies in the way to go about the prevention of trafficking and the entry of minors. Raid and rescue or trying to work from within the profession is being tried out by some collectives of women in sex work with moderate success. In the context of consent, trafficking and the entry of minors, self-regulation would involve some sort of self-regulatory boards of women in sex work and their associations rather than the coercive arm of the law.

The debate on prohibition, regulation and de-criminalization apart, the law on sex work in India needs to emphasize the distinction between adults and minors, especially with regard to consent. No matter whether a person may have come into sex work voluntarily or coercively, if he or she is an adult, their wishes must be taken into account before any prosecution or "rescue" goes forward—an adult, could well choose to remain in sex work, even accounting for the fact that the person might initially have been trafficked, illegally and unwillingly. Meanwhile, discriminatory provisions—giving powers to order the removal of a sex worker from a particular area—need to be weeded out. The legislation on sex work must be brought in line with the fundamental rights of people in sex work to live and work in liberty and dignity, the right to move unhindered, the right to reside in a place of their choice and the right to migrate—in short, the right to live freely as a full-fledged adult citizen of the country.

Is a Prostitute a Woman?

In the early 1960s, Kaushailiyabai and six other women were alleged to be prostitutes carrying on their trade in the city of Kanpur, and were issued notices by the City Magistrate of Kanpur to show cause why they should not be required to remove themselves from where they were residing under Section 20 of SITA. The Magistrate and the Additional Sessions Judge of Kanpur rejected the objection of Kaushailiyabai and others that the proceedings were not legally maintainable. In a rare instance of putting aside bias and prejudice, the Allahabad High Court set aside the proceedings, holding that Section 20 of the Act violated the right to equality of the women under Article 14 and the right to move freely and reside in a place of choice under Articles 19(1)(d) and (e) of the Constitution. The matter reached the Supreme Court in appeal.

The main arguments presented on behalf of Kaushailiyabai in the Supreme Court are telling of the sexism, dominant norms of respectability and the stigmatizing of women in sex work that pervade the jurisprudence in this arena.

The argument presented was that Section 20 of SITA is violative of equality as it gave uncontrolled power to the Magistrate to "discriminate between prostitute and prostitute" in the matter of restricting their movements and deporting them to places outside his jurisdiction. It was further argued that the section enables the Magistrate on flimsy and untested evidence to "interfere with the lives of respectable women by holding them to be prostitutes" and therefore violates equality. Implicit in the arguments presented on behalf of women in sex work seems to be the assumption that it would be valid to deport prostitutes, and the objection is to discrimination inter-se between prostitutes. The second line of argument expressed the apprehension that "respectable women" would be termed prostitutes and deported is in a similar vein.

However, even arguments of this genre seem to have made little headway with the Supreme Court. The judgment takes it as a given that the differentiation of women into prostitute and non-prostitute is reasonable for the purpose of making law, and did not offend the right to equality under Article 14 of the Constitution. The judgment observes that there were "pronounced and real" differences between a woman who is a prostitute and one who is not and these were held to be sufficient to justify the two being placed in different classes.

The main reasoning of the judgment upholding Section 20 is to establish that the provision does not discriminate between prostitutes by arbitrarily placing some in the category to be deported. The judgment offers the reasoning that a prostitute who carries on trade on the sly or in the unfrequented parts of the town or in a town with sparse population may not be so dangerous to public health or morals as a prostitute who lives in a busy locality or an over-crowded town or in a place within easy reach of public institutions like religious and educational institutions. The Court holds the latter to be "far more dangerous to the public", particularly to the younger generation "during the emotional stage of their life". Freedom of uncontrolled movement of a sex worker in a crowded locality or in the vicinity of public institutions was held to "demoralize the public morals" and spread diseases not only affecting the present generation but also the future one. The judgment declares that Section 20, in order to prevent moral decadence, differentiates between two classes of prostitutes and restricting the movement of and deporting one category of prostitutes is not violative of the right to equality under Article 14 of the Constitution.

Addressing the argument of the right of a sex worker to move freely throughout India and reside in a place of choice, the judgment examines the issue of the reasonableness of the restrictions imposed on the right. The Court observes that the reasonableness of a restriction depends on the values of life in a society, the circumstances obtaining at the time of restriction, and the degree and urgency of the evil sought to be controlled. The judgment declares that if in a particular locality the vice of prostitution is "endemic", degrading those who live by prostitution and demoralizing others who come into contact with them, then the law may have to impose severe restrictions on the right of a prostitute to move about and to live in a house of her choice. The Court held that if "the evil is rampant, it may also be necessary to provide for deporting the worst of them from their area of operation." The restrictions imposed by a Magistrate on the right of women in sex work to move freely and reside in a place of choice were held to be reasonable restrictions in the interests of the general public. The judgment declared that Section 20 of SITA did not violate equality, imposed reasonable restrictions in public interest on the right of a sex worker to move freely and reside in a place of choice and was constitutional and valid.[53]

Import:
1. This is to date the only case where the challenge to a provision of ITPA by a sex worker reached the Supreme Court. The judgment negating the challenge to the provision giving power to a Magistrate to order removal of a sex worker from a geographical area delivered in 1964 continues to impact the community. The orders passed by magistrates directing removal of a prostitute are not collated and published. However, anecdotal evidence like that of Shabnam, a sex worker from Belgaum who waged a struggle against her removal, indicates the use of the provision, especially at the instance of "respectable" members of a locality.
2. The provision giving power of removal of a prostitute from a locality is blatantly discriminatory. The stigmatized position of women in sex work appears to be the major reason to uphold the provision. The legal rationale offered seems little more than a cloak to cover the implicit prejudice against the sex worker community as a class.

Notes

1. 'Veshya Vyavsay Kaidyachi Olakh", 2005; Veshya Anyay Mukti Parishad (VAMP)
2. See section "Statutory Framework" for details of SITA
3. Article 19(1)(g) of the Constitution of India, 1950 reads: "All citizens have the right (g) to practise any profession, or to carry on any occupation, trade or business."
4. Article 19(6) of the Constitution of India, 1950
5. Article 23(1) of the Constitution of India, 1950
6. Shama Bai versus State of U.P. AIR 1959 All 57
7. Section 6 of the Immoral Traffic (Prevention) Bill, 2006 suggesting insertion of Section 5 (c) titled "Punishment for visiting brothel"
8. 'Sex workers protest "attack on livelihood"', *The Times of India*, December 8, 2005
9. "MPs may be caught taking bribes on camera, NGOs may be caught fudging accounts and judges nabbed taking favours—yet parliamentarians, social workers and the robed fraternity take the high moral ground when it comes to prostitution. They arrogate to themselves to pontificate on what is in the best interests of these

"fallen women'"—"She is no outlaw" by Rakesh Shukla, *The Times of India*, December 19, 2005

10. According to the *Arthashastra* providing sexual entertainment using trained ganikas was standard. Kautilya, said to be the author of this work, was the advisor to the first Mauryan Emperor, Chandragupta. (340-293 BCE)

11. Tambe, Ashwini (2009), *Codes of Misconduct: Regulating Prostitution in Late Colonial Bombay*, New Delhi: Zubaan, p. xx-xxii :"In descriptions of prostitution in ancient and medieval India, prostitutes appear to have enjoyed a good standing before the State and even State support (Joardar 1984, Mukherjee 1931/1986; Sinha and Basu, 1933). It is only in the mid-nineteenth century that prostitutes became the target of punitive laws under British colonial administrators, and the term "common prostitute" was inaugurated in Indian legal texts."

12. Chatterjee Ratnabali, "Indian Prostitute as a Colonial Subject Bengal 1864-1883".

13. Kotiswaran Prabha, "Preparing for Civil Disobedience: Indian Sex Workers and the Law'—http://www.bc.edu/bc_org/avp/law/lwsch/journals/bctwj/21_2/01_TXT.htm

14. The icon of purity and virtue in Indian society

15. "It is proposed to change the name of the Act to "Immoral Traffic (Prevention) Act…", Proposed amendment (a) in Act 44 of 1986—Gazette of India, August 20, 1986, Pt II, S2, Ext, p 9 (No 38).

16. "In 1950 the government of India ratified an international convention for the suppression of traffic in persons and of the exploitation of the prostitution of others", Statement of Object and Reasons—Gazette of India, 1954, Pt II-S2, Ext, p 757.

17. Agreement for the Suppression of the "White Slave Traffic," 18 May 1904, 35 Stat. 1979, 1 L.N.T.S. 83, *entered into force* 18 July 1905.

INTERNATIONAL AGREEMENT FOR THE SUPPRESSION OF THE "WHITE SLAVE TRAFFIC"

His Majesty the King of the United Kingdom of Great Britain and Ireland and of the British Dominions beyond the Seas, Emperor of India; His Majesty the German Emperor, King of Prussia, in the name of the German Empire; His Majesty the King of the Belgians; His Majesty the King of Denmark; His Majesty the King of Spain; the President of the French Republic; His Majesty the King of Italy; Her Majesty the Queen of the Netherlands; His Majesty the King of Portugal and of the Algarves; His Majesty the Emperor of all the

Russias; His Majesty the King of Sweden and Norway; and the Swiss Federal Council, being desirous of securing to women of full age who have suffered abuse or compulsion, as also to women and girls under age, effective protection against the criminal traffic known as the "White Slave Traffic", have decided to conclude an Agreement with a view to concerting measures calculated to attain this object, and have appointed as their Plenipotentiaries, that is to say:

Who, having exchanged their full powers, found in good and due form, have agreed upon the following provisions:

Article 1

Each of the Contracting Governments undertakes to establish or name some authority charged with the coordination of all information relative to the procuring of women or girls for immoral purposes abroad; this authority shall be empowered to correspond direct with the similar department established in each of the other Contracting States.

18. "Trafficking in persons" is defined in Article 3(a), Protocol to Prevent, Suppress and Punish Trafficking in Persons, Especially Women and Children, 2000, supplementing the United Nations Convention against Transnational Organised Crime.

19. Proposed Section 5A of the Immoral Traffic (Prevention) Act, 1956

20. Section 3 of [The] Immoral Traffic Prevention Act, 1956.

21. Section 8 of [The] Immoral Traffic Prevention Act, 1956.

22. Section 4 of [The] Immoral Traffic Prevention Act, 1956.

23. 'person" was substituted for the words "woman or girl" and such other consequential amendments as the rules of grammar required also made in the Suppression of Immoral Traffic in Women and Girls (Amendment) Act (44 of 1986), Section 4(26-1-1987).

24. Section 6 of [The] Immoral Traffic Prevention Act, 1956.

25. Section 5 of [The] Immoral Traffic Prevention Act, 1956.

26. Section 16 of [The] Immoral Traffic Prevention Act, 1956.

27. Section 20 of [The] Immoral Traffic Prevention Act, 1956.

28. The author was a member of the fact-finding team.

29. "Rights or the Wrongs—A Case Study of G B Road Rescue-Rehabilitation Operation", Choudhary, Banamallika, National Network of Sex Workers and Centre for Feminist Legal Research, May 2002.

30. On the similarity of certain Traffickers and Anti-Traffickers: A Report by Education Means Protection of Women Engaged in Recreation (EMPOWER), Chiang Mai on the Human Rights Violations women are subjected to when "rescued" by anti-trafficking groups who

employ methods using deception, force and coercion—*Namaskar*, Vol 6, No 2, January 2004, Durbar Prakashini.

31. Recommended Principles and Guidelines on Human Rights and Guidelines on Human Rights and Human Trafficking
32. International Convention on the Protection of all Migrant Workers and Members of their Families
33. "States will ensure the rights of women to protection and working conditions as well as the right to choose a profession", Convention on the Elimination of all forms of Discrimination against Women
34. In the case of a female offender found guilty of prostitution in the vicinity of a public place the court can order the detention of the person in a corrective institution for a minimum of two years and maximum of seven years—Section 10A of the Immoral Traffic (Prevention) Act, 1956
35. In the Name of Rescue, Report on the arrest of 75 sex workers in Delhi, www.pudr.org –unpublished report.
36. Section 7(2) of the Immoral Traffic (Prevention) Act, 1956
37. Section 10A of the Immoral Traffic (Prevention) Act, 1956
38. Section 17(4) of the Immoral Traffic (Prevention) Act, 1956
39. Advocates practising in courts find it easier to file petitions and at times there may be an element of personal publicity in PILs, which is frowned upon by courts.
40. Gaurav Jain versus Union of India, (1990) Supp 3 SCC 709
41. Vishal Jeet versus Union of India, 1990 AIR 1412 1990 SCR (2) 861 1990 SCC (3) 318 JT 1990 (2) 354 1990 SCALE (1)874
42. Section 366-A of the Indian Penal Code, 1860
43. Section 372 of the Indian Penal Code, 1860
44. Section 373 of the Indian Penal Code, 1860
45. Kothi: a self-identifying label for men who might feminize their behaviour and Hijra,a transgender person who is biologically male who takes on the gender role of a female.
46. Indian Penal Code, Section 375
47. Indian Penal Code, 1860, Section 377
48. Naz Foundation versus Government of NCT, Delhi judgment dated 2 July, 2009
49. "In view of the aforesaid suggestions, it is proposed to widen the scope of the Act to cover all persons, whether male or female who are exploited sexually for commercial purposes and to make further amendments in the Act", Statement of Object and Reasons to the Amendment Act 44 of 1986 to the Suppression of Immoral Traffic Act—Gazette of India, August 20, 1986, Pt II, S2, Ext, p 9 (No 38).

50. Interview with author
51. Human Rights Violations against the Transgender Community: A PUCL Report; A Study of Kothi and Hhijra Sex Workers in Bangalore, September 2003
52. 'Baina Beach Demolitions: What about the Sex Worker's Right to Shelter" by Rakesh Shukla, InfoChange News & Features, August 2004.
53. State of Uttar Pradesh versus Kaushailiya AIR 1964 SC 416

Notes on Contributors

Srilatha Batliwala is a feminist activist and researcher who is currently Scholar Associate with the Association for Women's Rights in Development (AWID). Since the 1970s, Srilatha has worked for gender equality and women's empowerment through grassroots activism, advocacy, teaching, research, training, grant-making and organizational development. Later, and till the mid-90s she focused on building movements of poor urban and rural women in India. She then moved on to work in several premier international institutions—including as a Program Officer in the Ford Foundation, New York (1997-2000), and as Civil Society Research Fellow at the Hauser Center for Nonprofit Organizations, Harvard University (2001-2009), and since 2007, with AWID. Srilatha has published extensively on a range of women's issues. Her current work focuses on the concepts and practices of feminist movement building worldwide, and supporting young women activists in the South. She lives and works in Bangalore, India.

Sonia Corrêa's imagination was captured by feminism in Paris in the 1970s and, with her colleagues from the university, she used to roam the red light district of Rue Saint-Denis, to "observe" prostitutes. Back in Brazil in the early 1980s, Sonia analysed how monetized sexual exchanges are not substantially distinct from selling muscles and brains in the capitalist labour market. Since 1994, she has closely followed United Nations negotiations in relation to gender, sexuality and reproductive health. Sonia has been energized by feminist intellectual curiosity around the birth of the Brazilian prostitutes' movement. She has since worked to break the troubling silences at the international level around issues related to sex work at a time when, under the impact of global anti-trafficking policies, these silences had spiralled towards open conflict among feminists working at the United Nations. Sonia is also the co-coordinator of Sexuality Policy Watch and a research associate at ABIA (Brazilian Interdisciplinary Association for AIDS) in Rio. Among her published works are *Development with a Body* with Andrea Cornwall and Susan Jolly (2008) and *Sexuality, Health and Human Rights* with Richard Parkers and Rosalind Petchesky (2008).

Joanne Csete is Associate Clinical Professor at the Columbia University Mailman School of Public Health. She focuses her research and teaching on health and human rights, particularly the impact of criminalization, marginalization and gender-based subordination on access to health services for people who use drugs, sex workers, and others vulnerable to HIV. She was the founding director of the HIV/AIDS Program at Human Rights Watch and executive director of the Canadian HIV/AIDS Legal Network.

Adrienne Germain's pioneering work for women's equality began in the 1970s with the Ford Foundation, including four years in Bangladesh. Her work has revolutionized the way the world views population policy and funding by making women's sexual and reproductive rights and health central. Under Adrienne's leadership, the International Women's Health Coalition has created international policy innovations, led global advocacy for sexual and reproductive rights and health, and helped build local organizations in countries of Africa, Asia and Latin America. Adrienne is a member of the Council on Foreign Relations, the editorial board of *Reproductive Health Matters*, the Human Rights Watch Women's Division Advisory Committee, and the International Health Partnership (IHP+) Monitoring and Evaluation Advisory Group. She served on the Commission on the Federal Leadership in U.S. Health and Medicine; Millennium Development Goals Project Task Force on Child Mortality and Maternal Health; the BRAC-USA board; and the Human Rights Watch Asia Division Advisory Committee. Adrienne received an Honorary Doctorate from Bard College in 2001 and was named a Woman of Distinction by the Girl Scouts of Greater New York in 2005.

Laxmi Murthy is Consulting Editor with *Himal Southasian*, the region's only political review magazine, published from Kathmandu. She also heads the Hri Institute for Southasian Research and Exchange. Laxmi has worked with the International Federation of Journalists, managing South Asia programmes on press freedom and journalists' rights. Till 2002, Laxmi was an editor at the Women's Feature Service, an international news-feature agency specializing in development issues from a gender perspective. Among her publications are: "Reporting Conflict: A Handbook for Media Practitioners" (edited) (2005) and "Reporting Safe Migration and Trafficking" (2008), *Our Pictures Our Words: A Visual Journey Through the Women's Movement* (Zubaan, 2011, co-authored with Rajashri Dasgupta). She is a journalism trainer, and has also contributed chapters to several books on journalism, the most recent being *Missing: Half the Story, Journalism as if Gender Matters* edited by Kalpana Sharma (Zubaan, 2010). Laxmi is one of the national co-ordinators of the Network of Women in Media, India, and is currently co-coordinator of a Zubaan-IDRC project on sexual violence and impunity in South Asia and has been active in the autonomous women's movement in India for about 25 years.

Cheryl Overs has worked since 1983 to promote the health and human rights of male, female and transgender sex workers, and as a founder of the one of the world's first community-based sex workers' organizations to provide services and advocate on sex work issues, the Prostitutes Collective of Victoria (PCV), which successfully advocated for reform of prostitution law and provided legal and welfare services and referrals to Melbourne sex workers in brothels, escort agencies and streets. Cheryl has participated in key international policy-making forums, cutting-edge research and provided technical support to NGO, UN and government HIV prevention and care programmes. In 1990 Cheryl co-founded the International Network of Sex Workers with Paulo Henrique Longo and led global advocacy on sex work issues. She is currently a Senior Research Fellow at Monash University in Melbourne, Australia.

Sandhya Rao is a freelance consultant and editor based in Bangalore. She works in the areas of gender, human rights and sexuality. She does research, training and media work. Her latest work is the monograph *Who Stole the Tarts*. She has written extensively on women's rights. She was the founder director of Hengasara Hakkina Sangha, a women's rights organization. In addition, she has written scripts for award-winning films. She has written radio plays on women's rights. She works as a translator from Kannada and Hindi to English for researchers and film makers. Sandhya has been part of the women's movement for over three decades. Her passion is reading and watching films. She relaxes by making patchwork quilts.

Rohini Sahni teaches at the Department of Economics, University of Pune, India. As a development economist, her research interests have diversified from transition economics and area studies of Soviet Russia into grassroot experiences of development in India. She has also been actively researching the 'sex-as-work' paradigm in India, conducting spatial studies to place sex work in its urban contexts and engaging in ethnographic studies to explore its changing economic and cultural dimensions. She is the co-editor of the volume *Prostitution and Beyond: An Analysis of Sex Work in India* (2008). Presently, she is involved in a pan-India survey, the first of its kind, which seeks to multi-dimensionally map sex work in India as practised by female and transgender sex workers. She is also an established writer in Marathi fiction, with her short stories published in leading journals and also translated into English.

Meena Saraswathi Seshu is the general secretary of SANGRAM, an organization that works on the rights of sex workers and people living with HIV/AIDS, based in Sangli, Maharashtra, India. In 1996 this work broadened into the organization of a collective of women in sex work, VAMP (Veshya Anyay Mukti Parishad). SANGRAM's Centre for Advocacy on Stigma and Marginalization (CASAM) advocates for the reduction of stigma, violence and harassment of marginalized communities, especially those who have challenged dominant norms. Meena works with marginalized populations, particularly rural women, adolescents and people in sex work, on HIV and AIDS, sexual and reproductive health, violence against women, and gender and sexual minority rights through grassroots, rights-based organizations in Karnataka and Maharashtra. She has more than a decade's experience with global movements addressing violence against women and sex workers' rights. In 2002, Meena was awarded the Human Rights Defender Award from Human Rights Watch.

V. Kalyan Shankar is currently a Doctoral Student at the Department of Economics, University of Pune. He has been working in the areas of international economic theory, WTO agreements and several inter-disciplinary strands of development economics relevant in the Indian context—extending into gender studies, urban studies, higher education and social history/ anthropology. He is the co-editor of the volume *Prostitution and Beyond: An Analysis of Sex Work in India* (2008). Presently, he is the principal investigator of a pan-India survey, the first of its kind, which seeks to multi-dimensionally map sex work in India as practised by female and transgender sex workers. He hails from a family of social reformers, scholars and poets in Andhra Pradesh. This background has profoundly influenced his concerns and sensibilities, leading him to work on issues of social concern.

Rakesh Shukla is a practising advocate of the Supreme Court of India, does clinical psychotherapeutic work, is an Affiliate of the Indian Psycho-Analytical Society, a Member of the Indian Association of Family Therapy and is associated with the Centre for Psychoanalytic Studies, University of Delhi. As part of exploring the interface of law and psychology, he has conceptualized and conducts regular workshops for judges on 'Minimizing the Impact of Biases, Prejudices and Stereotypes in the Judicial Decision Making Process' at the Delhi Judicial Academy. He has also designed interventions from a psychoanalytic perspective, for mediators and conciliators. He has been writing in the major dailies on issues of law and psychology. His publications include a booklet on the law regarding sex work meant for sex workers titled *Vaishya Vyavsay Kaidyachi Olakh* in Marathi which has also been translated into Telegu. Other publications include two monographs *Sex Work Laws in South Asia* and *Bail not Jail*, a volume entitled *'Misrepresentation and Fraud'* in *Halsbury's Laws of India* as well as booklets on 'Disciplinary Enquiry', the Contract Labour (Abolition and Regulation) Act, 1970 and 'Equal Pay for Equal Work'.

Cath Sluggett is an independent social researcher based in Goa. Her work focuses on sexuality, gender, and marginalization in South Asian contexts. With more than 17 years of experience in the capacity of researcher and activist in India, she has worked with both non-government and international development sectors, and a wide range of populations, including people in sex work, children, same-sex desiring and transgender individuals. Her recent area of research includes a study on how same-sex desiring women live in relation to the 'lesbian' identity and the politics of visibility in urban India. Cath also illustrates for various magazines and journals.

José Miguel Nieto Olivar worked in education and communication with NGOs and the United Nations System in relation to sexual and reproductive rights in Colombia. During his doctoral work in social anthropolgy at the Universidade Federal do Rio Grande do Sul in Porto Alegre (Brazil), he looked at the "politics of street prostitution", examining the trajectory of four prostitutes' activists, the sex workers' movement itself, its legal and policy demands and its relations with gender, family, kinship, sexual and body values. In so doing he engaged with the Brazilian Network of Prostitutes, in particular the NEP (Nucleus for the Study of Prostitution) in Porto Alegre and Davida in Rio de Janeiro. He is presently studying the dynamics of the sexual market in the Amazonian border between Brazil and Colombia, as a postdoctoral researcher at PAGU Nucleus for the Study of Gender (Universidade de Campinas, São Paulo, Brazil). He is also a member of the Center of Research on Society, Health and Culture (CISSC) in Colombia.